福建省社会科学规划项目（2011B244）成果

本书获厦门理工学院学术专著出版基金优先资助

THE CONSTRUCTION AND APPLICATION OF
THE BILINGUAL FUJIAN WORLD HERITAGE CORPUS

福建世界遗产双语语料库构建与应用

余 军 王朝晖 著

厦门大学出版社 国家一级出版社
XIAMEN UNIVERSITY PRESS 全国百佳图书出版单位

图书在版编目(CIP)数据

福建世界遗产双语语料库构建与应用/余军,王朝晖著.—厦门:厦门大学出版社,
2018.11
ISBN 978-7-5615-7184-2

Ⅰ.①福…　Ⅱ.①余…②王…　Ⅲ.①文化遗产—语料库—福建　Ⅳ.①K295.7

中国版本图书馆 CIP 数据核字(2018)第 262823 号

出 版 人	郑文礼
责任编辑	王扬帆　高奕欢
封面设计	李嘉彬
技术编辑	朱　楷

出版发行	厦门大学出版社
社　　址	厦门市软件园二期望海路 39 号
邮政编码	361008
总 编 办	0592-2182177　0592-2181406(传真)
营销中心	0592-2184458　0592-2181365
网　　址	http://www.xmupress.com
邮　　箱	xmup@xmupress.com
印　　刷	虎彩印艺股份有限公司

开本	720 mm×1 000 mm　1/16
印张	14.5
插页	2
字数	261 千字
版次	2018 年 11 月第 1 版
印次	2018 年 11 月第 1 次印刷
定价	48.00 元

本书如有印装质量问题请直接寄承印厂调换

厦门大学出版社
微信二维码

厦门大学出版社
微博二维码

前　言

　　世界遗产作为文化传播的重要媒介，翻译在其中起了不可替代的作用。翻译促进了不同文化间的有效沟通，进而实现世界遗产文化符号的传播。世界遗产翻译的质量，在一定程度上影响了文化符号的传播进程，相关研究具有重要意义和价值。但目前世界遗产翻译的研究存在总量极少、视角有限、缺乏系统考察等问题，基于语料库的实证研究更是付之阙如。

　　有鉴于此，本书以翻译这一世界遗产文化传播的重要途径为视角，以福建世界遗产为对象，以语料库的实证语料为依据，探究世界遗产翻译存在的问题与对策。通过语料库的构建及应用，评估福建世界遗产翻译质量，探索CCAT平台下的世界遗产翻译模式，提高福建世界遗产翻译的质量，促进福建文化的传播和文化产业的发展。

　　本书将语料库与CAT两大翻译技术结合，将其应用于福建世界遗产翻译研究，提出了世界遗产翻译的"信、达、效"原则，阐述了福建世界遗产双语语料库的研制及其应用，并从福建申遗文本、景区文本、酒店介绍和导游词等角度评估福建世界遗产翻译质量，考察了福建世界遗产网站的本地化情况，分析了存在的问题并提出对策。这些探讨，对于世界遗产翻译质量的提高，具有一定的实用价值。

　　在本书成稿之际，我们要感谢所有关心、支持本书的机构和个人。本书获厦门理工学院学术专著出版基金优先资助，厦门理工学院外国语学院也为本书的出版提供了资助，在此一并致谢！感谢魏志成教授在学术上给予我们的帮助和激励。

　　本书部分章节由王朝晖撰写，约5万字，其他部分由余军撰写；全书由余军统稿。

我们希望本书能引起更多人对世界遗产翻译研究的关注。由于水平有限，不当之处在所难免，诚挚地希望广大读者批评指正。

余军　王朝晖

2018 年 5 月于厦门

目录

第1章 绪 论

1.1 引言

福建文化源远流长，闽南文化、客家文化、朱子文化、海丝文化，各具特色，在海内外颇具影响。在文化"走出去"战略及"一带一路"背景下，福建文化占据天时地利，其对外传播，可谓充满机遇，但仍不乏挑战。

以世界遗产为例，申报者众，一旦入选世遗名录，不仅扬名国际，而且游客将纷至沓来①，文化产业潜力无穷。竞争之激烈，自不难想象，但福建凭其深厚的文化底蕴和丰富的申遗经验，在拥有武夷山、土楼和泰宁丹霞3个世界遗产之后，2017年厦门鼓浪屿又在历经数年的申遗之路上修成正果——入选2017年世界文化遗产名录。

然而，福建世界遗产作为福建文化对外传播的重要媒介②，相关研究极少，不利于福建世界遗产核心文化符号的输出。

有鉴于此，本研究以世界遗产翻译这一福建文化传播的重要途径为视角，以语料库的实证语料为依据，探究其存在的问题与对策。

1.2 福建世界遗产翻译研究现状

目前有关福建世界遗产的翻译研究并不多见，论文仅有10余篇，涉及武夷山、土楼及鼓浪屿等3个世界遗产。这些研究可概括为以下几个方面：

（1）公示语翻译研究：针对武夷山景区标识用语翻译若干问题及其原因进行简要分析（陈孝静，2008）；实地采集武夷山市双语公示语资料及相关采访，发现其英译存在表达不当、中式英语、过度翻译等12类问题并予以剖析（何兰芳，张美君，张素芳，林丽端，2016）；调查留学生对武夷山市公示语英译的满意度，提出在改进现有公示语英译准确度的同时，增加重要公共场所双语向

---

① 例如，我国的黄山申报世界遗产成功之后，旅游收入从每年几百万元猛增到2亿元，地处云南的边陲小城丽江，仅2000年便接待了海内外游客258万人，旅游收入达到13.44亿元（刘红婴，王健民，2003：230）。

② 陈先元（2004：67）认为，从现代传播学的媒介理论来看，世界遗产是一种媒介，它的信息特征是历史阶段性和恒久性的统一，地域局限性和共享性的统一，文化汇聚性和延展性的统一。

导系统的设置及提供更多的诸如地图、各类宣传册及实时网络平台等双语信息媒介（何兰芳，2018）。

（2）外宣／旅游文本翻译研究：以福建土楼世遗申报报告为语料，以接受美学的视野融合为视角，探析对外宣传文本的翻译策略（韦忠生，2011）；提出"以信息为中心"的福建土楼旅游文本英译策略（潘涓涓，2010）；以目的论为指导，指出鼓浪屿旅游文本中的主要英译错误，提出译者在翻译实践活动中可采用的翻译策略（汪懿婷，2014）；从框架理论的视角，分析客家土楼摄影文本的英译问题，从语言框架的词汇、单句、语篇及文化框架中的文化缺省和文化冲突等方面对误译进行阐释并加以纠正（肖晓玲，2015）；基于翻译适应选择论和多维转换原则，审视福建土楼旅游外宣英译，引入翻译生态环境、适应选择、适者生存等生态学概念，并以此诠释和指导翻译实践（谢爱玲，2016）；以功能加忠诚的翻译理论分析漳州土楼旅游文本的汉英翻译，探讨有利于旅游文本翻译与本土文化对接的翻译策略和方法（李静雯，2017）。

（3）景点名称翻译研究：探析武夷山景点名英译中存在的问题，并分析其缘由，讨论景点名梯级翻译标准，论述与景点名翻译对应的 5 大类翻译方法（陈孝静，唐有胜，2011）；探讨中国世界遗产名称的英译策略，提出译音与译意及两者并用的翻译策略（曾咪，2014b）。

此外，还有武夷山景区门票英译问题研究（刘金水，吴婧，2013）以及土楼申遗文本的中国文化遗产特色词汇翻译研究（曾咪，2014a），等等。

以上研究就福建世界遗产翻译做出了一定的探索，但主要仍集中于公示语翻译、外宣／旅游文本英译、景点名称翻译等传统话题，对诸如世界遗产网站的本地化、申遗文本英译的质量评估、导游词的英译等问题则均未涉及。此外，在翻译研究的技术转向背景下，相关研究未与语料库及 CAT 等翻译技术结合，未见基于语料库的系统考察，也未从 CAT 的角度探讨翻译质量的提升之道。福建世界遗产翻译的研究存在总量较少、视角传统、缺乏基于翻译技术的系统研究等问题。

1.3　语料库与世界遗产翻译研究

近 20 年来，基于语料库的翻译研究日趋增多，构建的语料库主要分为译文语料库、类比语料库和双语对应语料库 3 类。3 种语料库多数以文学文本为主，或是以收纳百科文本为特色，而结合地域特点或针对某一文类而专门研制的双语专门语料库则较为少见（李德超，王克非，2010）。

世界遗产翻译涉及的文本以旅游文本为主，此外还包括申遗文本及其他类型文本。就旅游文本而言，国外的旅游专门语料库主要有 3 个，分别为芬兰、英国和日本学者所研制，其共同特点是都属于容量小于 100 万词的小规模语料库。而我国内地除中科院研制的旅游咨询口语对话语料库和旅馆预订口语对话语料库外，尚无专门研发的旅游语料库，香港则仅有香港理工大学中文及双语学系研制的新型双语旅游语料库，是香港以至全国第一个较大容量的英汉／汉英旅游语料库（李德超，王克非，2010）。该语料库由一个双语旅游翻译对应语料库与一个双语旅游翻译类比语料库组成，语料规模均为 100 万字／词。前者目前收录香港的英译汉和汉译英的旅游翻译文本，后者主要收录以香港为主的海峡两岸暨香港、澳门非翻译的中文和英文旅游原生性文本。该语料库可能包含一些与世界遗产有关的语料，但就整个语料库而言，并非以世界遗产为主，而且仅限于旅游类文本，没有包括申遗文本。

综上所述，目前国内外尚无以世界遗产为对象构建的专门用途双语语料库，而世界遗产翻译的研究应以文化交流和传播为目的，进行基于双语语料库的实证研究。

1.4 世界遗产翻译研究的 CCAT 视角

CCAT 是将语料库与 CAT 技术相融合的翻译研究范式（王朝晖，余军，2016）。所谓 CCAT，指的是 Corpus and computer-assisted translation（语料库及计算机辅助的翻译），其中计算机辅助部分指 CAT 软件，而 Corpus 主要指双语语料库，以专门用途双语语料库为主，也包括网络语料库。

CCAT 平台由参与人员、CAT 软件、语料及在线平台构成，是一个完整的系统。

第一，参与人员。包括译者、译文审查者、译评人、出版商、翻译研究者等等。

第二，CAT 软件。在国内外多款 CAT 软件中，雪人 CAT 是最适合 CCAT 平台的，因为其句子对齐功能强大，软件易用性突出，功能符合 CCAT 需要，且性价比高、支持定制。

第三，语料。包括单语料库、双语语料库，以及 CAT 软件的翻译记忆库及术语库，统称语料。语料库研究领域的语料库多用于翻译研究，CAT 领域的翻译记忆库和术语库则侧重于翻译应用。之前学界很少注意到两者的关系，其实两者是相辅相成的，代表同一事物的理论和应用两个方面。双语语料库与翻译记忆库可以轻易便捷地相互转化，CAT 的术语库也可以从双语语料库中提取。

第四，在线平台。在线平台指语料库及翻译记忆库、术语库的网络平台，可以是共享性质的，也可以是收费性质的，视将来的发展而定，可能两种都会存在，只是语料规模不一样。这一在线平台和 CAT 软件是联系 CCAT 系统中译者、译文审查者、译评人、出版商、翻译研究者的纽带。

CCAT 这一理论包括应用和研究两个层次的内涵。应用方面，不论是文学翻译，还是非文学翻译，如果在语料库及 CAT 的共同辅助下进行，在翻译准确性、翻译效率等方面都将有可观的改善。研究方面，不论是语料库翻译学研究，还是 CAT 研究，要深入下去，突破瓶颈，唯有二者融合，优势互补，方能开辟一方新的天地。

以上有关 CCAT 的阐述，详见《基于 CAT 及语料库技术的电子商务翻译研究》（王朝晖，余军，2016）一书。我们认为，CCAT 同样适用于世界遗产翻译研究。因此，本研究旨在构建以福建世界遗产翻译为研究对象的专门用途双语语料库，探讨双语语料库的构建及其与 CAT 技术融合为 CCAT 的途径，基于 CCAT 平台，评估福建世界遗产翻译质量，探索 CCAT 平台下的世界遗产翻译模式，提高福建世界遗产翻译的质量，促进福建文化的传播和文化产业的发展。

1.5　本书主要内容

全书共分 7 章。第 1 章是绪论，简要评述了福建世界遗产翻译的研究现状，在此基础上说明本研究的目标和意义。第 2 章阐述了福建世界遗产双语语料库的研制，包括设计思路、语料来源及建库类型、建库工具、语料标注、术语库制作、记忆库制作等方面的内容。第 3 章介绍了福建世界遗产翻译双语语料库的检索方式。第 4 章探讨了基于 CCAT 的世界遗产翻译的质量评估标准和模式，并以申遗文本、景区文本、酒店介绍及导游词等为个案，对福建世界遗产翻译质量进行了评估。第 5 章考察了福建世界遗产网站的本地化情况，分析了存在的问题并提出对策。第 6 章提出了 CCAT 平台下的世界遗产翻译模式，并以福建申遗文本翻译和酒店介绍翻译为例，论述其具体应用。第 7 章以申遗文本为例，分别说明了福建世界遗产双语语料库的精细修订与入库修订。

第 2 章　福建世界遗产双语语料库的研制

2.1　引言

世界遗产翻译 CCAT 系统构建的重要支柱是语料库，其研制是构建 CCAT 系统的第一步。福建世界遗产双语语料库以武夷山、泰宁、土楼、鼓浪屿的申遗文本、景点介绍、导游词、世界遗产本地化网站及相关图书等为主要语料来源，将 CAT 技术与语料库技术相结合，基于 CCAT 理念构建，属于一种新型的专门用途双语语料库。

本章介绍福建世界遗产双语语料库的研制，分为两部分内容。第一部分介绍福建世界遗产双语语料库的研制方案，包括该语料库的设计思路、语料来源及建库类型、建库工具、语料标注等；第二部分介绍术语库制作、记忆库制作及转换等。

第一部分是福建世界遗产双语语料库的构建个案，对其他类型的专门用途双语语料库也具有参考价值；第二部分是技术基础，适用于任何一种新型专门用途双语语料库的术语库及记忆库构建。

2.2　设计思路

基于 CCAT 系统的构建原则，我们认为，福建世界遗产双语语料库的研制应不仅包含传统的单语类比语料库及双语对应语料库，还应从语料库与 CAT 相互融合的理念以及 CCAT 的应用角度考虑，加入术语库和记忆库，以促进福建世界遗产翻译的术语统一，提高翻译效率和质量。因此，在福建世界遗产双语语料库的构建上，我们沿用了之前构建电子商务翻译语料库时设计的一种新型的专门用途双语语料库研制模式，与传统的双语语料库构建模式有很大的不同。

以往任何一种双语语料库一般都以一种文件形式存储（多为 TXT 或者 XML 格式），属于单一的形态，可用专门的检索工具检索分析，但由于文件格式不兼容，不能被计算机辅助翻译工具所利用（王朝晖，余军，2016：185）。而福建世界遗产双语语料库不仅包含兼容于语料库检索工具的 TXT 文件，也包含雪人 CAT 软件可以加载的术语库和记忆库文件。

这一新型的双语语料库，提供了与传统的双语语料库和当代 CAT 技术的双重接口，既有利于语料库翻译学研究向应用翻译领域转向，也有助于语言服务行业人工辅助机器翻译的发展（王朝晖，余军，2016：185）。

2.3 语料来源及建库类型

2.3.1 语料来源

福建世界遗产双语语料库全部语料限定在与福建世界遗产相关的范围，如申遗文本、世界遗产本地化网站、导游词、旅游线路、景点介绍、酒店介绍、景区公示语，以及民俗风情、历史文化、饮食文化、物产资源、人名地名等。

语料来源主要包括正式出版物（著作、教材、旅游指南、摄影集等），非出版物（网页及各类旅游宣传材料，如酒店介绍、旅行社传单、景点免费发放的旅游小册子等），及景区的景点介绍文字和公示语等。

福建世界遗产双语语料库包括土楼、武夷山、泰宁、鼓浪屿 4 个世界遗产。

2.3.2 建库类型

（1）类比语料库（单语）：包括英语国家（如美国、英国等）原生英文语料，如原生英文申遗文本、原生英文导游词等，以及福建世界遗产译文语料，包括申遗文本英文译文、导游词英文译文等，原生英文文本可与译文文本进行类比比较。该部分库容目前约 60 万词。

（2）汉英对应语料库：包括福建世界遗产汉英对应语料，如中英文对照申遗文本、导游词、酒店介绍、景区介绍、公示语等等。该部分库容目前约 40 万字／词。

（3）译文语料库（单语）：包括汉英对应语料库中的英文译文。该部分库容目前约 17 万词。

（4）术语及翻译记忆库：从已构建的汉英对应语料库中提取并校正了约 5 万字／词的术语库，以及大约 40 万字／词的记忆库，其中约 20 万字／词已审校纠讹完毕，其他亦在审校之中。

2.4 建库工具

语料库的制作涉及多个环节，需要利用各种软件工具才能完成（王朝晖，余军，2016：187）。本研究启动之初，便遇到了语料收集及加工困难的问题。以申遗文本的中文版为例，坊间流传的申遗文本中文版数量极为稀少，且版本不止一种，但仅有一种与联合国世界遗产网站公布的英文版一致，费力购买之后，可能版本不符，又需重新物色。收集到相符的申遗文本中文版之后，还需扫描，OCR 识别，人工校对，然后与英文版进行双语对齐，制作为双语语料库。整个过程涉及多个步骤及环节，耗时费力。由于经费有限，人力不足，世界遗产双语语料库的语料采集颇为艰难，历时数年才最终完成。

在双语语料库的构建过程中，一些非传统的建库工具起了重要作用，这些工具包括：

（1）网页文本采集工具：与手工采集或使用 offline explorer 之类的离线下载工具不同，我们使用了网络矿工进行网页数据的自动采集，极大地提高了网络语料的获取效率。具体操作方法详见《基于 CAT 及语料库技术的电子商务翻译研究》（王朝晖，余军，2016）一书。

（2）双语语料对齐工具：双语对应语料库构建的核心环节是原文和译文以句为单位配对，即句对齐，采用何种对齐工具以及该工具效率的高下，决定了语料库所能达到的规模和项目成本，有的语料库翻译学研究团队为此制作了高效率的句对软件，但仅限内部使用，外界无从获取（王朝晖，余军，2016：187）。我们采用雪人 CAT 软件对双语语料进行句对齐处理，其准确率比传统的 WinAlign 高很多，而且更为易用，不像 WinAlign 经常出现乱码。

（3）自主开发工具：雪人软件导出的句对文件可选择主流计算机辅助翻译软件都支持的 TMX 格式，也可以选择 HTM 格式。这两种格式都需要进一步的人工处理才能转换为一般语料库检索工具支持的格式。虽然步骤较为简单，但如果存在大量句对文件，总的工作量仍会非常巨大。为提高效率，我们自主开发了自动转换工具，可将雪人软件导出的 HTM 双语文件批量转换为可供检索的双语语料文件，节省了大量人力，加快了双语语料的入库速度。

2.5 语料标注

Leech（1997：2）认为，对语料库进行标注可以使语料库增值（added value）。经过标注的语料库，其实用价值要大于无标注的语料库。

我们对福建世界遗产双语语料库进行了以下标注：

（1）文本头：文本头标注包括中文标题、英文标题、作者／文本来源、原文字数、译文字数等。

（2）词性标注：英文文本采用ClAWS4进行词性标注，中文文本则采用ICTCLAS进行词性标注。

（3）错误标注：抽取了部分典型汉英对应语料进行错误标注，制定错误标注规范，包括错误标注分类、标注赋码、标注流程等，并实施严格的标注质量监控。

2.6 术语库制作

术语库是CCAT平台的一个极为重要的组成部分。在第4章的福建世界遗产翻译质量评估中，我们发现术语不统一是比较普遍和严重的问题。制作高质量的术语库并在CCAT平台中将其应用于福建世界遗产翻译，可以极大地避免术语不统一的问题。

下面简要介绍术语库的制作流程和方法。视乎文本的不同，术语库的制作流程和方法也存在差异。

（1）仅有原文的单语文本

在仅有原文、尚无译文的情况下，根据原文文本制作术语库，对于翻译过程中的术语统一至关重要。制作流程为先提取术语，然后筛选、翻译术语。下面以中文申遗文本为例，简要说明单语文本术语库的制作。

①提取术语

启动雪人CAT，建立中译英项目，如图2-1：

图2-1 雪人CAT建立中译英项目

导入中文申遗文本，如图 2-2 及图 2-3：

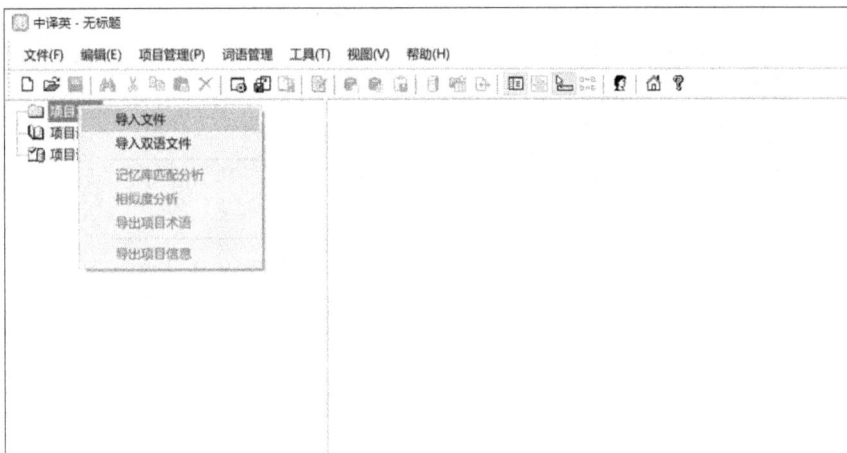

图 2-2　雪人 CAT 中译英项目导入文件 1

图 2-3　雪人 CAT 中译英项目导入文件 2

在软件"词语管理"菜单中点击"词频统计"，如图2-4：

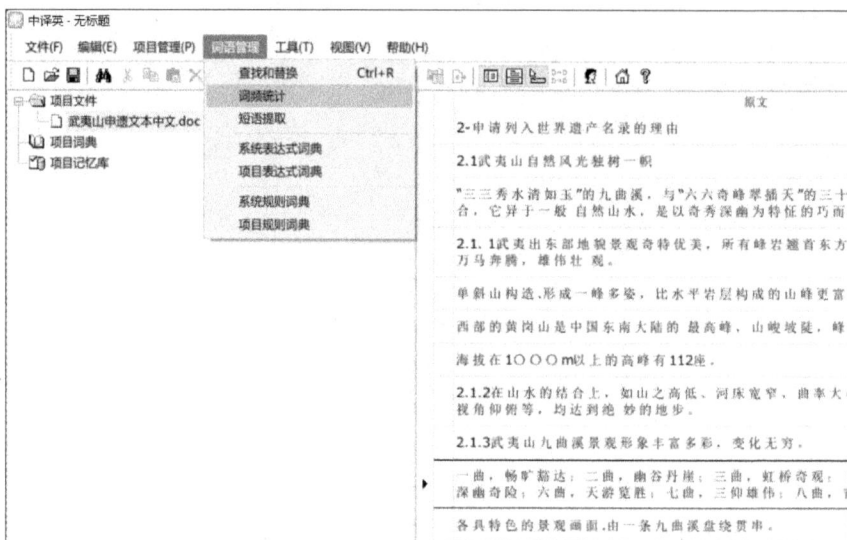

图2-4　雪人CAT词频统计操作1

在弹出窗口界面点击"提取词语"，在"最少出现频率"处填"2"，如图2-5：

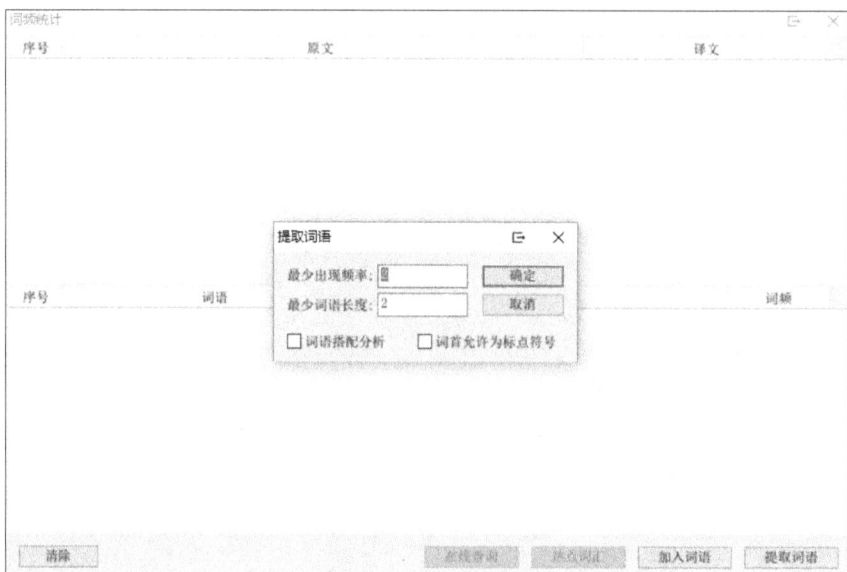

图2-5　雪人CAT词频统计操作2

点击"确定"，词频统计结果如图2-6：

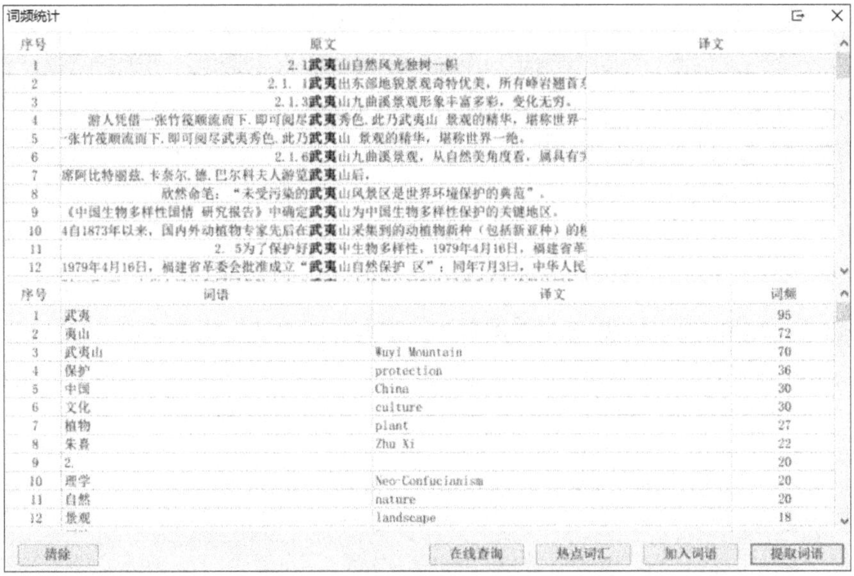

图2-6　雪人 CAT 词频统计结果

图2-6中的译文栏为雪人内置的词典翻译结果，可忽略。右键点击词语区，在弹出菜单中选择"导出词表"，如图2-7：

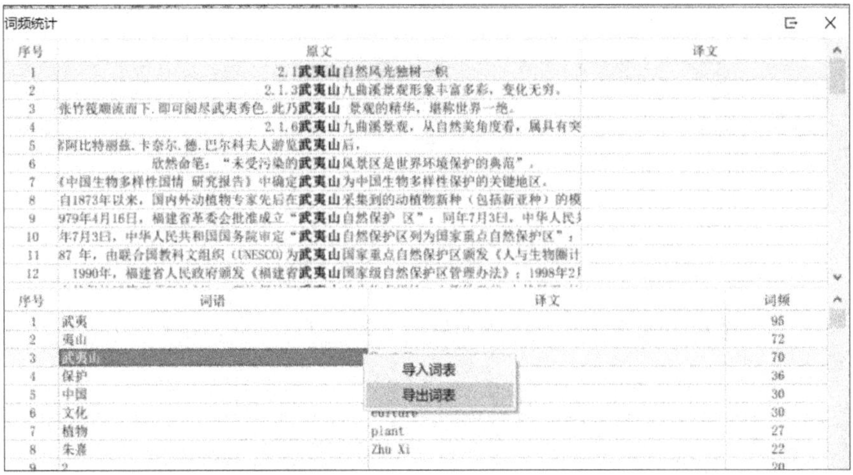

图2-7　雪人 CAT 词频统计导出词表

导出词表为 Excel 格式文件。

②筛选术语

导出后的术语需要筛选。筛选的原则主要有两点，一是出现频率2次以上，二是译文必须统一。如"九曲溪"一词的出现频率超过 2 次，网上有多种译文，包括"Nine-bend River"、"Jiuqu Xi"、"Nine-bent Stream"等等。如果不统一译文，势必造成混乱，因此要确定一个统一译名，收入术语库，以保持译文一致。有的表达并非术语，虽然频率超过 2 次，也不必统一译文。如"优美"、"景色"之类的表达，就无须收入术语库。

③翻译术语

筛选后的术语需要翻译，由于机器翻译术语的准确率已经较高（王朝晖，余军，2016：251），可采用机器翻译＋人工修订的方式。首先用 Bing 或 Google 等翻译引擎自动翻译所筛选出的术语，然后人工审核并修订机器译文。

④导入术语

右键点击"项目词典"菜单，选择"导入词典"，如图 2-8：

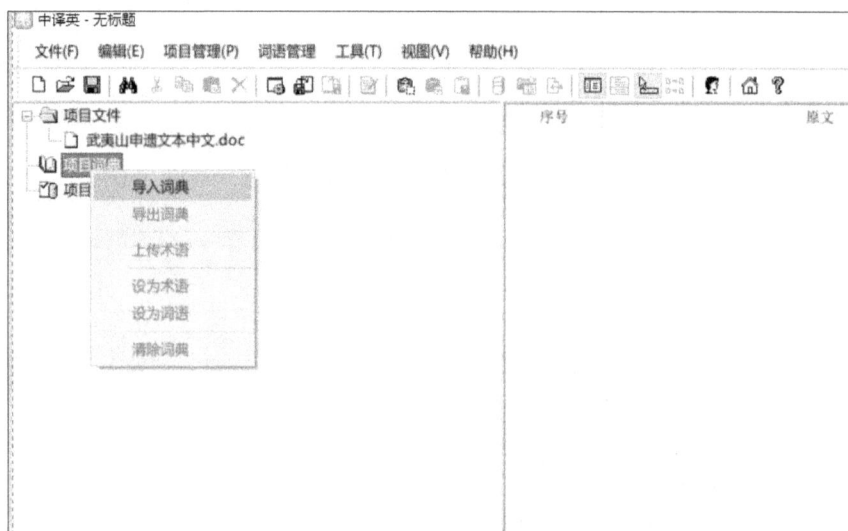

图 2-8　雪人 CAT 导入术语 1

在弹出窗口界面选择筛选并翻译后的 Excel 词表，将其导入雪人 CAT 软件，如图 2-9：

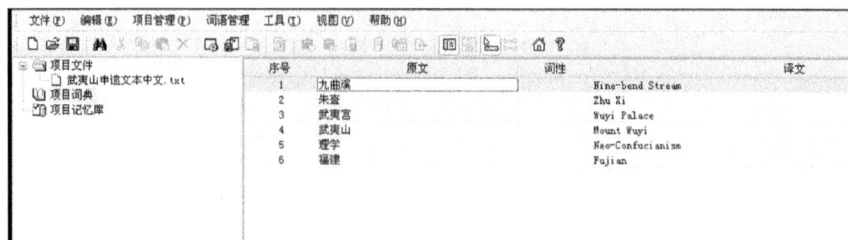

图 2-9　雪人 CAT 导入术语 2

右键点击"项目词典",选择"设为术语",如图 2-10:

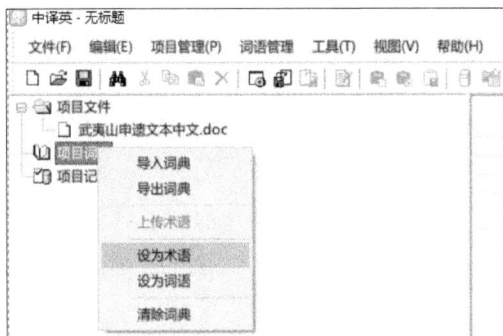

图 2-10 雪人 CAT 设置术语 1

设为术语后,之前导入的词语显示为加黑状态,如图 2-11:

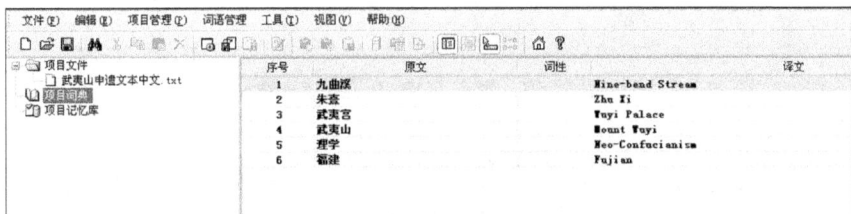

图 2-11 雪人 CAT 设置术语 2

右键点击"项目词典",选择"导出词典",即可将术语库导出。

(2)未句对齐的双语文本

此类文本属于双语语料库的原始语料,需要句对齐后入库。其术语库制作可在句对齐的过程中进行,步骤如下。

①建立双语对齐项目,导入双语文本,如图 2-12 及图 2-13:

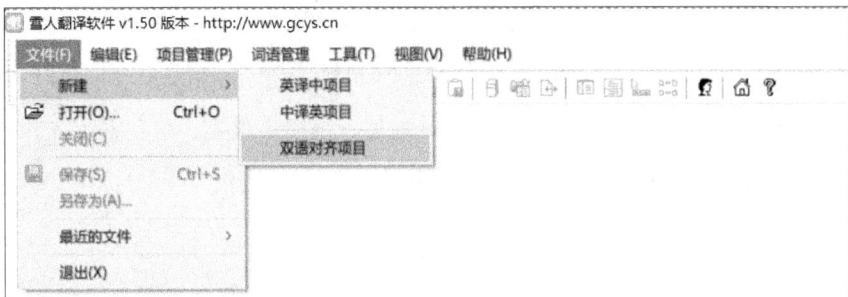

图 2-12 雪人 CAT 建立双语对齐项目

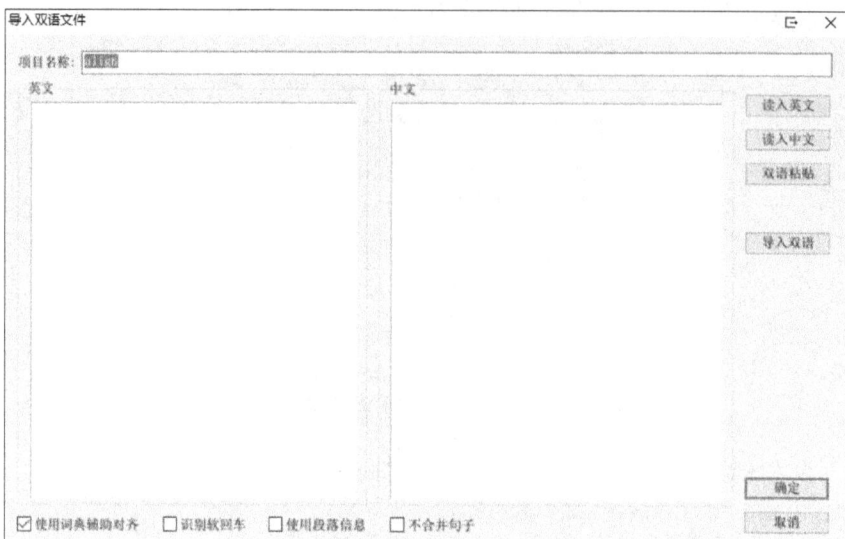

图 2-13　雪人 CAT 导入双语文本

②自动句对齐后人工审核句对，如图 2-14：

图 2-14　雪人 CAT 自动对齐

　　导入双语文本后，雪人 CAT 会自动对齐，准确率极高，但仍需人工审校，纠正错误。在审校过程中，可顺带设置术语。

③划词设置术语，如图2-15：

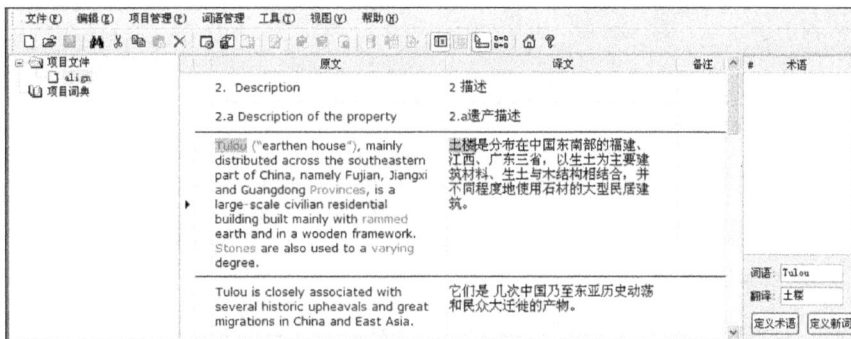

图2-15　雪人CAT划词设置术语

鼠标分别划中图2-15中英文栏的"Tulou"及中文栏的"土楼"，软件右侧底部会出现词语"Tulou"及其翻译"土楼"，点击"定义术语"即将其设为术语。

对齐过程中依次设置术语，完毕后导出术语即可。

（3）已句对齐的双语文本

此类文本为已经构建的双语语料库，提取术语并制作术语库的方式可参照上述（1）、（2）两种方式。既可按照（1）中所述步骤，提取并筛选术语后，通过语料库检索，获取术语的译文，制作为术语库，也可按照（2）中所述步骤，建立句对齐项目，将双语文本导入，人工划词，设置术语。

2.7　记忆库制作及转换

2.7.1　记忆库制作

福建世界遗产双语语料库的记忆库分为两种。一种是未经审校的生记忆库，利用雪人软件对齐双语语料，即可导出记忆库，语料来源主要为武夷山、土楼和鼓浪屿申遗文本以及缤客网的酒店介绍，等等。译文质量相对属较高水平。另一种记忆库是我们在生记忆库上人工审校修订的记忆库。生记忆库的制作方式简要介绍如下。

（1）双语对齐

建立双语对齐项目，导入双语文本，自动对齐后人工审核，见上一小节图2-12、图2-13、图2-14。需要注意的是，人工审校发现错误时需要调整句对，雪人 CAT 支持键盘快捷键操作，句对调整效率极高。如要合并两个句子，将光标移到句子末端，按 Del 键，即可将该句和下一行的句子合并。如要分割句子，将光标移到分割处，按回车键，即可将光标后的部分移至下一行。

（2）导出记忆库

人工审校完毕，确认无误后，可导出记忆库，如图 2-16：

图 2-16   雪人 CAT 对齐项目导出记忆库

2.7.2   记忆库转换

CAT 软件的记忆库只能由 CAT 软件加载使用，一般的双语语料库检索工具不能对其进行检索，因此需要将其转换为双语语料库支持的双语文件。所谓双语文件，主要包括两种类型：一种是原文及译文在同一文件中，一般是一行原文，一行译文，或者是原文与译文在同一行，我们称之为单文件型；另一种是原文在一个文件，译文在另一文件，原文与译文在各自的文件中位于同样的行数，如原文在 A 文件中位于第 3 行，译文在 B 文件中也位于第 3 行，我们称之为双文件型。两种类型的文件都有相应的检索工具，双文件型较为知名的检索工具是 ParaConc，单文件型的检索工具见第 3 章。

下面简单介绍将雪人 CAT 的记忆库转换为单文件型及双文件型双语文件的方法。

（1）雪人 CAT 记忆库转换为单文件型双语文件

在雪人 CAT 中双语对齐完毕后，选择"导出双语对照文件"（见图 2-16），可将记忆库导出为 HTM 文件，其中包含了已对齐的双语语料。鼠标左键双击打开 HTM 文件，如图 2-17。

align	
原文	译文
2. Description	2 描述
2. a Description of the property	2. a遗产描述
Tulou ("earthen house"), mainly distributed across the southeastern part of China, namely Fujian, Jiangxi and Guangdong Provinces, is a large-scale civilian residential building built mainly with rammed earth and in a wooden framework. Stones are also used to a varying degree.	土楼主要分布在中国东南部的福建、江西、广东三省，以生土为主要建筑材料、生土与木结构相结合，并不同程度地使用石材的大型民居建筑。
Tulou is closely associated with several historic upheavals and great migrations in China and East Asia.	它们是 几次中国乃至东亚历史动荡和民众大迁徙的产物。
Among the Tulou buildings of various descriptions, Fujian Tulou is the best-preserved with the broadest coverage, largest quantity and richest variety.	其中分布最广、数量最多、品类最丰富，保存最完好的，是福建土楼。
Fujian Tulou concentrates in the southwestern region of Fujian Province and a total of three thousands Tulou Buildings have been found across this province.	福建土楼分布范围以福建西南地区尤为集中，总数达3000多座。
The region is full of hills and valleys covered by bushy vegetation, enjoys subtropical and marine climate and rich rainfall. The Hakka and the Fulao, two branches of the Han nationality, live in the region, carrying forward the traditional customs of the Han's and taking farming as their main mode of production.	所处自然环境以丘陵谷地为主，南亚热带海洋性季风气候，气候温暖，雨水充沛，植 被茂密；居住着汉民族的客家民系和福佬民系，生活方式沿续着汉民族的传统习俗，生产方式以农耕为主。

图 2-17　雪人 CAT 对齐项目导出的 HTM 文件

将原文及译文全部选中，复制并粘贴到 TXT 文件中，即可获得单文件型双语文件。

（2）雪人 CAT 记忆库转换为双文件型双语文件

选中 HTM 文件中的原文及译文后，复制并粘贴到 Excel 表格中的两栏，则一栏为原文，一栏为译文，选中原文栏，粘贴到 TXT 文件，选中译文栏，粘贴到另一个 TXT 文件，两个文件即可形成双文件型双语文件，支持 ParaConc 的检索。

雪人 CAT 对齐功能强大，而且其记忆库极易转换为双语语料库检索工具支持的文件格式，在 CCAT 平台中起到了桥梁作用，非常重要。

2.8　小结

福建世界遗产双语语料库的研制过程采用了之前构建电子商务双语语料库时所发掘的一些技术，并有所发展和创新。

目前国内的双语语料库研究取得了很多成果，但传统的语料采集以及句子对齐方式已经不能满足构建大规模双语语料库的需要，推动技术革新、提高双语语料库研制的效率是当务之急（王朝晖，余军，2016：67）。两年前的这段话，目前仍未过时。

希望更多同行关注语料库与 CAT 技术的融合，创新双语语料库的建库方案及技术，共同推动双语语料库构建研究的发展以及大型专门用途双语语料库的构建。

第 3 章　福建世界遗产双语语料库的检索

3.1　引言

语料库的检索工具对于语料库语言学研究具有极其重要的作用，检索软件功能是否强大、完备，是否能够满足各种统计需要，对于语料库语言学研究的影响是非常大的（王朝晖，余军，2016：198）。

语料库的检索工具主要分为两类。第一类是桌面版检索工具，其中单语检索软件有著名的 WordSmith，相关介绍较多（王立非，梁茂成，2007；毛赟，邱天河，2007；尚琼，2011），此外还有 AntConc，以及许家金、贾云龙开发的 PowerConc（2013）。桌面版双语检索软件不如单语检索软件丰富，较为知名的有 ParaConc，常用的有贾云龙开发的检索工具。第二类是网络版检索工具，如中国英汉平行语料库的检索平台（王克非，2012）以及许家金等推介的 CQPweb（2014）。

我们在《基于 CAT 及语料库技术的电子商务翻译研究》（2016）一书中对语料库检索工具做了较为详尽的介绍，如 WordSmith、PowerGrep、ParaConc，等等。本章仅介绍福建世界遗产语料库中双语对应语料库的检索。所用工具为贾云龙编制的桌面版检索工具（以下简称贾云龙工具）以及我们基于 PHP 自主开发的网络版语料库检索平台（以下简称网络检索平台）。

3.2　双语对应语料库的检索

3.2.1　贾云龙工具

贾云龙开发的检索工具支持单语和双语检索，功能较为简单，但对于双语对应语料库的检索而言，不但实用，而且易用。

该检索工具为绿色软件，无须安装。软件目录内有一个 data 文件夹，将 TXT 文本文件置于 data 文件夹内，即可运行"检索 .exe"。输入检索关键词后，该检索工具会对 data 文件夹内的全部 TXT 文件进行检索，检索结果以网页的形式呈现。检索的方式是逐行检索，包含检索关键词的文本行会被提取出来，显示在检索结果中，支持中英文单语及双语检索，如图 3-1 和图 3-2。

No	Text	Line	File
1	同时，佛教信仰也有着广泛的信徒，在明代即已存在的**日光岩**寺建筑格局规整，且具有典型的闽南传统佛教寺庙的特点，见证了佛教信仰在当地的源远流长。 Meanwhile, Buddhism also attracts numerous followers. The Sunlight Rock Temple, built as early as in the Ming dynasty, has a regular architectural layout with the characteristics of typical traditional Buddhist temples in southern Fujian.	25	鼓浪屿世界遗产双语语料库.txt
2	1927年由鼓浪屿华人议事会会众多医院牵头筹委，以越南黄仲训主动捐献**日光岩**附近地产改造而成的延平公园，为厦门第一处公园，至今仍是最受欢迎的游览场所。 Yanping Park, the first park in Xiamen and still a place most visited today, was an initiative led by Kulangsu Chinese Council, and built on the land near Sunlight Rock which was donated by the Indonesian Overseas Chinese Huang Zhongxun in 1927.	87	鼓浪屿世界遗产双语语料库.txt
3	同样，镌刻于**日光岩**延平文化遗迹周边岩石上的摩崖题记，也以诗歌的形式表达其奋斗志业的雄心。 The poetry inscriptions on Sunlight Rock as part of Yanping Cultural Relics were also written by local and returned Chinese to show their aspiration.	99	鼓浪屿世界遗产双语语料库.txt
4	同时，工部局时期还在《鼓浪屿工部局规例》中特意将**日光岩**、鼓浪石、鸡母石、笔架山、燕尾石等标志性的自然景观要素认定为"名胜石"，明确提出不得对其进行破坏。 During the period of the Municipal Council, Kulangsu Municipal Council Regulations specially regarded Sunlight Rock, Kulang Stone, Jimu Stone, Bacon Hill, Yanwei Stone and other symbolic natural landscape elements as "Scenic Stones", clearly indicating that no damage was allowed to these stones.	127	鼓浪屿世界遗产双语语料库.txt
5	**日光岩**、燕尾山、升旗山等标志性的自然景观要素，以及依托自然山体而形成的延平文化遗迹等要素，都成为遗产构成的重要组成部分，它们在今天仍发挥着重要的景观价值，在社区发展中得到了妥善的保护。 Sunlight Rock, Yanwei Hill, Flag Raising Hill, and Yanping Cultural Relics are still with great landscape values, and are well-protected in today.	161	鼓浪屿世界遗产双语语料库.txt
6	a)**日光岩**、燕尾山、升旗山等自然景观要素均保持着其原有位置、景观形态的历史特征，延续了周边环境的主要特征和感受；相关文化遗迹则保持其原有位置、形态和材料特征，以及周边环境的历史特征。 a) Sunlight Rock, Yanwei Hill, and Flag Raising Hill retain the historic features as a natural landscape on the original location as well as the surrounding setting; related cultural relics still in their original forms and material stand on the original location and surrounded by the historic setting.	213	鼓浪屿世界遗产双语语料库.txt

图 3-1　贾云龙工具双语检索

No	Text	Line	File
1	Various architectural styles including traditional southern Fujian style, veranda colonial style, western classical revival style, modern style and Art Deco met together here and formed the unique **Amoy** Deco Style integrating vernacular architectural features in the multicultural island, and exerting influence to other coastal areas.	13	鼓浪屿世界遗产英文文库.txt
2	The mansions and home gardens built by returned overseas Chinese on Quanzhou Road and Anhai Road, especially the buildings of the 1920s with **Amoy**-deco style have vividly exhibited the great creativity of integration of Eastern and Western cultures in architecture design, construction techniques and landscape design.	20	鼓浪屿世界遗产英文文库.txt
3	Western-style buildings of overseas Chinese were developed in two phases – localization of veranda style and **Amoy**-Deco Style, best representing communication and fusion of diverse cultures of Kulangsu.	44	鼓浪屿世界遗产英文文库.txt
4	In 1920s to 1930s, the unique **Amoy**-Deco style became quite popular on Kulangsu, inscription which was a more brave combination of the traditional southern Fujian architectural style and foreign veranda type.	48	鼓浪屿世界遗产英文文库.txt
5	**Amoy**-Deco Style was represented by the Kulangsu Huang Cimin Villa, the middle building of Hai Tian Tang Gou Mansion, Yang Family Mansion, which further influenced the modern architecture design on Xiamen island, Zhangzhou and Quanzhou area of southern Fujian.	50	鼓浪屿世界遗产英文文库.txt
6	In terms of construction techniques, the villa or western-style buildings in the early period and **Amoy**-Deco mansions in the late 20th century all exhibit the combinations between western structure with the traditional material, masonry techniques and decorative techniques of the southern Fujian.	54	鼓浪屿世界遗产英文文库.txt

图 3-2　贾云龙工具单语检索

贾云龙工具支持同时检索 data 文件夹内所有文件并呈现结果，此外还支持正则检索，可以用于翻译文本的质量评估。例如，我们用"闽南"作为关键词，检索鼓浪屿申遗文本双语语料，得到检索结果 59 条，如图 3-3：

No	Text	Line	File
54	在特殊的管理模式作用下，通过**闽南**本土居民、外来多国侨民和还乡华侨群体的共同管理，鼓浪屿发展成为具有突出文化多样性和近代化生活范式的国际社区，成为活跃在东亚和东南亚地区各国侨民、各界精英的理想居所，是19世纪中叶到20世纪中叶这一地区体现现代人居环境理念的独特范例。 Under the special Sino-foreign joint management mode, through the concerted construction of local Chinese, returned overseas Chinese, and foreign residents from many other countries, Kulangsu developed into an international settlement with outstanding cultural diversities and modern living quality, as an ideal dwelling place for the overseas Chinese and elites who were active in East Asia and Southeastern Asia as well as a unique demonstration that embodies modern habitat concepts of the period between mid-19th century and mid-20th century.	433	鼓浪屿世界遗产双语语料库.txt
55	鼓浪屿的发展历程，不仅可以清晰地追溯外来文化的传播过程，更展现出历经海外闽落的**闽南**移民群体对近代土早期现代化基本特征的塑造。 The development process of Kulangsu not only demonstrates clearly the spread of foreign cultures but also the shaping of the basic characteristics of early modernization by the southern Fujian people who returned from their oversea lands.	436	鼓浪屿世界遗产双语语料库.txt
56	**闽南**传统风格、殖民地外廊式、西方古典复兴式、现代主义风格、装饰艺术风格等建筑风格汇聚于此，并在多元文化交流的土壤中生发出具有本土建筑特征的"厦门装饰风格"，影响福厦则沿海其他区域。 Various architectural styles including traditional southern Fujian style, veranda colonial style, western classical revival style, modern style and Art Deco met together here and formed the unique Amoy Deco Style integrating vernacular architectural features in the multicultural island, and exerting influence to other coastal areas.	441	鼓浪屿世界遗产双语语料库.txt
57	在早期全球化的浪潮中，鼓浪屿从19世纪中期到20世纪中期的发展轨迹是中国步入近代化历程的缩影，更是**闽南**移民文化开拓性和包容性的突出见证。 During the early waves of globalization, the development track of Kulangsu from the mid-19th century to the mid-20th centurymis an epitome of China's stepped in the contemporary times, and culture of southern Fujian.	444	鼓浪屿世界遗产双语语料库.txt
58	衍生自中原汉文化，吸收了当地海洋精神的**闽南**文化，自古以来就具有对汉文化核心价值的坚守和对异质文化的开放。 The migration culture of southern Fujian, an outstanding evidence of the pioneering and inclusive migration for originating from the ancient Chinese culture in the central plainsand absorbing the local maritime spirit, has featured the adherence to the core values of the ancient Chinese culture and the openness to heterogeneous cultures.	445	鼓浪屿世界遗产双语语料库.txt
59	19世纪后，大批**闽南**本土居民移民海外，成为全球化浪潮中文化、资本、信息交流的重要桥梁，构建了更具时代特色的移民文化。 Since the 19th century, a great number of people from southern Fujian emigrated, became an important bridge for the communications of cultures, capital and information during the globalization wave and built the immigration culture with the characteristics of the epoch.	446	鼓浪屿世界遗产双语语料库.txt

图 3-3　贾云龙工具检索"闽南"

从图 3-3 可以看出，“闽南”一律翻译为“southern Fujian”，那有没有翻译为“Minnan”的例子呢？当然可以用人工查看的方式将 59 条检索结果逐一查看，或者是在网页页面搜索“Minnan”，但贾云龙工具的正则检索功能提供了更直接的检索方法，即多个关键词组合检索，检索方式为“关键词 1. * 关键词 2. * 关键词 3”，余类推。

输入“闽南 . *Minnan”，检索结果如图 3-4：

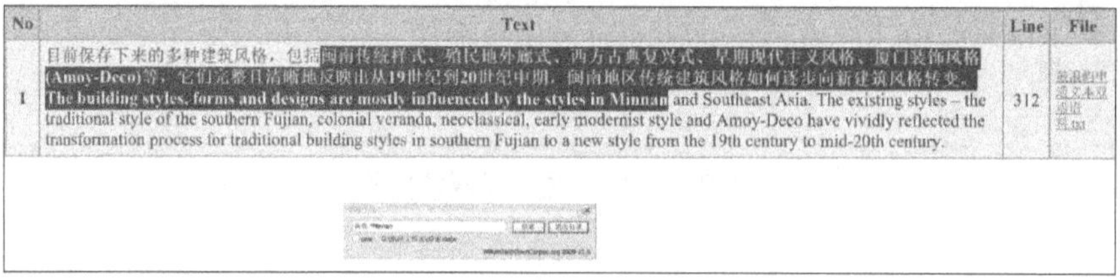

No	Text	Line	File
1	目前保存下来的多种建筑风格，包括闽南传统样式、殖民地外廊式、西方古典复兴式、早期现代主义风格、厦门装饰风格(Amoy-Deco)等，它们完整且清晰地反映出从19世纪到20世纪中期，闽南地区传统建筑风格如何逐步向新建筑风格转变。The building styles, forms and designs are mostly influenced by the styles in Minnan and Southeast Asia. The existing styles – the traditional style of the southern Fujian, colonial veranda, neoclassical, early modernist style and Amoy-Deco have vividly reflected the transformation process for traditional building styles in southern Fujian to a new style from the 19th century to mid-20th century.	312	鼓浪屿申遗文本双语语料.txt

图 3-4　贾云龙工具检索“闽南 .*Minnan”

图 3-4 仅一条检索结果，其文字内容为：

目前保存下来的多种建筑风格，包括<u>闽南</u>传统样式、殖民地外廊式、西方古典复兴式、早期现代主义风格、厦门装饰风格（Amoy-Deco）等，它们完整且清晰地反映出从 19 世纪到 20 世纪中期，闽南地区传统建筑风格如何逐步向新建筑风格转变。

The building styles, forms and designs are mostly influenced by the styles in ***<u>Minnan</u>*** and Southeast Asia. The existing styles—the traditional style of the southern Fujian, colonial veranda, neoclassical, early modernist style and Amoy-Deco have vividly reflected the transformation process for traditional building styles in southern Fujian to a new style from the 19th century to mid-20th century.

该句译文并未将“闽南”译为“southern Fujian”，而是译为“Minnan”，从该检索结果我们似乎可以得出一个结论，即鼓浪屿申遗文本在术语统一方面做得不错，但仍存在术语不统一的现象。以下是鼓浪屿申遗文本中“闽南”的 59 条检索结果中的 50 条，摘录于此，供参考。

鼓浪屿申遗文本“闽南”检索样例 50 条：

1. 在特殊的管理模式作用下，通过闽南本土居民、外来多国侨民和还乡华侨群体的共同营建，鼓浪屿发展成为具有突出文化多样性和近代化生活品质的国际社区，成为活跃在东亚和东南亚地区各国侨民、各界精英的理想居所，是 19 世纪中叶到 20 世纪中叶这一地区体现现代人居环境理念的独特范例。

Under the special Sino-foreign joint management mode, through the concerted construction of local Chinese, returned overseas Chinese, and foreign residents from many other countries, Kulangsu developed into an international settlement with outstanding cultural diversities and modern living quality, also became an ideal dwelling place for the overseas Chinese and elites who were active in East Asia and Southeastern Asia as well as a unique demonstration that embodies modern habitat concepts of the period between mid-19th century and mid-20th century.

2. 鼓浪屿的发展历程，不仅可以清晰地追溯外来文化的传播过程，更展现出历经海外闯荡的闽南移民群体对故土早期现代化基本特征的塑造。

The development process of Kulangsu not only demonstrates clearly the spread of foreign cultures but also the shaping of the basic characteristics of early modernization by the southern Fujian people who returned from their overseas adventures.

3. 闽南传统风格、殖民地外廊式、西方古典复兴式、现代主义风格、装饰艺术风格等建筑风格汇聚于此，并在多元文化交流的土壤中生发出具有本土建筑特征的"厦门装饰风格"，影响辐射到沿海其他区域。

Various architectural styles including traditional southern Fujian style, veranda colonial style, western classical revival style, modern style and Art Deco met together here and formed the unique Amoy Deco Style integrating vernacular architectural features in the multicultural island, and exerting influence to other coastal areas.

4. 本土宗教在鼓浪屿的传承源远流长：供奉闽南地方守护神——保生大帝的种德宫，是一座规模不大却极富闽南传统装饰色彩的宗教场所，至今依旧香火鼎盛。

Kulangsu's local religion has been passed down from ancient times: The Zhongde Taoist Temple, enshrining the local guardian of southern Fujian, the God of Medicines, is a small religious place with a unique southern Fujian decorative style. Today many people are attracted to burn incense and worship there.

5. 同时，佛教信仰也有着广泛的信徒，在明代即已存在的日光岩寺建筑格局规整，且具有典型的闽南传统佛教寺庙的特点，见证了佛教信仰在当地的源远流长。

Meanwhile, Buddhism also attracts numerous followers. The Sunlight Rock Temple, built as early as in the Ming dynasty, has a regular architectural layout with the characteristics of typical traditional Buddhist temples in southern Fujian. It witnessed the long history of development of Buddhism in this area.

6. 另一方面，早在19世纪40年代，美国公理会传教士雅裨理、美国圣公会传教士文惠廉（1842年）、英国伦敦会传教士施约翰夫妇（1844年）等人即以鼓浪屿为基地向闽南内陆地区传播基督教。

On the other hand, David Abeel of the American Congregational Church, William Jones Boone of American Episcopal Church (1842) and Mr. and Mrs. John Thie of the British London Missionary Society (1844) took Kulangsu as a foundation to spread Christianity in southern Fujian in the 1840s.

7. 于1934年动工兴建的三一堂，为厦门港礼拜堂、新街礼拜堂和竹树脚礼拜堂三个基督堂会联合修建，且专门聘请中国建筑师进行建筑设计，该礼拜堂至今仍为鼓浪屿社区基督教徒所使用，强有力地彰显了闽南基督教的本土化。

The Trinity Church built by the three Christian congregations at Xiamen Chapel, Xinjie Chapel and Zhushujiao Chapel in 1934 was designed by a Chinese architect and is still used today by Christians living on Kulangsu, a strong evidence of the localization of western religions in southern Fujian.

8. 根据风水堪舆学"背山面水"的选址原则，早期中国传统住区主要集中在今内厝澳、岩仔脚、鹿耳礁三片区域，街区肌理由闽南红砖大厝形成的合院式建筑构成，现海坛路的四落大厝、大夫第等院落式建筑即是岩仔脚片区传统闽南住区的典型代表。

As accordance with the principle of Chinese feng shui theory, it is best to select a residential place that is "facing water with hills on the back". So early Chinese settlements on Kulangsu mainly lived in three areas at Neicuo'ao, Yanzaijiao, and Lu'erjiao where urban fabric was comprised by red-brick courtyard buildings of southern Fujian. The existing Four-courtyard Mansion, Dafudi Courtyard and other courtyard building complexes on Haitan Road are typical examples of the traditional southern Fujian residential courtyard buildings in Yanzaijiao area.

9. 以四落大厝、大夫第为代表的闽南红砖厝民居是清代地方传统民居的典型代表，建筑采用院落式布局，材料上使用当地常见的红砖，以燕尾脊等构件或灰塑工艺进行细部装饰。

The red-brick courtyard mansion represented by the Four-courtyard Mansion and Dafudi Courtyard Mansion was the typical example of local traditional residence of Southern Fujian in Qing Dynasty. The building complex, built with red bricks, a common local building material, was organized by courtyards and decorated with swallow-tail spinal or grey-model technique.

10. 早期洋楼的设计在模仿殖民地外廊式建筑风格的同时，还受到东南亚地区华侨建筑，以及闽南红砖厝等传统建筑的影响。

In the early phase, overseas Chinese mansions imitated the colonial veranda style, and were influenced by the overseas Chinese residences in Southeast Asia and traditional red-brick courtyard mansions in southern Fujian.

11. 建筑外廊平面形式的处理逐渐与闽南红砖厝民居中的"塌岫"、"出龟"手法相结合，增加外廊空间的丰富性；建筑立面的柱、梁、楣、檐、栏杆等位置多采用中国吉祥图案，或以斗拱、垂花、雀替、挂落等中国传统建筑元素进行装饰，而建筑屋脊和起翘则配以闽南传统灰塑装饰。

The plan design combined the plan of veranda with the plan of "Ta You" (indent in the entrance door) and "Chu Gui" used in red-brick courtyard mansions, to enhance the spatial variation of the porch. Pillars, girders, lintels, eaves and handrails on the elevation were decorated with traditional Chinese auspicious patterns such as brackets, tassels, queti, or KULANGSU hanging fascia. Ridge and shelling were decorated by the traditional grey-models of southern Fujian.

12. 而在20世纪20到30年代，鼓浪屿形成了极具当地建筑特色的厦门装饰风格建筑，这一建筑风格可以说是对闽南传统建筑与外廊式建筑形式、中西方装饰手法更加大胆的结合。

In 1920s to 1930s, the unique Amoy-Deco Style became quite popular on Kulangsu, inscription which was a more brave combination of the traditional southern Fujian architectural style and foreign veranda type.

13. 建筑形态以正面外廊为突出特征；"四房一厅"的平面布局延续红砖厝的平面格局，强调不同功能房间的秩序性和等级性；立面构图继承红砖厝"出砖入石"的装饰习俗，多采用烟炙红砖铺面配以白石沟边；屋顶将殖民地外廊式建筑常见的坡屋顶改为屋顶平台，成为家庭重要的交往空间；细节装饰则自由地将柱式等西方传统装饰元素、现代装饰艺术风格元素和闽南装饰手法并置、结合，是鼓浪屿20世纪初至20世纪中叶最为流行的建筑样式，并充分体现出闽南华侨热烈而富于表现的民族个性。

The front veranda was the outstanding element on the facade. The plan layout as "four rooms and one hall" referenced that of red-brick courtyard to highlight that rooms of different functions were arranged in strict order. The composition of facade followed the decoration tradition of "filled with red bricks and framed with white stone" used in red-brick courtyards, taking the smoky red bricks as filling material together with margins of white stones. Slope roof commonly used in colonial veranda architectures were changed to roof deck for family public spaces. For the detail decorations, the column orders from the western style, the decorative elements from art deco style, and traditional techniques from southern Fujian were freely combined and integrated to express the warm and expressive personality of overseas Chinese in southern Fujian.

14. 厦门装饰风格建筑以鼓浪屿黄赐敏别墅、海天堂构中楼、杨家园最具代表性，进而影响到厦门本岛以及闽南漳州、泉州地区近代建筑的创作。

Amoy-Deco Style was represented by the Kulangsu Huang Cimin Villa, the middle building of Hai Tian Tang Gou Mansion, Yang Family Mansion, which further influenced the modern architecture design on Xiamen island, Zhangzhou and Quanzhou area of southern Fujian.

15. 与建筑设计相似，鼓浪屿华侨宅园的景观营造既表现出对闽南传统园林"诗情画意"山水意境的塑造，大量采用假山装饰，又结合西方古典园林的几何式格局，加入花圃、喷泉与雕塑等造园要素。

Similar to architectural design, returned overseas Chinese on Kulangsu adopted both Chinese and western landscape design measures and elements to create a unique character of home gardens, such as the artificial hill which was used in southern Fujian traditional gardens to create a "poetic" imagery, and the geometrical layout, flower nursery, fountains and sculptures which were common used in western classical garden.

16. 在具体的建造技术上，鼓浪屿早期的别墅洋楼式建筑和 20 世纪后的厦门装饰风格建筑均表现出西方建筑设计、结构和闽南传统材料、砖石砌筑工艺和装饰工艺的结合。

In terms of construction techniques, the villa or western-style buildings in the early period and the Amoy-Deco mansions in the late 20th century all exhibit the combinations between western structure with the traditional material, masonry techniques and decorative techniques of the southern Fujian.

17. 毓德女学堂中的"三落住宅"即是这类被动技术融合的产物，为解决建筑屋顶跨度过大的问题，本地工匠迫于技术所限只能将闽南红砖厝民居坡屋顶组合形式和外来的三角支架结构相结合，如此形成了一种有趣的屋顶形态。

The buildings with "three connected roofs" in the former A.R.C.M. Girls' School is a case in point. Restricted by the limited techniques, local craftsmen had to combine the slope roof of the red-brick courtyard residence with the foreign A-frame structure, as a solution to the exaggerated span of roof.

18. 在早期全球化的浪潮中，鼓浪屿从 19 世纪中期到 20 世纪中期的发展轨迹是中国步入近代化历程的缩影，更是闽南移民文化开拓性和包容性的突出见证。

During the early waves of globalization, the development track of Kulangsu from the mid-19th century to the mid-20th century is an epitome of China's stepped in the contemporary times, and an outstanding evidence of the pioneering and inclusive migration culture of southern Fujian.

19. 衍生自中原汉文化，吸收了当地海洋精神的闽南文化，自古以来就兼具对汉文化核心价值的坚守和对异质文化的开放。

The migration culture of southern Fujian, originating from the ancient Chinese culture in the central plains and absorbing the local maritime spirit, has featured the adherence to the core values of the ancient Chinese culture and the openness to heterogeneous cultures.

20. 19 世纪后，大批闽南本土居民移民海外，成为全球化浪潮中文化、资本、信息交流的重要桥梁，构建了更具时代特色的移民文化。

Since the 19th century, a great number of people from southern Fujian emigrated, became an important bridge for the communications of cultures, capital and information during the globalization wave and built the immigration culture with the characteristics of the epoch.

21. 在这漫长的历史过程中，经由中原移民携带的汉民族文化与土著文化不断融合，经过沉积、发酵后形成了在中国传统文化中举足轻重的一支亚文化——闽南文化，这种移民文化也因此兼具深厚的民族特性、宽阔的包容力以及开放的海洋精神，闽南地区很早就与东南亚地区、西方国家之间建立了密切的海上商贸往来，即是这种文化传统的突出表现。

In this long historical course, the Han national culture brought by migrants from the central plains and the indigenous culture kept integrating, and after sedimentation and evolution, an extremely important subculture in the central plains' traditional culture—the southern Fujian culture was formed. As a result, this migrant culture also has profound national quality, broad inclusiveness and open maritime spirit: the establishment of close business and trade ties between the southern Fujian area and the Southeast Asia and Western countries is a prominent manifestation of such cultural traditions.

22. 1727 年清政府取消南洋禁航令后，厦门成为中国与东南亚地区海上贸易唯一的合法口岸，目前鼓浪屿岛上保存完好的 18 世纪西班牙船商墓碑，即默默地为本土闽南居民与西方文化的早期接触提供了佐证。

When the Qing dynasty lifted the ban on maritime trade with the Southeast Asia in 1727, Xiamen became the only legitimate port for maritime trade between China and Southeast Asia. The tombstone of a Spanish merchant of the 18th century well preserved on the Kulangsu Island now is a silent witness to the early contact between southern Fujian's local inhabitants and the Western culture.

23. 然而在第一次鸦片战争之前，这种因移民带来的文化交往过程是缓慢而温和的，此时鼓浪屿仍是一个处于闽南文化影响下的传统住区，集中于内厝澳、岩仔脚、鹿耳礁的中国社区以四落大厝、大夫第、黄氏小宗为代表的闽南红砖厝建筑组成，周围分布有大片农田。

However, before the First Opium War, the course of such cultural exchange brought by migrants was slow and mild. At that time, Kulangsu was still a traditional settlement under the influence of the southern Fujian culture. The Chinese settlements at Neicuo'ao, Yanzaijiao, and Lu'erjiao were formed by the typical red brick courtyard houses, represented by the Four-courtyard Mansion,

Dafudi Courtyard Mansion and Huang's Ancestral Hall, surrounded by a large area of farmland.

24. 岛内现存众多海关建筑和商贸类建筑和遗址，包括海关理船厅公所、海关验货员公寓、英国和记洋行仓库遗址、英商亚细亚火油公司、汇丰银行公馆等，以及提供跨国通讯服务的丹麦大北电报公司旧址，都展示出鼓浪屿这一时期与海上跨国贸易的紧密联系，以一系列显著改善了鼓浪屿的卫生条件和环境质量的道路网络、基础设施和住区建设，记载了这一时期外国侨民初步推动其从一个闽南传统住区向着近代社区转变的足迹。

The close ties Kulangsu had with maritime multinational trade during this period are reflected by many existing buildings and sites used for customs and commerce on the island, including the former Residences of Amoy Deputy Commissioner of Customs, Amoy Maritime Affairs Office, Amoy Customs Tax Officers' Quarters, the site of former Boyd & Co Warehouse, former Office Building of British Asiatic Petroleum Company, former Residence of HSBC Bank, and former Office of Great Northern Telegraph Company (Denmark) providing multinational telecommunication services. They took a series of initiatives to construct the roads network, infrastructure and residences to improve the sanitary condition and environment quality on Kulangsu. This marked the beginning of its transformation from a traditional settlement in southern Fujian to a modern settlement pushed forward by foreign residents in this period.

25. 在西方人眼中，19世纪末的鼓浪屿已经"像欧洲南部城市一样呈现出一幅悦人心目的图画"，这无疑与闽南文化自身具有的开放性、进取性与包容力密不可分。

In the eyes of Westerners, at the end of the 19th century, Kulangsu had turned into "a city as in Southern Europe with charming scenery". This was undoubtedly inseparable from the openness, progressiveness and inclusiveness of the southern Fujian culture.

26. 同时，这里也孕育了具有鲜明地方特点的闽南移民文化，一方面继承了本土传统文化，又在此基础上吸收了西方和东南亚文化中的近代思想，以此实现对中国传统文化的革新与改良。

The southern Fujian migrant culture was also born here, with distinctive local characteristics, western cultures and modern ideas from southeastern Asian countries, manifesting reform and improvement on traditional Chinese culture.

27. 据1921年厦门海关税务司统计，"1912至1913年，在厦门和海峡殖民地之间就有50829人（华侨）返回"，与此同时，大批侨汇资金也流入厦门，成为当地乃至闽南地区城乡建设的经济支柱。

According to the statistics of the Amoy Commissioner of Customs in 1921, "a total of 50,829 persons (overseas Chinese) returned to Xiamen between 1912 and 1913". Meanwhile, influx of overseas remittances to Xiamen provided strong financial support to urban construction of Xiamen and southern Fujian.

28. 这些返乡侨民从外国，尤其是东南亚区域带回的外来文化和积极学习的态度，和自身对中国传统价值观的支持，以及因受到20世纪初"实业救国"观念的影响而将家乡市政建设改造和工商业发展作为推动社会近代化核心工具的理念，也进一步滋养了鼓浪屿独特的闽南移民文化。

The foreign cultures brought back by these returned overseas Chinese from foreign countries, especially Southeast Asia, their attitude of active study and support for traditional Chinese values as well as the idea of taking the hometown's municipal construction and industrial and commercial development as the core tool for promoting social modernization under the influence of the view of "saving the country with industry" in the early 20th century further nourished Kulangsu's unique southern Fujian migrant culture.

29. 鼓浪屿现存大量社区公共设施建筑，全面地展示出上世纪20至30年代在华侨群体的推动下社区公共生活的革新成果，见证了闽南移民文化中的开放性与进取性。

Many existing settlement and public facilities on Kulangsu fully manifesting the achievement in settlement and public life improvement promoted by returned overseas Chinese in the 1920s-1930s are witnesses to the openness and progressiveness of the southern Fujian migrant culture.

30. 鼓浪屿在形成过程中受到西方国家、东南亚区域和海外华侨文化等多元文化的影响，其文化来源的丰富性在中国近代历程中是少有的，成为闽南地方传统和外来文化的重要交汇点。

Kulangsu is influenced by the cultures of western countries, Southeast Asia and overseas Chinese during the process of development. The rich sources of culture are rare in the modern journey of China. It becomes an important intersection of local Southern Fujian traditions and foreign cultures.

福建世界遗产　双语语料库构建与应用

31. 与之相似的表现手法在鼓浪屿众多华侨洋房和宅园景观中均有体现，并在厦门装饰风格建筑中得到更为系统的展现，成为闽南移民文化标志性的美学取向。

The features as exemplified by many other similar buildings and home gardens of overseas Chinese, became mature in Amoy-Deco style, showed that overseas Chinese regarded the local characteristics as an important aspect of identity, presenting the aesthetics orientation of southern Fujian migrant culture.

32. 正是由于还乡精英群体的存在，使闽南移民文化在吸取外来文化影响后，仍表现出对传统文化的不断革新与发展，令鼓浪屿成为这种文化独特性的突出见证。

Thanks to the great efforts of the elite overseas Chinese group to renovate the traditional culture after southern Fujian migrants absorbed the essence of foreign cultures, Kulangsu became an important evidence for such cultural characteristics.

33. 闽南移民文化在鼓浪屿历史国际社区的发展历程中得到了独特的见证，其在全球化早期阶段中表现出的巨大创造力和活力为鼓浪屿百年来的迅速发展提供了真正动力，深刻地推动了鼓浪屿自闽南传统社区向近代化社区的急剧变革；尤其是20世纪后还乡华侨群体在鼓浪屿的城市建设与社区营造，集中地展示出其在社区治理、公共生活、经济、文化等方面寻求社会近代化的种种努力和成就，是闽南移民文化开放性、民族性和包容力的最佳见证。

The southern Fujian migrant culture was uniquely witnessed in the course of development of Kulangsu's historic international settlement. The great creativity and vitality shown by it in the early stage of globalization provided real momentum for Kulangsu's rapid development in about 100 years, and promoted Kulangsu's drastic change from a traditional settlement of southern Fujian to a modern settlement in depth; in particular, Kulangsu's urban construction and settlement building by returned overseas Chinese after the beginning of the 20th century epitomize their efforts to pursue modernization and achievements with respect to settlement governance, public life, economy, culture, etc., and are the best witness to the openness, nationality and inclusiveness of the southern Fujian migrant culture.

34. 不过，正是闽南移民文化特殊的形成过程，闽南本土居民、外来多国侨民和还乡华侨群体共同塑造的文化特征，使鼓浪屿的建成环境、文化品格与亚太地区同时期历史城区存在显著的不同：兼具多元性、开放性、进取性的同时深刻地体现了包容性与本土性，在对外来文化进行吸收的过程中不断寻求对传统文化的彰显，这在世界范围内是极为独特的。

However, just because of the special course of formation of the southern Fujian migrant culture and the cultural features jointly shaped by southern Fujian's local inhabitants, foreign residents from many countries and returned overseas Chinese, Kulangsu's built environment and cultural character are notably different from historic urban areas of the same period in the Asia-Pacific region: it has diversity, openness and progressiveness, meanwhile deeply reflects inclusiveness and localness, and keeps pursuing demonstration of the traditional culture in the course of absorbing foreign cultures, which is unique in the world.

35. 这里是闽南地区最早引入西医实践的地方之一：1883 年由美国归正教会创办的救世医院是厦门的第一家西式诊所，医院规模不断扩大，至 1898 年迁入现址时已在闽南地区享有盛名，而其创办者郁约翰神父也深得当地社区的爱戴，在其去世后在医院北侧建有郁约翰纪念堂。

It is one of the places in southern Fujian where practice of Western medicine was first introduced: the first western clinic of Xiamen was the Hope Hospital established by the American Reformed Church in 1883, which was expanded in scale and gained great reputation in southern Fujian when relocated to the current place in 1898. A Memorial Hall was built on the north of the hospital in memory of the founder, priest John Otte, who was respected by the local community.

36. 蒙学堂旧址（吴添丁阁）、毓德女学校旧址、安献楼等遗存则突出地见证了其完善的教育制度：蒙学堂旧址（吴添丁阁）为 1908 年由教会所创办的"蒙学堂"，即幼教机构的所在地；毓德女学校旧址为 1847 年由美国归正教会创办的女子小学和中学学堂，是闽南地区早期教会女学的代表性实例，也是厦门现代基础教育的重要基石，对于该区域女性人口素质的提升和社会地位的提升具有重要意义；安献楼则为美国安息日会所创办的美华学校的后期校舍；救世医院护士学校旧址为美国归正教会在救世医院的基础上于 1926 年开办的护士职业学校。

The site of the Enlightenment School (Wu Tianding's House), the site of A.R.C.M. Girls' School, the Anxian Hall and other relics are prominent witnesses to its sound educational system: the site of the "Enlightenment School" was the location of the "Enlightenment School" (Wu Tianding's House) established by the church in 1908 for preschool education; the Former A.R.C.M. Girls' School was established by the American Reformed Church in 1847 to provide primary and secondary education for girls, a representative example of early women's education organized by the church in southern Fujian; the Anxian Hall served as the buildings of Sino-American Primary School established by the American Sabbath Club; the Former Hope Hospital Nurses' School was set up in 1926 by the American Reformed Church following the Hope Hospital to provide vocational nursing education.

37. 1871 年在鼓浪屿开办的大北电报公司最先将电报服务引入闽南地区，是中国最早引进电报的地区之一，实现了与长崎、香港等的通信；由华侨兴办的鼓浪屿自来水公司和鼓浪屿电话公司，均引进处于当时世界范围先进水平的机电设备。

The Great Northern Telegraph Company established on Kulangsu in 1871 first introduced the telegraph service into southern Fujian, which became one of the first Chinese areas to introduce the telegraph service, and realized telecommunication with Nagasaki and Hong Kong; Kulangsu Water Supply Company and Kulangsu Telephone Company established by returned overseas Chinese had the world's advanced mechanical and electrical equipment at that time.

38. 完善且先进的公共设施使 20 世纪 30 年代的鼓浪屿成为亚太地区具有示范作用的高品质社区，进而经验推广、影响到 20 世纪的厦门，乃至闽南地区，成为近代城市化和市政建设的样板，有力地连接起当代生活与历史记忆。

The complete and advanced public facilities made Kulangsu a demonstrative high-quality settlement in the Asia-Pacific region in the 1930s, further promoted its experience and influenced Xiamen and even southern Fujian in the 20th century, and became a model influencing their urbanization and municipal construction.

39. 鼓浪屿近代居住建筑丰富的建筑风格和多样的功能形态，反映出与闽南传统红砖厝式的院落住宅截然不同的生活方式和审美取向，揭示出近代百年中国东南沿海区域城市居住建筑代表性的发展演变方向，也是构建理想人居环境的核心要素。

Rich architectural styles and diversified functional layouts of Kulangsu modern residential buildings present a lifestyle and aesthetic orientation which are totally different from traditional red brick courtyard in southern Fujian, and discloses typical development of urban residential architecture in southeast coastal regions in China over the past 100 years, which is the core elements for constructing ideal human settlement enironment.

40. 数量众多且风格多样的居住建筑和宅园景观是鼓浪屿近代国际社区的核心遗产构成要素，它们不仅展示出不同于传统闽南住区的居住习惯、形态特点，更反映出不同文化群体、不同历史时期差异化的生活理念和审美取向。

The numerous residential buildings and home gardens of different styles are the key heritage attributes in Kulangsu settlement, reflecting the living habits, forms which were different from the traditional southern Fujian residences, and the living philosophy and aesthetic orientation owned by the people of different cultures in different historic periods.

41. a) 本土文化沉淀时期的闽南传统民居、宗教建筑和相关文化遗存，展示出鼓浪屿在清代受到了闽南地区特有红砖文化传统的影响。

a) Historic Buildings constructed during the period of the local culture, including the traditional residential houses of southern Fujian, religious buildings and cultural relics, reflect that Kulangsu was influenced by the special red-brick culture traditions of southern Fujian during the Qing dynasty.

42. 随后在本土闽南文化族群、外来多国侨民和返乡华人华侨的共同推动下，鼓浪屿成为中外精英向往的理想居所，这一功能一直较好地保存并延续至今。

Later, under the joint push of local cultural groups in southern Fujian, foreign residents from many countries and returned and overseas Chinese, Kulangsu became an ideal place where Chinese and foreign elites aspired to live. This function has been well preserved and continued till today.

43. 鼓浪屿形成发展的特殊地理、历史背景，以其保存完整的自然景观、道路结构、街区肌理、社区公共建筑和设施遗存、风格多样的居住建筑，集中地展现出 19 世纪中叶至 20 世纪中叶百年间中国传统文化与外来多元文化急剧的交流和融合，见证了多元文化群体在传统社会近代化历程中的

福建世界遗产 双语语料库构建与应用

重要作用，及闽南移民文化具有的开放性、包容性和革新力，成为亚太地区体现现代人居理念国际社区的独特实例。

The unique geographic location, historic background, and well-preserved natural landscape, roads, urban fabrics, public buildings and facilities, residential houses of different styles have exhibited the drastic communication and fusion between the traditional Chinese culture and the foreign cultures during the 100 years since the mid-19th century to the mid-20th century. It has witnessed the important role played by multicultural groups in the modernization of the traditional society in the early 20th century, the unique open, inclusive and innovative culture held by the southern Fujian migrants. It is an extraordinary example of the international human settlement in modern times in the Asian-Pacific region.

44. 也正是闽南移民文化具有的强大活力，使鼓浪屿在繁荣时期的文化特性不是单纯地模仿、照搬西方思想，而是在此基础上加入了闽南本土居民、华侨群体对中国传统文化的认识与革新。

The dominant culture of the overseas Chinese of southern Fujian was showing strong vitality. For the development of Kulangsu, people did not simply copy the western thought but rather learned the good points to combine with the understanding of traditional Chinese culture of local residents in southern Fujian and groups of overseas Chinese.

45. 建成环境：鼓浪屿多种风格的历史建筑，反映出广泛的文化交流，并系统地呈现了 19 世纪到 20 世纪中期闽南地区本土建筑传统与外来文化的碰撞与融合历程。

Built environment: The historic buildings of different styles on Kulangsu bears testimony to the extensive cultural exchange, and collision and fusion between the architectural traditions of southern Fujian and western cultures from the 19th century to the mid-20th century.

46. 目前保存下来的多种建筑风格，包括闽南传统样式、殖民地外廊式、西方古典复兴式、早期现代主义风格、厦门装饰风格（Amoy-Deco）等，它们完整且清晰地反映出从 19 世纪到 20 世纪中期，闽南地区传统建筑风格如何逐步向新建筑风格转变。

The building styles, forms and designs are mostly influenced by the styles in Minnan and Southeast Asia. The existing styles—the traditional style of the southern Fujian, colonial veranda, neoclassical, early modernist style and Amoy-Deco have vividly reflected the transformation process from traditional building styles in southern Fujian to a new style from the 19th century to mid-20th century.

47. 而在鼓浪屿，多种文化相互融合，都在一定程度上吸收了其他文化的影响，发展出新的形态，即一种独特的闽南移民文化。

While on Kulangsu, multiple cultures mixed with each other under mutual influences and developed into new forms unique to Kulangsu, namely an unique southern Fujian migrant culture.

48. b. 鼓浪屿是闽南移民文化的见证——在全球化早期进程中，以华侨为代表的具有移民特质的多元文化群体，显著地推动了鼓浪屿城市发展和近代化进程，在体现开拓性和包容性的同时兼具传统文化和本土性的表达，塑造出独特的城市历史景观和以厦门装饰风格为代表的建筑样式，这一特殊的近代化进程在中国近代史中是极其特殊的。

b. Kulangsu is a witness to southern Fujian migrant culture—During the early stage of globalization, multicultural groups with immigrant characteristics represented by overseas Chinese greatly promoted the modernization of the city and development of Kulangsu. Great attention has been paid to the expression of the traditional culture and local culture and demonstration of innovation and inclusiveness, which resulted in the unique urban historical landscapes and the architectural styles as represented by the Amoy-Deco style. This is special in the modern history of China.

49. 鼓浪屿所处的地理区位、历史和政治背景，使之形成了独特的社区管理方式；来自欧美地区、东南亚地区的文化和地方传统闽南文化相互碰撞与融合，在文化方面形成了罕见的多元性和杂糅的特点。

Kulangsu settlement was under a unique management scheme applicable to the geographic location, history and political background. Cultures from Europe, America and the Asian-Pacific region collided with the local traditional Southern Fujian culture.

50. 鼓浪屿与中国近代同主题文化遗产在发展时期上存在相似性，但它在很多方面具有自身的特殊性：在社区管理方式上采用的华洋共管模式；在文化特征上反映出的多元文化的互鉴、影响和融合，以及闽南移民文化的开拓性、包容性与本土性特征；在城市功能上，展示出近代社区生活公共设施和人居环境理念的先进性；在建成环境形态上表现出整体的完整性；在建筑风格上表现出多样性和对地方传统的表达。这使它在中国近代城市发展历程中具有极高的独特性，成为中国反映多元文化相互融合特征的近代社区的罕见实例。

Kulangsu and Chinese modern cultural heritage with the same theme are similar in terms of development period. Kulangsu was managed similar to an autonomy where multinational expatriates and Chinese worked together reflecting the mutual reference, influence and fusion of multiculture, and the innovation, inclusiveness and local characteristics of southern Fujian migrant culture. With the advanced public facilities and concepts in human settlement environment, integrity of built environment, expression of the diverse cultures and local traditions in the architecture style, help demonstrate the uniqueness of Kulangsu in the development process of a Chinese modern city, an extraordinary modern settlement which reflected the fusion of multinational cultures in China.

从以上样例，可以看出，"闽南"一词，在鼓浪屿申遗文本中绝大多数情况下都译为"southern Fujian"，偶尔不译。故"Minnan"这一孤译，可判定为译者疏漏所致。

3.2.2 网络检索平台

为了 CCAT 平台的语料库资源利用，我们自主开发了语料库网络检索平台，支持单语及双语检索，平台登录界面如图 3-5：

该检索平台支持用户注册，即可以对外部用户开放，但目前仅在教学中面向学生开放。

该平台已开发的功能较多，如支持多个关键词组合检索，支持正则检索，等等。此外，还支持一些自主学习功能。其检索结果界面如图 3-6。

图 3-5 语料库检索平台登录界面

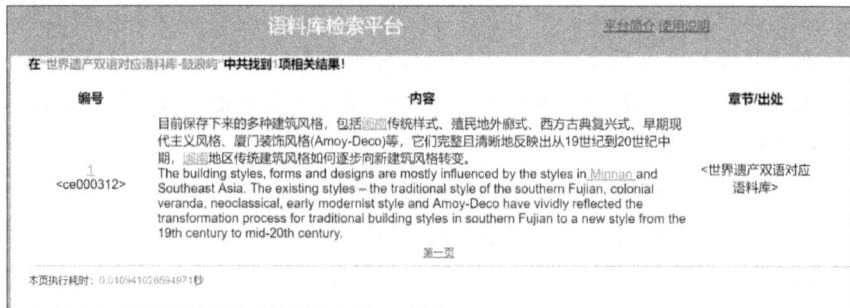

图 3-6　语料库检索平台 "闽南" 和 "Minnan" 组合检索

3.3　小结

本章介绍的双语对应语料库检索工具，其特点是简单易用。我们认为，检索工具不一定是越复杂越好，应尽量简单易用。同理，双语语料库的构建也应考虑构建的效率和格式的兼容性，以能支持简单易用的检索工具为佳。

目前双语语料库检索工具仍以桌面版居多，但未来网络版双语语料库检索平台的开发和应用将成为趋势，它们将更具开放性、兼容性、易用性。

第 4 章　福建世界遗产翻译质量评估

4.1　引言

构建福建世界遗产双语语料库并与 CAT 结合，主要目的和作用之一是对福建世界遗产翻译质量进行基于实证语料的评估。本章的评估对象包括福建世界遗产的申遗文本、景区文本、酒店介绍、导游词。评估根据世界遗产翻译的"信、达、效"原则，采用基于 CCAT 的评估模式，基于大量语料展开，发现了一些不易察觉的问题，如术语不统一、申遗译文文本与申遗原生英文文本在风格方面的差异，等等。

4.2　世界遗产翻译的"信、达、效"原则

我国翻译活动最早可追溯到周朝时期，迄今已有 3000 多年的历史，提出了众多的翻译标准和原则，如佛经翻译的"五不翻原则"，严复的"信、达、雅"，傅雷的"重神似不重形似"，钱钟书的"化境论"，刘重德的"信、达、切"，许渊冲的"新译论"，等等（王朝晖，余军，2016：49）。

但这些翻译标准和原则主要是针对文学翻译提出的，对于应用翻译范畴内的世界遗产翻译而言，并不完全适用。

应用翻译主要指商贸、法律、金融、广告、医药、旅游、新闻等各类应用文本的翻译。

十几年来，有关应用翻译的理论及原则标准，学界的探讨层出不穷，提出了各种相关理论和原则标准。

（1）商务翻译："忠实、准确、统一"（刘法公，2002）；"忠实、通顺和地道"（叶玉龙，等，1998）；"创译原则和功能主义原则"（张新红，李明，2003）；"达意、传神和表形"（恒齐，隋云，2003）；"变通原则"（李明清，2009）；借鉴国外翻译理论的"目的论"（谭美云，2011）；"准确性原则、功能性原则、规范性原则和文化调适原则"（姜荷梅，2011）；等等。

（2）法律翻译："使用庄严词语、准确性、精练性、术语一致性、使用专业术语"（邱贵溪，2000）；"准确严密、庄重得体、地道规范"（栗长江，2005）；"法律翻译合适性"（杜金榜，2005）；"公正性、准确性、合适性"（余婷，2007）；"模糊度对等"

（夏远利，2007）；"译名同一律原则"（刘迎春，王海燕，2008）；"静态对等策略"（李克兴，2010）；"专业性、严谨性、准确性和等效性"（熊德米，熊姝丹，2011）；"精准性、规范性、简明性"（李楠，2012）；"一致性"（吕万英，2018）；等等。

（3）旅游翻译："主题信息突出策略原则"（曾利沙，2005）；"合作原则的数量准则、质量准则、关联准则和方式准则"（袁式亮，2011）；景点名称翻译的"全名译音＋通名译意原则"（牛新生，2013）；"信息再创造原则"（乌永志，2012）；"模糊对等"（张慧，2010）；等等。

此外，有关应用翻译的原则标准还有："目的指导下的功能原则与规范原则"（杨清平，2007）；"目的—需求原则、文本优化—重写原则、平行文本对照修改原则"（刘红新，2014）；"合规、达意、识别、有为、异为"（赖德富，2015a）；等等。

这些翻译原则或标准面向具体应用翻译领域，针对性强，具有可操作性和应用性。尤其是方梦之提出的应用翻译"达旨、循规、喻人"三原则（2007），"从语言文化的框架内脱离出来，主要从翻译效果角度界定应用翻译的原则，是一大进步"（王朝晖，余军，2016：62）。

在应用探讨上，文军等（2007）从语篇功能的角度创建了博物馆解说词适度摘译的基本模式；李德超和王克非（2009）提出了"旅游英译的平行文本比较模式"，在 Werlich 文本语法的基础上，提出了一种适用于非文学翻译，特别是旅游英译的平行文本比较模式。

在理论建构上，黄忠廉之"变译理论"、胡庚申之"翻译生态学"、周领顺之"译者行为研究"，已为研究者所熟知（杨荣广，黄忠廉，2016）；曾利沙、李燕娜（2011）提出了"翻译研究的经验模块与理论模块的建构"这一范畴理论；黄忠廉提出"应用翻译学创建论"的构想，在应用翻译研究系统性理论的创建上有了重大突破（贾文波，2014：88）。

以上应用翻译的理论探讨主要是在语言文化框架内展开的，推动了应用翻译研究及实践的发展。但在大数据、"互联网＋"、云时代的技术背景下，语言服务行业翻译技术的发展远远超过了传统讨论的步伐。理论的探讨终归要应用于实践，要落到实地，有益于语言服务行业的发展，有利于翻译产品质量的提高，这才是理论研究的应有之义，但在应用翻译研究领域，结合翻译技术的探讨非常之少。王华树（2012：62）认为，也许译学研究在信息化时代的背景下会出现"Technological Turn"。谢天振（2012：13）则认为，当今的翻译发展已经进入了以实用文献为主流翻译对象的"非文学翻译阶段"，"已经从'书房'进入到了'作坊'，对翻译史而言，我们今天所处的时代已经是翻译的职业化时代了"。

应用翻译标准的探讨应将翻译技术包括在内，并与语言服务行业相结合，注重实用，真正能对应用翻译实践起到促进作用。

我们曾在前人理论的基础上，提出电子商务翻译的"信、达、效"三字原则，并予以这三字新的解释（王朝晖，余军，2016：64）。这一原则，也适用于世界遗产翻译。

（1）信

在传统译论中，"信"指忠实于原文。对于世界遗产翻译而言，"信"，既指忠实于原文信息，也包括信息的传递力度。以土楼申遗文本为例，内有多个土楼的介绍，其文本格式如图4-1和图4-2：

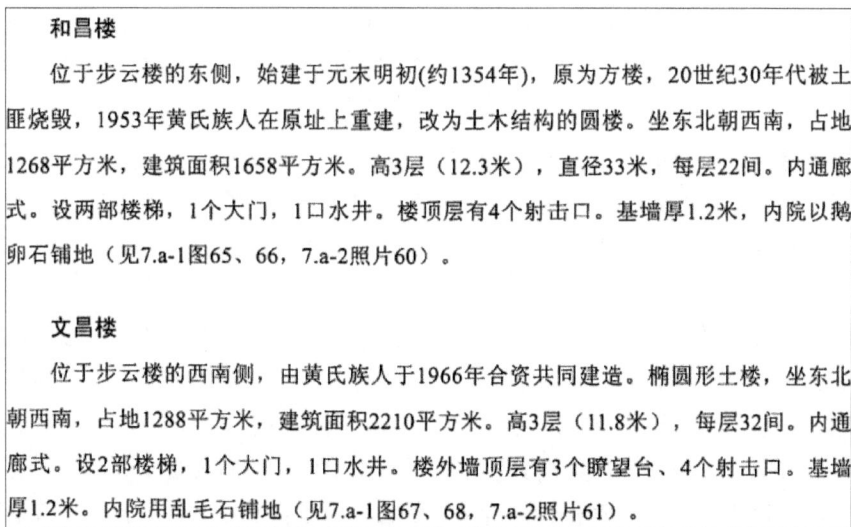

和昌楼

位于步云楼的东侧，始建于元末明初(约1354年)，原为方楼，20世纪30年代被土匪烧毁，1953年黄氏族人在原址上重建，改为土木结构的圆楼。坐东北朝西南，占地1268平方米，建筑面积1658平方米。高3层（12.3米），直径33米，每层22间。内通廊式。设两部楼梯，1个大门，1口水井。楼顶层有4个射击口。基墙厚1.2米，内院以鹅卵石铺地（见7.a-1图65、66，7.a-2照片60）。

文昌楼

位于步云楼的西南侧，由黄氏族人于1966年合资共同建造。椭圆形土楼，坐东北朝西南，占地1288平方米，建筑面积2210平方米。高3层（11.8米），每层32间。内通廊式。设2部楼梯，1个大门，1口水井。楼外墙顶层有3个瞭望台、4个射击口。基墙厚1.2米。内院用乱毛石铺地（见7.a-1图67、68，7.a-2照片61）。

图4-1　土楼介绍文本格式1

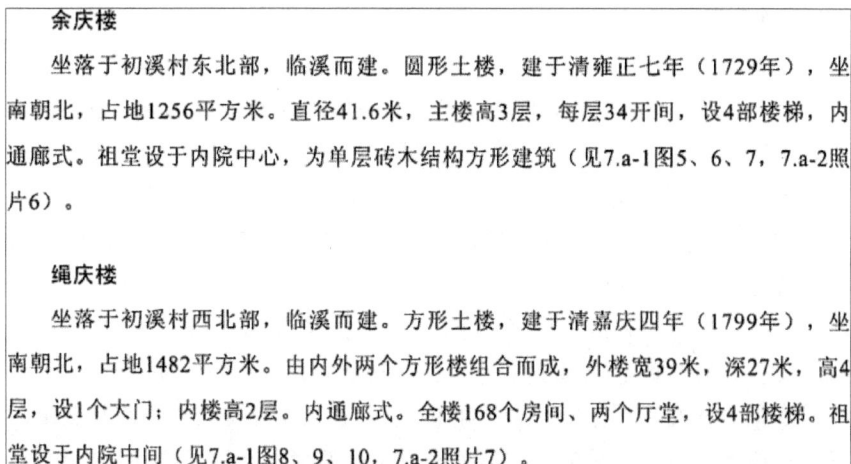

余庆楼

坐落于初溪村东北部，临溪而建。圆形土楼，建于清雍正七年（1729年），坐南朝北，占地1256平方米。直径41.6米，主楼高3层，每层34开间，设4部楼梯，内通廊式。祖堂设于内院中心，为单层砖木结构方形建筑（见7.a-1图5、6、7，7.a-2照片6）。

绳庆楼

坐落于初溪村西北部，临溪而建。方形土楼，建于清嘉庆四年（1799年），坐南朝北，占地1482平方米。由内外两个方形楼组合而成，外楼宽39米，深27米，高4层，设1个大门；内楼高2层。内通廊式。全楼168个房间、两个厅堂，设4部楼梯。祖堂设于内院中间（见7.a-1图8、9、10，7.a-2照片7）。

图4-2　土楼介绍文本格式2

从图片中可以看出，其格式为楼名单独一行，下一行的介绍文字一律不重复楼名，直接用"位于"或"坐落于"。以图 4-1 中的绳庆楼为例，如译为：

Shengqing Lou

Shengqing Lou is located…

就会受到译评家的批评，因为犯了重复的毛病，应该改为"It"。官方译文为：

Shengqing Lou

It is situated beside the creek in the northwest of Chuxi Village. Built in 1799, the 4th year of the reign of Emperor Jiaqing of the Qing Dynasty, the square Tulou facing the north occupies an area of 1482 square meters. It is composed of two square buildings, one of which is the inner building and the other is the outer building. The outer building is 39 meters in width, 27 meters in depth and 4 storeys in height, provided with a main gate, while the inner building is 2 storeys

---

图 4-3 土楼申遗文本英文译文示例

果然用的是"It"。但其实从"信"的角度即信息传递来看，这并不是一个好的译文，因为"Shengqing Lou"这个文化符号没有重复，未被凸显，削弱了其信息传播的力度。具体理据及分析见本书 6.4.2.2。

（2）达

在传统译论中，"达"指文字通顺流畅。对于世界遗产翻译而言，"达"，并非仅限于文字层面，还指信息的"达"，即"达"于受众眼中／耳中，并为其所理解。二者缺一，皆不能称之为"达"。例如，有的福建世界遗产英文网站的网站入口在易达性方面较弱，网页较难被受众检索到，故而其文本难以达于受众（见本书 5.4.1）。又如，有的导游词英文译文虽然忠实于原文，但忽略了口语和书面语的差异，导致"信"而不"达"，不为受众所理解（见本书 4.7.3 有关"明十三陵"的案例）。

（3）效

"效"，包括基本的时效，即一定时间内的翻译效率；在满足时效的前提下，还包括无效、有效、高效三个依次递进的层次。

①时效。为满足时效要求，世界遗产翻译必须重视翻译技术的应用，如 Google、Bing、有道、百度等机器翻译工具，以及雪人、Trados 等 CAT 工具。

②无效。有的译文由于忽视了文化差异，可能导致无效，例如，"Golden Cock"这一商标译名，因其译者不了解文化差异而造成失误，从"效"的角度评判，就属于无效译文（王朝晖，余军，2016：64）。

③有效。译文在"信"、"达"的基础上，在跨文化交流中不会导致障碍或误解，一般而言就是有效的。这需要多方位的努力，尤其是要注意文化差异。以上述"Golden Cock"这一无效译文为例，如果将其改为"Golden Rooster"，则

为有效译文。

④高效。指译文能取得较好效果。如土楼申遗文本将"土楼"翻译为"Tulou"，而不是"earthen building"之类的名称，对于文化符号的传播就起到了很好的作用，属于"高效"译文。

三字原则呈递进关系，相互冲突时，以最后一原则为准。以武夷山"九曲溪"的译名为例，译为"Jiuqu Stream"，忠实于原文，也符合翻译常规，合乎"信"的原则，但由于"九曲溪"已有了另一个较为通用的译名"Nine-bend Stream"，"Jiuqu Stream"在"到达"受众的时候，受众会觉得疑惑，以为是另一条溪流，从而可能导致信息传递效率变低甚至失效。由于违背了"效"这一原则，该译文就需要修改，改为通用译名"Nine-bend Stream"。就"信、达、效"的原则而言，术语统一非常重要。

4.3　基于 CCAT 的世界遗产翻译质量评估模式

翻译质量评估的研究有 40 多年的历史，相关讨论较多，如 House（1997），Reiss（2004）和 Williams（2004），尤其是 House 新出的《翻译质量评估：过去和现在》（2014），更是一部力作。国内的研究或是关于豪斯模式的介绍述评、评估参数的讨论及评估模式的修改，如屠国元、王飞虹（2003）、司显柱（2007）等人的研究；或是从不同角度阐释翻译质量评估模式，如功能语言学（司显柱，2004）、功能翻译观（周学恒，2011）以及关联理论（何三宁，2010）等。上述质量评估模式多用于文学类翻译作品的评估，与应用翻译实践联系不甚紧密。

基于 CCAT 的世界遗产翻译质量评估侧重于对语言错误、一致性的全面考察，以及与类比语料库的比较。

下面根据世界遗产翻译的"信、达、效"原则，从申遗文本、景区文本、酒店介绍、导游词等方面对福建世界遗产翻译质量进行评估。

4.4　评估个案 I——申遗文本

申遗文本的评估包括武夷山申遗译文文本和土楼申遗译文文本。考察的内容分为语言错误、一致性以及与类比语料库的比较。

4.4.1　语言错误

经考察，我们发现两个申遗译文文本都存在较多的语言错误，部分错误例证可参看第 7 章。

（1）标点

① Thus, Tulou is also called a "bustling small city" or a "little kingdom for the family"．（土楼）

说明：句号应在引号内。

② The ancestral halls within the buildings are tasteful and mostly adopt a combined style of "column and tie construction" and "post and lintel construction"．（土楼）

说明：同上。

（2）冠词

① The Tulou is located on the eastern end of this Tulou cluster and was built during the reign of Emperor Longqing in ***Ming Dynasty*** (1567-1572). （土楼）

说明：前应加"the"。

② Facing ***the*** south, this rectangle building covers an area of 3,600 square meters without stone-made wall foundation.（土楼）

说明：删除"the"。

③ The middle hall takes the shape of Chinese character 口 (Kou) and is of ***single storey***.（土楼）

说明：前加"a"。

④ The peak rises vertically like ***city wall***.（武夷山）

说明：前加"the"。

以上 4 例错误中 3 例皆来自土楼申遗文本，其中冠词错误可谓不胜枚举。如图 4-4。

N	Concordance	Set Tag Word # Ser Ser Par Par Hea Hea
1	Longqing in Ming Dynasty (1567-1572). Facing the south, this rectangle building	14,71 55 11 26 54
2	to the west of Nanxun Lou from 1958 to 1961. Facing the west, it covers an area of 870	21,83 90 10 26 90
3	west of Dongsheng Lou from 1967 to 1970. Facing the west, it covers an area of 1808	22,04 92 10 26 91
4	northeast of Yuchang Lou from 1969 to 1971. Facing the east, it covers an area of 907	22,25 93 10 26 92
5	the south of Chaoshui Lou from 1967 to 1972. Facing the north, it covers an area of 1661	22,14 93 10 26 91
6	well as 7.a-2 photos 29, 30, 31, 32 and 33). Facing the south and covering an area of	12,63 45 99 26 44
7	in the central part of Hongkeng villiage and facing the East, , the rectangular Tulou was	9,620 32 29 26 29
8	with it. The podium building has three arches facing the patio. There are some place names	18,79 76 80 26 74
9	land between mountains and besides creeks. Facing the sun, the neatly arranged Tulou	34,67 1, 10 27 64
10	and carvings, with its entrance directly facing the patio in the front. On its back wall	11,16 39 89 26 36
11	the gate of the building, so as to avoid directly facing the mountain. Thus, it produced a	32,90 1, 95 27 54
12	has a front entrance door with stone doorframe facing the front gate of the Tulou on the south	13,40 49 57 26 48
13	Guangxu (1875-1908) of the Qing Dynasty. Facing the west, this single-ring	12,36 44 79 26 42
14	the Hongchuan stream on the east. Facing the east and covering an area of 4000	10,53 36 69 26 33
15	Tulou and links with the outer front gate. Facing the Southeast, the outer front gate is	18,95 77 12 26 75
16	Chuxi Village, to the southeast of Jiqing Lou. Facing the north and covering an area of 400	8,388 26 69 26 22
17	part of Chuxi Village, south of Jiqing Lou. Facing the north and covering an area of	8,757 28 11 26 24
18	for every one or two rooms, with front one facing the ancestral hall and the back one	7,707 23 56 26 19
19	office for sales and management personnel. Facing the entrance hall are two gates opened.	18,53 74 22 26 73
20	beautiful engraved beams and painted pillars, facing the front gate of the Tulou. The door of	15,64 60 75 26 59
21	the wind and proximity to the road or river. Facing the south, most of the buildings are	4,695 10 11 26 49
22	is enclosed with one-storey supporting rooms facing the main building complex. In the case	5,035 12 73 26 69
23	one well 10 Chungui Lou 1963-1968 Square Facing the northeast, taking up a total area of	20,56 83 69 26 83
24	one well 9 Dongsheng Lou 1958-1961 Square Facing the west, taking up a total area of 870	20,53 83 63 26 83
25	and one well Yuchang Lou 1943-1947 Square Facing the southeast, taking up a total area of	20,50 83 57 26 83
26	and one well 13 Yuxing Lou 1969-1971 Square Facing the east, taking up a total area of 907	20,64 83 89 26 84
27	one well 12 Yongqing Lou 1967-1972 Square Facing the north, taking up a total area of	20,61 83 82 26 84
28	one well 11 Xiaochun Lou 1967-1970 Square Facing the west, taking up a total area of	20,58 83 76 26 83
29	Emperor Yongzheng in Qing Dynasty) Square Facing the west, taking up a total area of	20,34 83 19 26 82
30	the reign of Kangxi in Qing Dynasty) Square Facing the north, taking up a total area of 676	20,30 83 12 26 82
31	Emperor Jiangqing in Ming Dynasty) Square Facing the south, taking up a total area of	20,27 83 59 26 82
32	of Emperor Qianlong in Qing Dynasty) Square Facing the north, taking up a total area of 525	20,37 83 27 26 82
33	of Emperor Guangxu in Qing Dynasty) Square Facing the north, taking up a total area of	20,47 83 50 26 83
34	of Emperor Guangxu in Qing Dynasty) Square Facing the northeast, taking up a total area of	20,44 83 43 26 83
35	Emperor Daoguang in Qing Dynasty) Square Facing the south, taking up a total area of	20,41 83 35 26 82
36	floor of the Tulou there are four watch towers facing the four directions. Its framework is	22,60 95 82 26 93
37	Jiaqing of the Qing Dynasty, the square Tulou facing the north occupies an area of 1482	8,015 24 70 26 21
38	of the Qing Dynasty, the circular Tulou facing the north covers an area of 660 square	8,286 26 70 26 22
39	of the Qing Dynasty, the rectangular Tulou facing the north covers an area of 480 square	8,160 25 70 26 21

图 4-4　土楼申遗文本"facing the"检索

（3）词序

① This ***open entrance large cave*** is caused by a protruding peak.（武夷山）

说明：改为"large open cave"（既然"open"，"entrance"就是多余的）。

（4）数词

① Fujian Tulou concentrates in the southwestern region of Fujian Province and a total of three ***thousands*** Tulou Buildings have been found across this province.（土楼）

说明：应为"thousand"。

（5）主谓一致

① And the rainwater ***fall*** from the cliff, creating several long parallel marks like long pieces of cloth.（武夷山）

说明：应为"falls"。

4.4.2 一致性

本小节主要考察术语的一致性。经考察，土楼申遗译文和武夷山申遗译文在术语一致上总体做得不错，说明译者花了较多功夫审核校对，如武夷山申遗文本通篇"Mount Wuyi"都保持一致，没有"变异"为其他译名。土楼申遗文本也是如此，通篇都保持了"土楼"译为"Tulou"、"楼"译为"Lou"的原则。虽然如此，两者在术语一致上仍存在问题，如武夷山"九曲溪"出现多种译文（见本书6.4.1.1）。而土楼申遗译文也在几个楼名的翻译上出现问题，导致术语不一致，如图4-5：

No.	Name	Time	Type
1	Guangyu Lou	1775 (the Fortieth year of the reign of Emperor Qianlong in the Ming Dynasty)	Rectangle
2	Fuxing Lou	1821-1850(under the reign of Emperor Daoguang in the Qing Dynasty)	Rectangle
3	Guiju Lou	1834(the fourteenth year of the reign of Emperor Dongguang in the Qing Dynasty)	Square

图4-5　土楼申遗译文文本术语错误1

图4-5中"Guiju Lou"应为"Kuiju Lou"（奎聚楼），另外，该图中的"Emperor Dongguang"也错了，应为"Emperor Daoguang"。

再如：

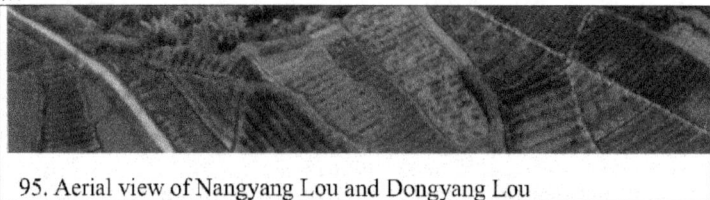

95. Aerial view of Nangyang Lou and Dongyang Lou

图4-6　土楼申遗译文文本术语错误2

图4-6中"Nangyang Lou"应为"Nanyang Lou"（南阳楼）。

术语不一致的原因有两种，一是未统一术语译名，如武夷山"九曲溪"译名，二是即便统一译法，但由于没有使用 CAT 软件，纯人工翻译，难免出错。

4.4.3 类比语料库比较

通过与原生英文申遗文本进行比较，可以考察申遗译文文本的语言特征是否与原生英文申遗文本一致或者接近一致，如差异较大，则说明译文在文体的把握上存在偏差。类比库选用的是美国及英国的原生申遗文本，美国为 San Antonio Missions，英国为 the Forth Bridge。由于申遗文本包含内容较多，例如，有一部分内容是有关遗产的保护，会附上一些法律文件，其原文／译文可能取自其他来源，并非是为申遗撰写或者翻译的，因此，为了使之具有可比性，本小节从申遗文本的遗产描述部分分别选取 10000 词进行比较。申遗译文文本与类比库中原生文本的比较主要通过语料库软件的检测进行，检测分为以下 2 类。

4.4.3.1 Readability Analyzer 易读性检测

Readability Analyzer 为许家金等编写的检测文本易读性指数的软件。4 个文本的检测数据如表 4-1：

表 4-1　武夷山、土楼申遗文本及二个类比文本的 Readability Analyzer 易读性数据

File	Reading Ease	Sentences	ASL	AWL	Word STTR	Word Types
武夷山 -10000.txt	55.8	284	16.3	4.7	0.2441	2272
土楼 -10000.txt	54.8	196	21.6	4.6	0.1859	1630
英国 -10000.txt	42.4	195	24.1	4.9	0.243	2447
美国 -10000.txt	35.5	195	24.3	5	0.1942	2028

从表 4-1 可以看出，4 个文本中，英国和美国的原生文本易读性指数最低，即难度最大，这与其作为申遗文本的特性相符；而武夷山和土楼申遗译文则难度较低，平均句长和平均词长都低于英美原生文本。该类文本是给评审专家看的，文本难度过低，则显得阐述不够深入。

4.4.3.2 Readability Studio 易读性检测

Readability Studio 软件与 Readability Analyzer 一样，可以检测文本的易读性。4 个文本的检测结果如图 4-7。

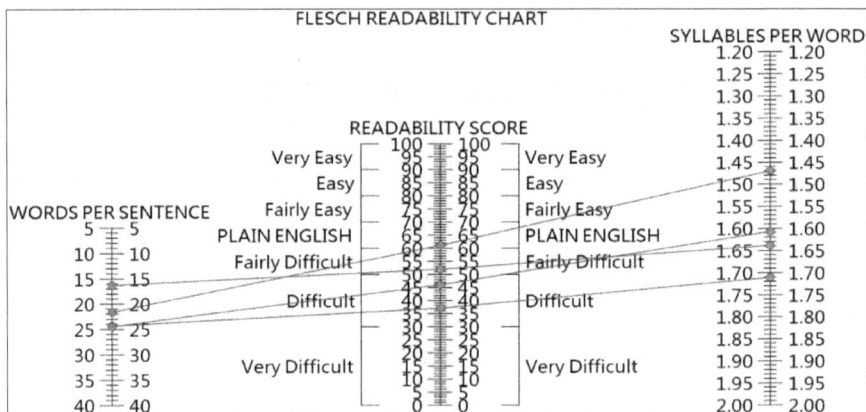

图 4-7　武夷山、土楼申遗文本及 2 个类比文本的 Readability Studio 易读性检测

易读性指数（Flesch）从高到低依次为：土楼（61），武夷山（52），英国 The Forth Bridge（46），美国 San Antonio Missions（36）。与 Readability Analyzer 的数据有些差异，但总体结论一致，即译文文本的难度低于原生文本较多。究其原因，与译文不够紧凑、用词简单有关。

4.5　评估个案 Ⅱ——景区文本

景区文本指景区实地获取的文本，如景点介绍、景区公示语、景点名称等等。有关景区文本翻译的评析，国内较为多见。其中有关福建世界遗产景区文本翻译质量评估的，就我们所见，仅 2 篇。一篇探析了景点名英译中存在的问题，并分析其缘由，讨论景点名梯级翻译标准，论述与景点名翻译对应的 5 大类翻译方法（陈孝静，唐有胜，2011）。另一篇针对武夷山景区标识用语翻译若干问题及其原因进行了简要分析（陈孝静，2008）。

本节也是以武夷山为例，评析福建世界遗产景区文本的翻译质量，评估侧重于两个方面，一是术语一致，二是语言错误。

4.5.1　武夷山景区文本的翻译质量评估

国内有关景区公示语和景点名称翻译的探讨虽然极多，但总体而言仍存在一些问题，如：有的未对景区做全面考察，个别甚至将引用过滥的例证移植到景区上；有的只是集中在孤立例证的语言表达方面，未将不同例证关联起来考察；大多只从语言层面或者语言加交际／文化层面考察，视野较窄；有的只是举出几个有问题的例证，未深入分析问题的成因，也未提出问题的有效解决办

福建世界遗产

双语语料库构建与应用

法；等等。

我们认为，景区文本的翻译应该明确其目的和功效，一是为外国游客提供服务，使其有"a home from home"的感觉，二是介绍、传播本地文化，扩大其国际影响和知名度。要实现这两个目的，需要解决目前旅游景区文本翻译普遍存在的几个问题，这些问题是我们对在武夷山景区实地考察收集的语料进行分析后得出的，真实性和代表性没有问题。

4.5.1.1 公示语翻译错误

武夷山景区的公示语翻译，据我们实地考察，并不存在太大的问题，我们在景区拍了200多张照片，图4-8是唯一一个有问题的：

"export"应改为"exit"。

图4-9中的这幅照片拍于武夷山九曲溪，"禁止游泳"译为"No Swimming"并没有问题。

这个例证非常有趣，因为陈孝静的文章提到，武夷山天游峰边的九曲溪有一则公示语，写着"Prohibit playing with water or swimming strictly beside river"

图 4-8　武夷山景区公共标识错误

图 4-9 武夷山景区"九曲溪"公示语示例

（"溪边禁止嬉水游泳"），认为该公示语出现"严禁……"等祈使、命令句，对中国普通游客来说是司空见惯，但对国外游人却过于生硬（2008：155）。我们看到的与此不同，说明景区的公示语也在改进。

4.5.1.2 英文标识不全

英文标识不全是景区文本翻译中存在的一个较为严重的问题，因为会给外国游客带来不便，如图4-10和4-11：

左边的图4-10"玉女峰"有英文标识，右边的图4-11则没有。

这种情况在景区颇为多见，就不一一举例了。

图 4-10　中英文标识完整

4-11　中英文标识不全

4.5.1.3 译名混乱

除英文标识不全外，武夷山景区文本英译存在的另一个严重问题是译名混乱，如图 4-12 和图 4-13：

图 4-12 "大红袍"译名 1

图 4-13 "大红袍"译名 2

图 4-12 中，"大红袍"译名为"Dahongpao (Scarlet Robe)"，图 4-13 中则为"Dahongpao (Big Red Robe Tea)"。但这并不是最糟糕的，著名景点"一线天"的译名多达 3 个：

① One-line-sky

② A Thread of Sky

③ Yixiantian

图 4-14 "一线天"译名 1 　图 4-15 "一线天"译名 2 　图 4-16 "一线天"译名 3

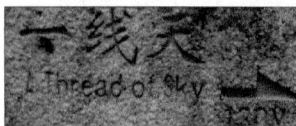

前两个会造成混淆，第三个则会让外国游客感到无助。

武夷山景区译名混乱的问题较为严重，亟须景区管理部门给予重视，予以纠正。

4.5.1.4 译与不译

与缺少英文标识、只有中文的标牌不同的是，还有一类标识的上面有字母，但只是拼音而非英文，而且与有英文的标识并置，如图4-17：

图 4-17 "音译"与意译

4.5.1.5 拼写不规范

图 4-18 拼写不规范

图4-18中的"WuYi"应为"Wuyi"。

4.5.1.6 标点错误

图 4-19 标点错误

图4-19中的顿号应改为逗号。

4.5.1.7　拼音代替译文

图 4-20　拼音代替译文

图 4-20 的"音译"没有意义，不如不译。

4.5.1.8　译文错误

图 4-21　译文错误

图 4-21 的译文错误还不算严重，因为左侧有警示图形，外国游客大体还是能理解其意。图 4-22 的景点介绍错误更多：

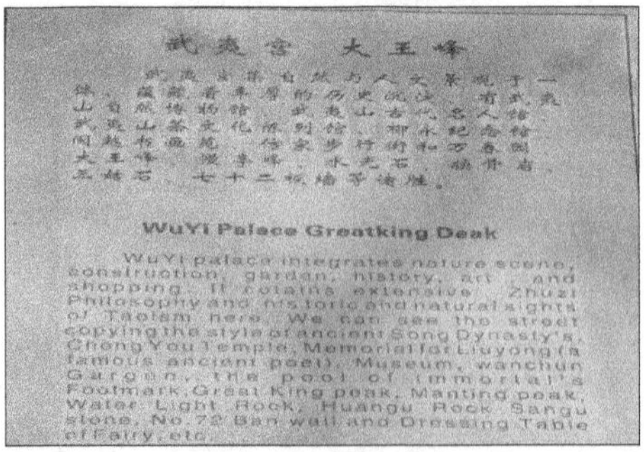

图 4-22　景点介绍

4.5.2　问题成因与对策

景区文本翻译问题是由多种因素造成的，如译者水平低下、不负责任、缺少监管，景区管理部门不懂翻译、缺少翻译质量意识、缺乏管理，等等。

景区文本翻译应像政府采购一样采取招标的方式，在一定程度上避免粗制滥造的译文流入景区。此外，在国际化发展目标下，政府应成立专门部门，对城市公示语和景区英文标识实行统一管理。

另外，景区的英文标识应设计为可以替换的纸质或者塑料制品，发现有问题的标识抽取替换即可。景区英文标识既是为了给外国游客提供便利，也是为了促进中外交流和文化传播，可以请到景区的外国游客收集错误译文，核实后进行修改。

从文化符号的传播角度来看，建议英文标识加上统一的世界遗产标志，让中英文标识都带有此标志。

文化的交流以及文化符号的传播是多渠道的，加强景区英文网站的建设，制作英文音频导游材料，如 MP3，都有助于促进景区的宣传与推广，从而吸引更多外国游客。

最后，就译员而言，应多搜集类比语料用于景区文本的翻译，例如，图 4-23 是武夷山景区票价的中英文标牌及迪士尼乐园的票价标牌，比较之下，会发现迪士尼乐园的票价标牌可给我们制作英文票价标牌提供颇多借鉴。如该标牌中并无"／人"这种用语，因为标明的价格自然就是一人一票的，无须说明。

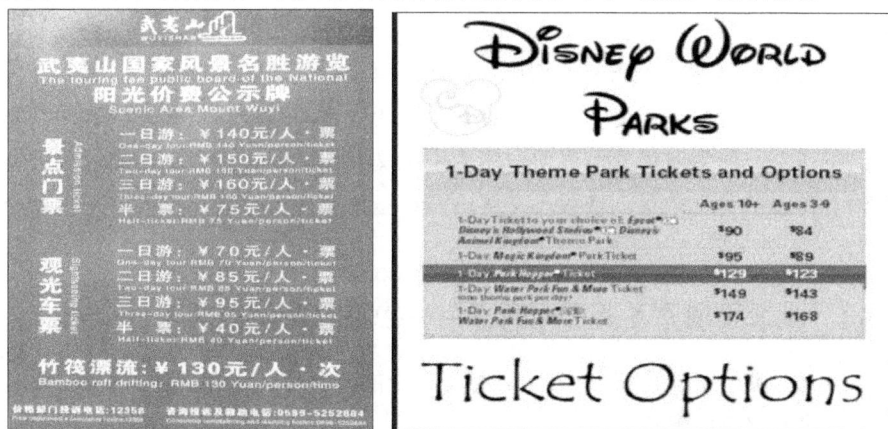

图 4-23　武夷山景区票价中英文标牌及迪士尼乐园票价标牌

根据迪士尼的票价标牌，图 4-23 武夷山景区的票价标牌标题可改为：

The Mount Wuyi National Scenic Area

Tickets and Options

4.6　评估个案Ⅲ——酒店介绍

外宾来中国，不论是公干还是旅游，都需要定好行程，选好酒店。为了吸引宾客，酒店介绍往往突出自身特色，凸显当地的文化符号，如名胜景点。以土楼为例，缤客网南靖土楼 32 家酒店共 4979 字的介绍文字中，"土楼"一词共出现 33 次，其他土楼名称共出现 26 次，对于浏览这些酒店介绍的人而言，无疑是一种密集轰炸。可见，酒店介绍是外宾了解一地文化的重要途径之一，其译文质量对文化传播有较大影响，相关研究值得重视。

目前有关酒店介绍翻译的研究数量不多，其研究视角包括语用对比（陈静，2012）、目的论（胡佳炜，姜诚，2015）、生态翻译学（赖德富，2015b）、功能翻译理论（莫红利，2009）、平行文本比较（李德超，王克非，2009）、质量评估模式（莫红利，2011）。以上探讨中，李德超、王克非从平行文本的角度比较酒店介绍翻译，具有语料库的基因，颇具启发意义。其他多是从单个或数个语篇、甚至数个例证切入，并无基于语料库实证语料的翻译质量评估。缺乏语料库的支撑，便无法对术语统一问题进行统计分析。而术语统一对于文化"走出去"、"国际化"等目标而言，极其重要。因为如果术语不统一，除了造成混淆之外，原本统一的文化符号，如"土楼"（Tulou），在译语中会"变异"为各种符号，如"earth building"、"round house"、"earth castle"、"earthen building"、"earthen castle"等等，在对外传播中令人无从辨识，失去传播优势。

本节以语料库实证语料为依据，考察武夷山、南靖和鼓浪屿三地酒店介绍的翻译质量，考察重点为术语的一致性。酒店介绍的双语语料来自缤客网，属于质量较高、较为难得的世界遗产酒店中英文介绍材料，因为三地酒店绝大多数没有自己的英文网页，携程英文网站虽有三地酒店预订服务，但并无英文介绍。

4.6.1　缤客网酒店英文介绍特点——以鼓浪屿酒店为例

缤客网的鼓浪屿酒店介绍，中英文齐全的共 40 篇，从结构、信息、语言等方面来看，有以下几个特点：

（1）结构统一，长度适中

英文和中文介绍都遵循"位置—交通（景点）—设施—服务—（特色）—酒店所在区域特色概括—语言服务"的模块式结构，不同酒店的介绍，"交通（景点）、设施、服务"3 个模块的先后位置可能不完全一致。特色模块要看酒店情况，有的酒店没有。介绍以旅客为中心（Customer-oriented），将旅客关心的问题一一回答，如下例。

①鼓浪屿玫瑰小镇旅馆介绍

英文：

Accepting only Mainland Chinese citizens, Gulangyu Rose Town offers accommodation on Gulang Island. （说明位置在厦门的鼓浪屿）

Free WiFi is accessible throughout the entire property. Zhonghua Road is a 15-minute walk from Gulangyu Rose Town. Xiamen Railway Station is a 23-minute drive from the property. Xiamen Gaoqi International Airport is a 40-minute drive away. （首先回答旅客最关心的 WiFi 问题，然后是交通）

Each room in Gulangyu Rose Town is fitted with a flat-screen TV. Free toiletries and slippers can be found in the private bathroom. （设施介绍，侧重洗浴用品）

The 24-hour front desk can help with luggage storage and concierge service. Laundry is free. （24 小时服务、行李寄存等旅客关心的问题，突出免费服务）

Gulangyu is a great choice for travellers interested in architecture, gourmet food and street food. （对所在区域鼓浪屿的一句话概括，申遗成功之后，应该会更新，加上世界遗产这一广告）

We speak your language! （最后强调提供英文服务）

中文：

鼓浪屿玫瑰小镇旅馆位于鼓浪屿，旅馆各处设有免费 WiFi，仅接待中国大陆客人入住。

鼓浪屿玫瑰小镇旅馆距离中华路有 15 分钟的步行路程，距离厦门火车站有 23 分钟车程，距离厦门高崎国际机场有 40 分钟车程。

每间客房均设有平板电视，私人浴室提供免费洗浴用品和拖鞋。24 小时前台提供行李寄存和礼宾服务。旅馆还提供免费的洗衣服务。

旅友们喜爱鼓浪屿的理由：建筑艺术、高级美食和街头小吃。

住宿场所的员工使用您的语言！

中文介绍与英文介绍结构一致，中文 191 字，英文 102 词，长度适中。

（2）信息齐全，凸显特色

语料库中 40 个鼓浪屿酒店的中英文介绍都遵循上面的结构，在简短的框架内提供了较为齐全的信息，但并不千篇一律，而是尽量凸显酒店特色，如下例。

②厦门鼓浪屿六悦海景酒店英文介绍

Xiamen Gulangyu Liuyue Sea View Hotel is situated in the Gulangyu District in Xiamen.

It is located a 5-minute walk from Riguang Hill. Free WiFi is available in all areas.Xiamen Gulangyu Liuyue Sea View Hotel is a 10-minute walk from the Piano Museum. Gulangyu Ferry Terminal is located a 15-minute walk away.（交通＋景点）

Each room at this hotel is air conditioned and is equipped with a flat-screen TV with cable channels. Each room comes with a private bathroom equipped with a shower. For your comfort, you will find slippers, free toiletries and a hair dryer.

Xiamen Gulangyu Liuyue Sea View Hotel has a 24-hour front desk offering tour services. Staff at the front desk can also give trip advice to Xiamen, Gulangyu and nearby places. Free luggage storage space is available.（服务介绍）

Guests will find a garden which is a shared area to relax. The on-site restaurant offers delicious authentic Xiamen food.（特色模块）

Gulangyu is a great choice for travellers interested in architecture, gourmet food and street food.

We speak your language!

（3）英文地道，中文可读

40 个鼓浪屿酒店的中英文介绍中，英文表达流畅、地道，中文通顺可读，文字方面总体达到了较高的质量。

（4）英文简短，富于变化

缤客网的酒店介绍属网页文本，网页文本不宜过长，应尽量简短易读，我们用 Readability Studio 考察 40 篇酒店介绍英文文本的易读性，结果见图 4-24：

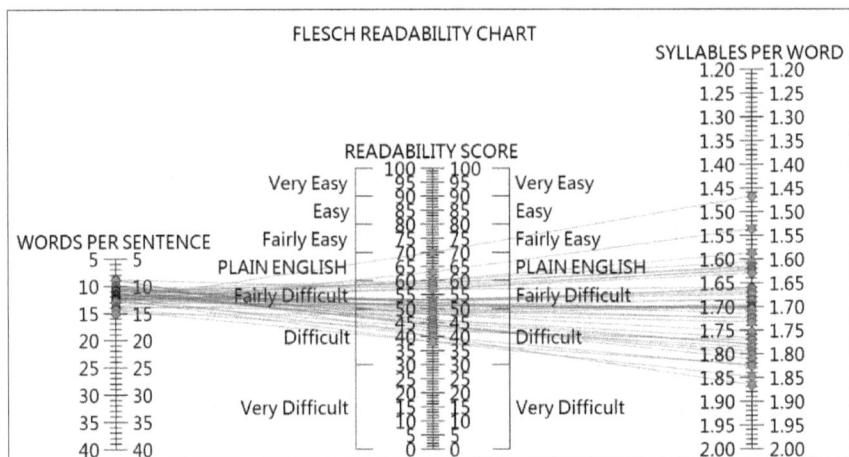

图 4-24　40 个酒店介绍文本的 Readability Studio 易读性检测

从图 4-24 可以粗略看出，40 篇酒店介绍中多数文本的 Flesch 易读性指数在 50 以上，绝大多数平均句长在 15 词以内。

下面使用许家金等开发的 Readability Analyzer 1.0 版具体统计 40 个文本的易读性指数、平均句长、标准类符形符比和平均词长，统计结果见表 4-2：

表 4-2　40 个酒店介绍文本的 Readability Analyzer 易读性分析值

File	Reading Ease	ASL	Word STTR	AWL
17.txt	63.1	11.4	0.7739	5
27.txt	63.1	12.8	0.7015	4.8
13.txt	61.6	11.1	0.7486	4.7
14.txt	60	13.3	0.7344	4.4
40.txt	59.7	11	0.6553	5.1
11.txt	58.5	11.6	0.6967	4.9
28.txt	57.8	13.6	0.6513	4.8
5.txt	57.5	14.3	0.6933	5.1
1.txt	56.3	16.8	0.6461	4.7
20.txt	56.1	11.5	0.7163	5
36.txt	56	11.6	0.7239	5.2
19.txt	55.5	17.2	0.704	4.9
34.txt	54.9	10.7	0.7017	5
22.txt	54.7	11.6	0.5998	5
2.txt	54.6	13.4	0.668	5.1
18.txt	54	11.1	0.6528	5
38.txt	53.8	15.1	0.7025	5
29.txt	53	12.1	0.6379	5.2
7.txt	52.6	14	0.6664	5.3
16.txt	52	9.8	0.59	5
9.txt	52	12.8	0.6728	5.1
39.txt	51.4	10	0.6985	5.2
23.txt	50.7	16.5	0.6651	4.9
35.txt	50.6	15	0.6317	4.9
15.txt	50.1	12	0.6262	4.8
4.txt	49.4	13.3	0.6776	5

File	Reading Ease	ASL	Word STTR	AWL
26.txt	49.1	11.1	0.6486	5.5
30.txt	46.2	14.5	0.7035	5.1
33.txt	45.4	15.1	0.68	4.9
12.txt	45	15.2	0.6591	5.1
32.txt	44.8	11.7	0.6589	5.1
37.txt	44.7	14.3	0.585	4.9
10.txt	44.6	11.8	0.7524	5.3
31.txt	41.7	13.4	0.6023	4.9
6.txt	40.5	11.5	0.7	5.3
3.txt	38.6	14.8	0.7291	5
24.txt	38	10.3	0.6983	5.5
25.txt	37.4	13	0.625	5.2
8.txt	33.6	13.5	0.6396	5.3
21.txt	30.6	13	0.7581	5.6
平均	50.48	12.92	0.677	5.045

据该表，25 个文本的易读指数在 50 以上，占 62.5%，由于酒店介绍文本中不可避免地会涉及地名之类的专有名词，软件词典没有收入该类词汇，会导致易读指数比实际的略高；55% 的文本平均句长在 13 词以内，85% 在 15 词以内，说明句子简短；92.5% 的文本标准类符形符比在 0.6 以上，说明单篇文本词汇较为密集，重复率低，富于变化，信息量大；92.5% 的文本平均词长在 5.3 以内，说明多数词汇简短。

4.6.2 酒店介绍翻译质量评估

从对缤客网鼓浪屿酒店介绍所做的特点分析来看，其酒店介绍英文文本质量达到了较高水平，如采用传统的评估模式，仅从单篇或者数篇文本分析，较难对其翻译质量得出全面客观的评价。因此，我们采取 CCAT 平台下翻译记忆库检索的考察方式，该方式能发现并且解决传统评估模式发现不了、解决不了的问题。考察所用 CCAT 工具为雪人 CAT 软件，语料为缤客网武夷山、永靖、鼓浪屿三地酒店中英文介绍记忆库。

4.6.2.1 操作流程简介

（1）建立中译英项目

启动雪人 CAT 软件，选择"文件"菜单下的"中译英项目"，如图4-25：

图4-25 雪人 CAT 新建中译英项目

（2）加载记忆库

右键点击"项目记忆库"，选择导入"记忆库"，如图4-26：

图4-26 雪人 CAT 导入记忆库

软件弹出文件选择框，如图 4-27：

图 4-27　雪人 CAT 导入记忆库文件选择

　　查找并选择构建福建世界遗产双语语料库时，利用雪人 CAT 对齐句对后导出的酒店介绍记忆库，如鼓浪屿酒店介绍记忆库，导入后如图 4-28：

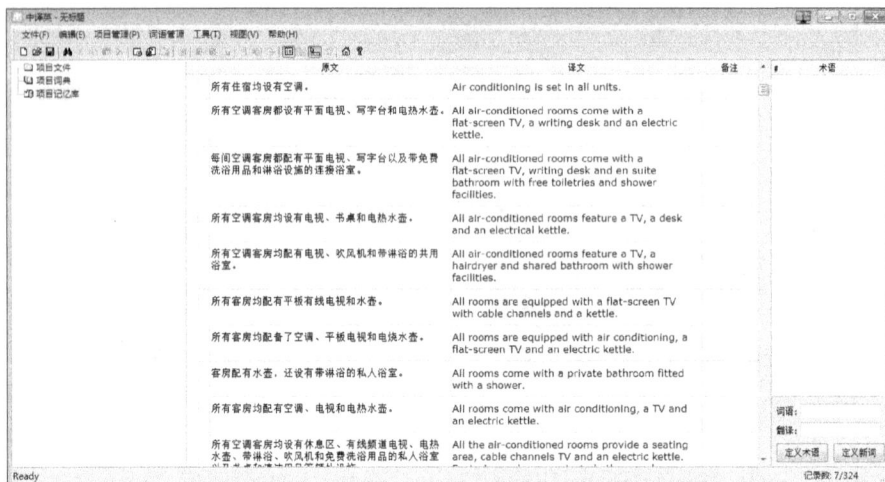

图 4-28　雪人 CAT 导入的鼓浪屿酒店介绍记忆库

（3）查看、检索记忆库

　　通过查看以及检索记忆库，可发现酒店介绍翻译中的各种问题，考察结果概括如下。

4.6.2.2　考察结果

（1）缤客网酒店介绍为中英、英中双向翻译

检索中发现，采集自缤客网的中英文网页数据配对对齐后，有的句对只有

英文，并无中文。查看酒店中文介绍原始页面，发现并无中文，如图4-29：

从图4-29来看，缤客网上的中国酒店介绍原始文本为英文，而中文介绍其实是由英文翻译而来的。由此可以推断该网站中国酒店介绍的翻译流程较为复杂，可能包括中文文本编译为英文及英文文本回译为中文两个过程，即涉及中英、英中双向翻译。

图 4-29　缤客网简体中文页面酒店介绍为英文

我们将对缤客网酒店介绍翻译的评估由汉英单向考察转为英汉、汉英双向考察。在雪人 CAT 中增加一个英译中翻译项目，导入酒店介绍翻译的记忆库，记忆库的语言对会自动调整为英—汉方向，如图4-30：

图 4-30　雪人 CAT 英—汉方向记忆库示例

以下结果基于对三地酒店汉英记忆库及英汉记忆库的双向考察。

（2）中文译名不一致

以"Huangu"一词为例，该词对应了多种不同的中文译名，如图4-31。

图 4-31　缤客网中文术语不统一

这些不同译文举例如下:

① Garden Dreamer offers the accommodation in Xiamen. Gulangyu Island is 500 m away, while *Huangu Ferry Marina* is 1.1 km away.

花庭旅馆（厦门鼓浪屿稚梦店）位于厦门，距离鼓浪屿岛有 500 米，距离环鼓轮渡码头有 1.1 公里。

② *Huangu Ferry Marina* is 1.3 km from Gulangyu Manmanyouyou Inn, while Nanputuo Temple is 3.4 km away. Xiamen Gaoqi International Airport is 13 km from the property.

鼓浪屿漫漫悠悠旅馆距离还鼓轮渡码头 1.3 公里，距离南普陀寺 3.4 公里，距离厦门高崎国际机场 13 公里。

③ It is 20 minutes' drive from Xiamen Railway Station. Alternative you can take 25 minutes' drive from Xiamen Gaoqi International Airport. For sightseeing, you can take around 5 minutes' walk from Gulangyu Island and *Huangu Ferry Marina*.

旅馆距离厦门火车站有 20 分钟车程，距离厦门高崎国际机场有 25 分钟车程，距离鼓浪屿岛（Gulangyu Island）和环鼓过渡码头（Huangu Ferry Marina）约有 5 分钟步行路程。

双语语料库构建与应用

（3）英文译名不一致

①厦门夏洛特旅馆地理位置优越，毗邻鼓浪屿笔架山，距离日光岩仅有不到 10 分钟的步行路程。

Ideally located close to Bijia Mountain on Gulangyu Island, Xiamen Charlotte Inn is within a 10-minute walk from ***Sunshine Rock***.

②著名的旅游景点如日光岩、鼓浪石、菽庄花园和皓月园均距离酒店仅有不到 15 分钟的步行路程。

Famous tourist spots such as ***Riguangyan***, Gulangshi, Shuzhuang Garden and Haoyue Garden are within a 15-minute walk of the hotel.

说明：例①、例②中"日光岩"的英文译名不一致。

③厦门鼓浪屿箜篌音乐酒店距离港仔后沙滩、菽庄花园和日光岩仅有 10 分钟的步行路程，距离厦门海底世界和鼓浪屿渡轮码头有 15 分钟的步行路程。

Conch of Xiamen Gulangyu is a 10-minute walk from Gangzaihou Beach, Shuzhuang Garden and Sunshine Rock. ***Xiamen Seabed World*** and Gulangyu Ferry is a 15-minute walk away.

④厦门海岛之家位于鼓浪屿，配有免费 WiFi，提供舒适的客房，距离厦门海底世界 100 米。

Featuring free WiFi, Island House offers comfy accommodation on Gulangyu Island. ***Xiamen Underwater World*** is 100 m away.

说明：例③、例④中"海底世界"的英文译名不一致。

⑤客栈距离南京土楼有 45 分钟车程，距离漳州火车站有 2 小时车程，距离厦门高崎国际机场有 2 小时 40 分钟车程。

You can reach Nanjing ***Earth Buildings*** in 45 minutes' drive. Zhangzhou Railway Station is located 2 hours' car journey away, while Xiamen Gaoqi International Airport can be reached in 2 hours 40 minutes' drive.

⑥围裙楼客栈 2 号店距离塔下土楼风景区有 5 分钟的步行路程，距离市中心有 54 公里。

Taxia ***Tulou*** Scenic Area is a 5-minute walk from Weiqunlou Inn No.2.

Downtown is 54 km from the property.

说明：例⑤与例⑥中"土楼"的英文译名不一致，应为"Tulou"。

（4）术语翻译错误

① It takes 10 minutes on foot to ***Sanqiutian Wharf*** and 20 minutes on foot to Neicuo'an Wharf.

旅馆距离<u>三秋天码头</u>约 10 分钟步行，距离内厝垵码头约 20 分钟步行。

说明："Sanqiutian"这一术语误译为"三秋天"；"Neicuo'an"有误，应为"Neicuo'ao"，中文名称应为"内厝澳"。

② The hostel is a 10-minute walk from Neicuo'ao Terminal. ***Sanqiutian Terminal*** is located a 15-minute walk away. It takes 20 minutes to walk to the Piano Museum.

这家旅舍距离内厝澳码头有 10 分钟的步行路程，距离<u>三丘田站</u>有 15 分钟的步行路程，距离钢琴博物馆有 20 分钟的步行路程。

说明："Sanqiutian Terminal"应译为"三丘田码头"。

③ Nanjing Yun Shui Yao Fu Chun Inn offers accommodation in ***Nanjing***. Liufang Temple and Defeng Tower can be reached within 200 m.

南靖云水谣福春客栈位于<u>南京</u>，距离流芳祠和德丰大厦不到 200 米，提供覆盖各处的免费 WiFi。

说明："Nanjing"一词对应的中文应为"南靖"，但土楼酒店中文介绍中 11 处误译为"南京"，如图 4-32。

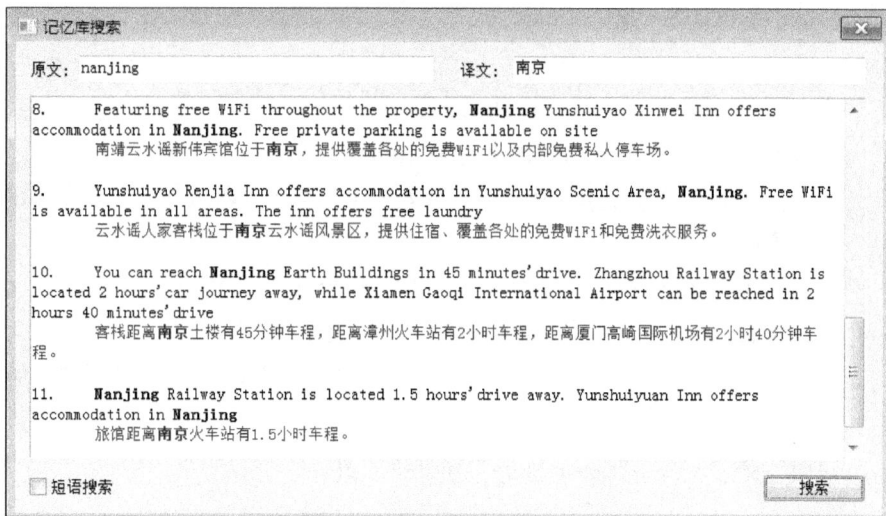

图 4-32 "Nanjing"误译为"南京"

（5）英文缺漏

①厦门鼓浪屿鼓浪朵拉旅馆距离日光岩有 3 分钟步行路程，距离菽庄花园有 7 分钟的步行路程，距离鼓浪屿轮渡码头有 5 分钟的步行路程，距离厦门火车站有 15 分钟的车程，距离高崎国际机场有 35 分钟的路程。

Dora' House is a 3-minute walk from Sunlight Rock and a 7-minute walk from Shuzhuang Garden. It is also a **_5-walk_** from Gulangyu Ferry Terminal. It takes 15 minutes by car to Xiamen Railway Station and 35 minutes to Gaoqi International Airport.

说明："5-walk"应为"5-minute walk"。

（6）中文缺漏

① The hotel is 1.5 km from Wuyishan Scenic Zone. It takes **_7 minutes by car to Binglian Mountain and_** 23 minutes by car to Wuyishan Railway Station. The city centre can be reached in 34 minutes' drive.

民宿距离武夷山风景区 1.5 公里，距离武夷山火车站有 23 分钟的车程，距离市中心有 34 分钟车程。

说明："7 minutes by car to Binglian Mountain and"无对应中文。

（7）中文译文不一致

① Featuring free WiFi in all areas, Weiqunlou Inn No.1 offers *pet-friendly* accommodation. Free private parking is available.

<u>允许客人携带宠物入住</u>的围裙楼客栈 1 号店提供覆盖各处的免费 WiFi 和免费私人停车场。

② Featuring free WiFi throughout the property, Weiqunlou Inn No.2 offers *pet-friendly* accommodation. Free private parking is available.

围裙楼客栈 2 号店各处均设有免费 WiFi，提供<u>宠物友好型的</u>客房和免费私人停车场。

说明：例①、例②"pet-friendly"译文不一致。

4.6.3 问题分析及对策

从以上考察结果来看，缤客网存在术语不一致、译文不一致、术语翻译错误、译文缺漏等问题。其中最为严重的是中文术语不一致及误译问题，如"Nanjing"（南靖）误译为"南京"，且多达 11 次。

究其原因，可能是因为缤客网注重英文介绍文本的体例一致、风格统一，英文是由中文改写编译而来，这是值得国内像携程这样的酒店预订平台借鉴的做法。由于中文文本须与英文在格式、内容、长度等方面大体一致，不能再使用原来的中文，须由英文文本回译为中文，故而在回译中出现了失误。

此类失误不一定是因为缤客网没有使用 CAT 软件等翻译工具。在质量考察中，我们发现缤客网酒店的中英文介绍采用了比较固定的模式，有时甚至采用了完全相同的句式，如：

① Gulangyu is a great choice for travellers interested in architecture, gourmet food and street food.

旅友们喜爱鼓浪屿的理由：建筑艺术、高级美食和街头小吃。

② We speak your language!

住宿场所的员工使用您的语言！

③ ... sells fast on our website.

……在我们网站上超热门。

此类句子在缤客网的酒店介绍中反复出现了多次，说明缤客网的译员可能

福建世界遗产

双语语料库构建与应用

也使用了 CAT 软件作为辅助翻译工具。

问题出在翻译质量的监控上，缤客网没有采取严格有效的管理措施及技术手段保持术语统一及译文一致。

缤客网的这种情况，需要采取基于 CCAT 的翻译模式，即架设服务器级别的 CCAT 平台，所有译者连线至该 CCAT 平台，译审人员通过服务器审校译员翻译的术语和句子，审核通过后将其加入共享术语库和记忆库，译员在翻译过程中连接共享术语库和记忆库，便可保持术语一致及译文一致。

最后需要说明的是，缤客网的酒店介绍文本虽然存在一些问题，但总体而言，其酒店介绍的中英文文本都遵循一定的结构，语言地道，质量较高，符合"信、达、效"原则，值得国内酒店及酒店预订网站学习、借鉴。

4.7 评估个案Ⅳ——导游词

据世界旅游组织预测，到 2020 年中国有可能成为世界上最大的旅游目的地。福建拥有丰富的旅游资源，如"海上花园"之厦门，"九曲仙境"之武夷山，"海上丝路"之泉州，"东方古堡"之土楼，无不独具特色，驰名中外。

福建的世界遗产数量位居中国前列，旅游文化产业发展迅猛，国际化步伐不断加快，来闽的外国游客日益增多，其中不少是慕名而来，探寻世界遗产奇境。外语导游介绍世界遗产景点所用的英文导游词，对于传播世界遗产的文化符号，如客家文化、朱子文化，具有重要作用，前提是英文导游词的译写符合其文本功能，能为外国游客所接受，从而有效传递信息，促进文化交流。

4.7.1 导游词翻译研究概述

虽然近年来随着旅游业的兴起，国内不少学者对导游词的翻译进行了研究，但系统性的专门研究较少，研究方向主要集中于导游词的语言因素和文化因素处理方式两个方面（王艳红，徐桂艳，2012：450）。其研究视角主要包括功能翻译理论（袁琼，2007）、目的论（陈淑霞，2008；张建英，闵西鸿，2011；李良辰，2013）、功能对等（廖为群，2010）、文本功能（王冬梅，2008）、会话合作原则（郭艳，2006）等等。研究对象或是导游词手册中的某些译例（曾丹，2006），如 *Touring China: Selected Tour Commentaries* 一书，或是某地景点的导游词，如河南景点（丁小月，2011）、武当山景区（徐珊，杨铭，2013）等等。

这些研究大多是结合理论分析实例，侧重点在翻译策略和技巧方面，一般都提倡"信"、"忠实"等原则，即要通过导游词的翻译传播本土文化，促进文化交融。不可否认，这些探讨促进了国内导游词翻译研究的发展。但亦存在不足之处。一是缺乏语料库数据的支撑，往往是通过列举几个例证进行分析，较少通篇／全盘考察，缺乏在一定数据规模上得出的结论。二是未与原生英文导游词进行语言特征上的比较，对于英文导游词作为一类特殊文体的语言特征缺乏重视。虽然部分研究也提到英文导游词要比较口语化（王冬梅，2008），但只是浅而论之，未作深入探讨。

本节以福建世界遗产双语语料库中的土楼英文导游词及原生英文导游词为实证语料，通过语料库的数据分析，对福建世界遗产英文导游词进行质量评估，侧重点为语言错误、翻译错误、术语一致以及文化符号的翻译策略，以及导游词译文与原生英文文本的易读性比较。

4.7.2　语料来源

英文导游词可分为 3 类：预制类（pre-translated type）、现编类（impromptu presentation type）和预制现编类（combined type），预制类导游词不同于即兴发挥的"现场导游"（on-the-spot introduction）和"途中导游"（on-the-way introduction），也不同于一般的笔译，文本类型属于信息型、表情型和指导型的结合体（陈刚，2002：68）。

现编类和预制现编类英文导游词极其罕见，除非是聘请外语导游在讲解时录音，然后再转写为文本，但目前尚未见此类试验。预制类英文导游词亦不多见，主要来自数量极少的英文导游词书籍，如 2000 年由中国旅游出版社出版的 *Touring China: Selected Tour Commentaries*，但该书译文质量欠佳，可用"错误百出"、"误人子弟"来加以描述（陈刚，2002：68）。由于此书未收入福建任何景点的导游词，故不在评估之列。

福建世界遗产双语语料库中所包含的中英文导游词来自《福建省主要旅游景区景点英语导游词》（陈洪富，2014）一书中有关土楼、武夷山及泰宁的章节。本小节从中选取了土楼部分进行质量评估，共约 14467 字／词，其中英文约 5800 词。除土楼中英文导游词外，还从类比语料库中选取了国外原生英文导游词 6 篇，作为参照语料。这些导游词皆为音频导游（Audio Tour）的文字材料（Script），涉及景点／设施分别为：

（1）Lady Bird Johnson Wildflower Center（3969 词）
（https://www.wildflower.org）
（2）The Regent's Canal Towpath（5632 词）
（http://www.canalmuseum.org.uk/visit/podcasts.htm）

（3）London Canal Museum（2868 词）

(http://www.canalmuseum.org.uk/visit/podcasts.htm)

（4）The High Museum I（4357 词）

(https://www.high.org/Educators/Teachers/Picasso-To-War hol-Teach er-Resources /Audio-Guide-Scripts)

（5）Randall Library（3645 词）

(http://library.uncw.edu/uploads/pdfs/Library%20Tour%20Script %202014. pdf）

（6）The High Museum II（9529 词）

(https://www.high.org/Educators/Teachers/Picasso-To-Warhol-Teacher-Resources /Audio-Guide-Scripts)

此类音频导游词属于预制类导游词，适于用作类比语料。

4.7.3 基于双语语料库的土楼导游词译文质量考察

本小节基于双语语料库对土楼导游词译文质量进行了考察，选择了语言错误、翻译错误、术语一致及文化符号的翻译策略等 4 个角度，考察的方式是利用检索工具对语料库进行批量检索，然后进行人工分析。

（1）语言错误

土楼英文导游词由多位译者合力完成，并由外国专家审校定稿，在语言方面错误较少，达到了较好水平，发现的少量问题列举如下：

①福裕楼是一座府第式的建筑，而奎聚楼则是宫殿式的建筑。奎聚楼建于 1834 年，外观呈方形状，里面是宫殿式的建筑，被人称为土楼中的"布达拉宫"。

Kuiju Lou is a rectangular structure built in 1834. While Fuyu Lou is a mansion-style architecture, Kuiju Lou is a palace-like one. It is nicknamed "the Potala Palace" among *Tulous*.

说明：目前国际惯例已将"Tulou/tulou"用作单复数同形名词，如：

They and the families in four **tulou** nearby all share one ancestor and surname, Huang. (*The New York Times*)[1]

因此，建议将"Tulous"改为"Tulou"。

②我们现在步入振成楼的中堂大厅，也称祖堂，祖堂的这四根石柱<u>粗</u>约 2 米，高近 7 米。

This is the main hall, also the ancestral hall of the earthen building. These four stone columns are seven meters high and 2 meters ***in circumference***.

说明：前为"high"，违反平行结构规则，建议改为"round"。

③与圆形土楼相比，方形土楼在福建的农村地区较为常见。

Square Tulou ***is*** actually more common than circular ones in the rural areas of Fujian Province.

说明：此处"Tulou"为复数，"is"改为"are"。

（2）翻译错误

翻译错误也较少，列举数例如下。

①另一种说法是来自一个民间传说——<u>田螺姑娘的故事</u>。

Some others would rather believe a folktale that involves a ***beautiful fairy tale of river snails***.

说明："fairy"有"仙女"之意，但"fairy tale"则只有"神话故事"之意，且与前面的"folktale"重复。建议整句改为：Some others would rather believe the story of a snail fairy.

"story of a snail fairy"构成头韵，"snail fairy"在西方文学中为常见形象。

②另外，我们还可以看到土楼人最原生态的生活附设建筑，比如鱼塘和牛舍等。

And we could also find such ***living facilities*** as cowsheds and a fish pond.

---

① http://www.nytimes.com/2008/04/27/travel/27heads.html?_r=0

说明："living facilities" 意为"生活设施"，与"鱼塘"、"牛舍" 冲突，属误译，改为"facilities"。

③振成楼是由清末秀才<u>林逊之</u>设计，他多才多艺，精通书法、易经，及其他中国传统技艺。<u>林逊之</u>是洪坑村当时最富有的林氏家族的子孙。林氏家族从事烟草生意而发家，多年来致力于洪坑村的基础建设。<u>林逊之</u>的父亲林仁山想兴建一栋浩大的土楼，却因病搁浅。仁山去世后，<u>逊之</u>继承父志，开始建造振成楼。

This building was designed by ***Mr. Lin Xunzhi***, a versatile government official in the late Qing Dynasty who was specialized in calligraphy, research of *The Book of Changes*, and many other traditional Chinese arts. ***Mr. Lin*** came from the once richest family in Hongkeng Hakka Village. The Lin Family accumulated a great fortune by doing tobacco business, and was committed to the development of local infrastructure.

Lin Renshan, ***Lin Xunzhi***'s father, aspired to build a huge Tulou in his village. However, his aspiration failed because of his health problems. After his death, ***Xunzhi*** decided to continue his father's dream and started constructing Zhencheng Lou.

说明：该段原文由"林逊之" 及"逊之" 这两个名字衔接，合乎中文习惯。译文先后用"Mr. Lin Xunzhi"、"Mr. Lin"、"Lin Xunzhi"、"Xunzhi" 4 个不同的称谓，对于不熟悉汉语拼音的外国游客而言，会造成理解上的负担。据说，在参观明十三陵时一导游对外国游客说："This is Ding Ling, the tomb of Zhu Yijun and his empresses, Xiao Duan and Xiao Jing."（这是定陵，是朱翊钧和他的皇后孝端和孝靖的寝陵。）结果当即有外国游客抱怨说："What is he talking about！"（王连义，1990：147）。这句话如果是笔译文字，读者琢磨一下之后是能明白的："Ding Ling" 就是"tomb"，"Xiao Duan" 和"Xiao Jing" 是"empresses"，"Zhu Yijun" 自然就是"emperor"。但导游词信息靠听觉获取，游客还会分心观赏风景，加上对汉语拼音不熟悉，听不明白是正常的。导游词的译者要思考这个问题。以上例而言，4 个不同的称谓依次译为 Mr. Lin Xunzhi、Mr. Lin、Mr. Lin、Mr. Lin 较好。此例属于衔接上的不当。

（3）术语一致

经语料库检索，发现土楼导游词在"土楼" 一词的译名方面不太统一，有时译为"Tulou"，有时译为"earth/earthen building"，下面列举两例。

①各位团友大家好！今天我们游览的第一站是田螺坑土楼群，俗称"四菜一汤"。

Ladies and gentlemen, our first stop of the Tulou trip today is the Tianluokeng ***Earth Building*** Cluster.

②田螺坑土楼群以其独特的视觉魅力和历史价值于 2001 年被评为国家重点文物保护单位。

With impressive and unique charm and high historical value, Tianluokeng ***Tulou*** cluster was included in 2001 as a key historical site under the state protection.

说明：例①的"Earth Building"应改为"Tulou"，以保持术语一致。

"Tulou"一词在国内外已被广为接受，建议在导游词中将"土楼"译名统一为"Tulou"。可以在需要的时候使用"earth building"解释"Tulou"，如"Hakka Tulou, also known as Hakka earth building"。

（4）文化符号的翻译策略

在文化"走出去"战略下，应打造一批具有影响力、竞争力的核心文化符号，多管齐下，提高核心文化符号在各种场合出现的频率，如网站、影视、图书、社交媒体等等，当然也包括导游词。

塑造核心文化符号，第一步是确立具有排他性的译名，而不是释义词，如"土楼"就是一个核心文化符号，曾有过多种译名，其中只有"Tulou"具有排他性，其他如"earth building"之类都是释义词。在上一节酒店介绍翻译质量评估中，我们认为，译名不一会导致文化符号异化，变异为多个符号，造成受众认知上的混淆，不利于文化符号的传播。

就"土楼"这一文化符号而言，"Tulou"的译名基本已经确立。例如，外国游客到访土楼之后，制作上传介绍土楼的视频到各类视频网站，使用的大多为"Tulou"，说明这一文化符号已经具备了较大的影响力，较为稳固。但其衍生词，即"某某楼"，如"承启楼"，译名仍处于纷乱状态，有完全音译的"Chengqilou、Chengqi Lou"，有音译加意译的"Chengqi building、Chengqi castle、Chengqi house"没有一个词能脱颖而出，占据统治地位。我们认为，既然"Tulou"已经成为一个为西方受众接受的名称，就像"Palace"一词，西方有各种"Palace"，如"Buckingham Palace"，以此为参照，为何不将土楼中的"某某楼"译法统一为"音译 + Tulou"，如"Chengqi Tulou"？这样就会形成以"Tulou"为核心的文化符号群。而且完全音译的官方译名（如"Chengqi Lou"，申遗文本译名）离开了介绍"Tulou"的语境，便不为西方受众所认知，如果译为"Chengqi Tulou"，便无须依赖语境，可以独立传播。做出这一思考，并非异想天开，实际上西方已有此种译法的先例，如下例：

The Zhengchang tulou spans 260 feet and has two concentric circles of different heights that contain 250 rooms.（*The New York Times*）[1]

土楼导游词对于"某某楼"这类文化符号中"楼"字的翻译策略与申遗文本相同，大多是译为"Lou"或"building"，建议统一译为"Tulou"。

以上为基于双语语料库数据的评估，属翻译视角的讨论。但导游词作为通过听觉传导信息的特殊文本，视觉上的译文质量高，并不一定等于听觉上的语言质量高。下面通过原生英语导游词的类比语料，使用语料分析软件 Readability Analyzer 1.0 及 Readability Studio 2015，评估土楼导游词译文的易读性。

4.7.4 基于类比语料库的土楼导游词译文易读性分析

导游词传递信息是通过游客的听觉，而非像阅读那样通过视觉，因此虽然导游词具有自身的专业性特点，但仍属于口语类文字。音频导游词作者 Lou Giansante 在 "Writing Verbal Descriptions for Audio Guides"[2] 一文中就音频导游词的写法提出了自己作为业内人士的见解：

Keep It Simple

Verbal Description writing is writing for the ear instead of the eye, and it has basic principles that writers use when writing for any presentation that uses the spoken word … whenever information is conveyed with the spoken word.

1. Use simple sentences. Sometimes a compound sentence is ok. But never, or almost never, use a complex sentence, that is, one with a subjunctive clause. These clauses begin with words like which, that, who, while, when.

2. Use active verbs. The passive voice is weak writing whether for the eye

---

[1] http://www.nytimes.com/2008/04/27/travel/27heads.html?_r=0

[2] http://www.artbeyondsight.org/mei/wp-content/uploads/Writing-for-Audio-Guides-short.pdf

or the ear, but it's especially troublesome for a listener.

他认为音频导游词的撰写，应以简洁为第一要义，能用简单句则不用复合句，绝不要用 which、that、who、while、when 等开头的从句。用主动语态，少用被动语态。

下面我们使用许家金等开发的 Readability Analyzer 1.0 对土楼英文导游词及 6 篇类比语料进行评测，结果见图 4-33：

Readability Analyzer 1.0 (Using Microsoft Office Word 199X)			
Settings Results About			
File	Reading Ease	Text Difficulty	Grade Level
HMA_Pic...	82.50	17.50	4.20
podcast-s...	70.60	29.40	7.80
HMA_Pic...	70.10	29.90	7.30
podcast-s...	66.70	33.30	8.30
Library T...	61.80	38.20	8.60
Wildflowe...	57.30	42.70	9.30
土楼导游...	54.80	45.20	9.20

图 4-33　土楼导游词及 6 篇类比语料的 Readability Analyzer 1.0 易读性数值

该图显示，土楼英文导游词在 7 个文本中的易读性指数最低，只有 54.80，最高为 82.50。具体数据如表 4-3：

表 4-3　土楼导游词及 6 篇类比语料的 Readability Analyzer 1.0 易读性数值

File	Reading Ease	ASL	AWL	Word STTR	Lemma Types
High Museum I	82.5	10.1	4.2	0.2535	958
Regent's Canal Towpath	70.6	18.1	4.1	0.286	1460
High Museum II	70.1	15.5	4.3	0.1969	1624
London Canal Museum	66.7	17.8	4.4	0.3348	854
Randall Library	61.8	16.1	4.6	0.1524	510
Wildflower Center	57.3	16.8	4.8	0.3105	1092
土楼	54.8	14.5	5	0.2478	1266

从表 4-3 可以看出，7 个文本的平均句长最高为 18.1 词，最低 10.1 词，土楼为 14.5；平均词长土楼最高，为 5；除易读性差别较大外，仅从表中难以看出其他明显区别。需要对具体的语言项进行分析，找出导致易读性差异的具体原因。

下面再用 Readability Studio 2015 软件分别统计 7 个文本的易读性，该软件可根据句子、词汇和语法等语言项对一个文本可读性进行分析，提供多种参数。本评估主要从 Readability Studio 2015 所提供的参数中选择 3 类，即难句（超过 22 个单词）比率、被动语态和累赘表达（wordy items），借此考察 7 个文本的可读性。

表 4-4　土楼导游词及 6 篇类比语料的 Readability Studio 2015 易读性数值

File	难句	被动语态	累赘表达	易读性分值
High Museum I	14(3.7%)	6(1.59%)	27	82
Regent's Canal Towpath	77(26.8%)	44(15.33%)	90	71
High Museum II	138(26.8%)	27(5.24%)	193	66
London Canal Museum	44(29.1%)	24(15.89%)	56	68
Randall Library	40(18.3%)	23(10.50%)	70	65
Wildflower Center	51(22.9%)	29(13.00%)	87	57
土楼	60(15.9%)	54(14.32%)	103	65

从表 4-4 来看，土楼英文导游词易读性指数排倒数第 2，但数值比 Readability Analyzer 1.0 的统计结果提升了一些，由于 Readability Studio 的考察涉及一些具体的语言项，如被动语态、累赘表达等，因此我们认为其统计结果应该更可靠一些。

就此结果而言，土楼英文导游词与排名前 4 的原生英文导游词的易读性差异值为 1～17，如果与第 1 名比的话，差距比较大。考虑到用于比较的原生英文导游词实际为音频导游的文本，音频导游由专业人士录制，语音纯正，而国内景点的英文导游词目前还是供外语导游讲解参考，如果与原生英文导游词相比难度都算大的话，由外语导游说出来，恐怕并不容易，也更不易为外国游客所理解，从"信、达、效"的角度来看，恐怕无法易达，效果打折。因此，仍需提高其易读性指数，方能真正派上用场。

4.7.5　提高易读性的对策

在编译导游词的时候，应参照易读性指数高的原生英文导游词，学习其写法。下面是易读性评估中排名第 1 的"High Museum I"导游词中的一段文字，从中可以看出导游词是如何做到简洁易懂的：

> This is Picasso, himself, painting a model. Can you find him? Look on the right for two eyes, one on top of the other. Picasso's model is on the left side. She's got a

long thin neck. In the middle is the painting he's working on. Can you see where he's painted the black line of her profile? It doesn't quite look like the model. She's got three eyes. And Picasso, I think he's got two noses. And his mouth? It runs down the middle of his head instead of side to side. I thought he was good at this? Why didn't he paint people to look like people? Isn't that what artists are supposed to do?

根据 Lou Giansante 的建议及 Readability Studio 2015 对被动语态和累赘表达的统计，可从被动语态、长词、复合句、累赘表达等方面入手，改写笔译痕迹明显的英文导游词。

具体如下：

（1）少用被动

①从观景窗往外看，二宜楼的选址非常考究。周围青山绿水环绕，是风水宝地，最适宜居住。

From the viewing window, we can see the well-located building ***is surrounded*** by green mountains and running rivers, which ***is believed*** by Chinese as a good geomantic omen.

改：From the viewing window, we can see the well-located building is among green mountains and running rivers. We believe it is a good geomantic omen.

②该楼始建于 1912 年，占地面积 5,000 平方米，耗时五年建成。

It covers an area of 5,000 square meters. The construction started in 1912 and ***was completed*** in 1917.

改：It covers an area of 5,000 square meters. The construction started in 1912 and ended in 1917.

③开门时，则卦卦相连，成为一个整体。

When the doors ***are opened***, all the eight sections ***are connected***.

改：When the doors open, they connect all the eight sections.

④楼上三个门顶都放置水箱，当遇到外敌火攻的时候，可用于防御。

Water tanks ***are placed*** on top of the three doors in preparation for possible fire attacks.

改：There are water tanks on top of the three doors in preparation for possible fire attacks.

（2）少用长词

①这个误解确实情有可原，同时也说明这些无辜的建筑具有多么奇特的外形！

This is an honest mistake, and it indeed shows us how **_unorthodox_** these harmless buildings appear!

改：This is an honest mistake, and it indeed shows us how curious these harmless buildings look!

②林氏家族从事烟草生意而发家，多年来致力于洪坑村的基础建设。

The Lin Family **_accumulated_** a great fortune by doing tobacco business, and was committed to the development of local infrastructure.

改：The Lin Family became very rich by doing tobacco business, and was committed to the development of local infrastructure.

（3）删除冗余

①关门时，每卦就自成一个院落，与其他的卦隔离开来。

When the residents close the **_communicating_** doors between the **_adjacent_** sections, each section becomes an independent house.

改：When the residents close the doors between the sections, each section becomes an independent house.

②土楼内的每一寸空间都被充分利用，生活设施齐全，住户的日常起居都可以在楼内解决。

Dwellers **_utilized_** every square inch of space **_for their domestic use_**. They could survive for quite some time without leaving the buildings.

改：Dwellers made full use of every square inch of space. They could survive for quite some time without leaving the buildings.

（4）少用复合句

①先生们、女士们，接下来，我将带领大家参观规模宏大，素有"土楼之王"美名的承启楼。

Ladies and gentlemen! Next, I will show you around Chengqi Lou, **_which_** is known as "the King of Tulou" owing to its large scale.

改：Ladies and gentlemen! Next, I will show you around Chengqi Tulou. We call it "the King of Tulou" because of its size.

②现在，我要带领大家参观洪坑客家村。洪坑村是永定众多知名土楼的所在地，比如振成楼、如升楼、奎聚楼等。

Now we are going to visit Hongkeng Hakka Village, _**where**_ such famous earthen buildings as Zhencheng Lou, Rusheng Lou, and Kuiju Lou are located.

改：Now we are going to visit Hongkeng Hakka Village. Here we will see some famous Tulou, such as Zhencheng Tulou, Rusheng Tulou, and Kuiju Tulou.

③关于土楼群有一个有趣的故事。冷战期间，土楼的卫星图片曾让一些西方国家忧心忡忡，他们以为这些蘑菇状的巨型建筑是核掩体，也怀疑这些建筑群是中国的导弹基地。

It's interesting to note _**that**_ the satellite images of Tulou clusters once made western countries nervous during the Cold War, _**because**_ they thought the giant mushroom-like structures resembled nuclear shelters and they also feared the complex was a Chinese missile base.

改：Here is an interesting story about Tulou. The American satellite once took pictures of Tulou clusters during the Cold War. These pictutres made western countries very nervous.They thought the giant mushroom-like structures looked like nuclear shelters and feared the complex was a Chinese missile base.

经过以上所示各项修改，土楼导游词在 Readability Analyzer 1.0 中检测的易读性指数由原来的 54.8 上升到 64.7%（见图 4-34）。

File	Reading Ease	Text Difficulty	Grade Level
土楼导游...	**64.70**	35.30	7.50
土楼导游...	54.80	45.20	9.20

图 4-34　改译的土楼导游词 Readability Analyzer 1.0 易读性数值

部分中英文对照修改样例如下：

永定土楼因历史悠久，风格独特，规模宏大，结构精巧而屹立于世界建筑艺术之林。

原译：They have won international renown for their long history, unique style, large scale and exquisite structure.

改译：They have won international fame for their long history, unique style, large scale and exquisite structure.

2008 年，它被联合国教科文组织列为世界遗产。

原译：In 2008, they were inscribed on the UNESCO world heritage list.

改译：In 2008, they entered the UNESCO world heritage list.

土楼为大型多层建筑，以竹条与木头为框架，用生土、沙、泥、糯米、红糖等材料层层碾压砌成。

原译：Most of the Tutous are multi-story huge structures, framed with bamboo strips and timbers. The walls were built with a mix of raw earth, sand, lime, glutinous rice and brown sugar, rammed into shape, layer by layer.

改译：Most of the Tutou are multi-story and huge. They are framed with bamboo strips and timbers. The walls are a mix of raw earth, sand, lime, glutinous rice and brown sugar, rammed into shape, layer by layer.

现在，我要带领大家参观洪坑客家村。洪坑村是永定众多知名土楼的所在地，比如振成楼、如升楼、奎聚楼等。

原译：Now we are going to visit Hongkeng Hakka Village, where such famous earthen buildings as Zhencheng Lou, Rusheng Lou, and Kuiju Lou are located.

改译：Now we are going to visit Hongkeng Hakka Village. Here we will see some famous Tulou, such as Zhencheng Tulou, Rusheng Tulou, and Kuiju Tulou.

首先，让我们先去参观圆形土楼的建筑典范：振成楼。

原译：Let's go to see one of the finest examples of circular Tulou, Zhencheng Lou.

改译：Let's go and see one of the finest circular Tulou, Zhencheng Tulou.

该楼始建于 1912 年，占地面积 5000 平方米，耗时五年建成。2001 年 5 月，振成楼与福裕楼、奎聚楼和承启楼一道被列入全国重点文物保护单位。

原译：It covers an area of 5,000 square meters. The construction started in 1912 and was completed in 1917. Together with Fuyu Lou, Kuiju Lou and Chengqi Lou, Zhencheng Lou was added to the list of key national cultural relics under state protection in May 2001.

改译：It covers an area of 5,000 square meters. The construction started in 1912 and ended in 1917. Together with Fuyu Tulou, Kuiju Tulou and Chengqi

Tulou, Zhencheng Tulou became key national cultural relics under state protection in May 2001.

大家眼前的就是振成楼。振成楼既有苏州园林的印迹，又有古希腊建筑风格的特点，堪称建筑奇葩。

原译：Zhencheng Lou is a combination of the classical architecture styles of Suzhou gardens and that of ancient Greek architecture, and is regarded as an architectural wonder.

改译：Zhencheng Tulou combines the classical architecture styles of Suzhou gardens and the architecture styles of ancient Greece, and becomes an architectural wonder.

振成楼是由清末秀才林逊之设计，他多才多艺，精通书法、易经，及其他中国传统技艺。林逊之是洪坑村当时最富有的林氏家族的子孙。

原　译：This building was designed by Mr. Lin Xunzhi, a versatile government official in the late Qing Dynasty who was specialized in calligraphy, research of *The Book of Changes*, and many other traditional Chinese arts. Mr. Lin came from the once richest family in Hongkeng Hakka Village.

改译：Mr. Lin Xunzhi designed this building. He was a versatile government official in the late Qing Dynasty. He is talented in many things, such as calligraphy, research of *The Book of Changes*, and many other traditional Chinese arts. He came from the once richest family in Hongkeng Hakka Village.

林氏家族从事烟草生意而发家，多年来致力于洪坑村的基础建设。

原译：The Lin Family accumulated a great fortune by doing tobacco business, and was committed to the development of local infrastructure.

改译：The Lin Family became very rich by doing tobacco business, and did a lot to develop local infrastructure.

林逊之的父亲林仁山想兴建一栋浩大的土楼，却因病搁浅。

原译：Lin Renshan, Lin Xunzhi's father, aspired to build a huge Tulou in his village. However, his aspiration failed because of his health problems.

改译：Lin Renshan, Mr. Lin's father, wanted to build a huge Tulou in his village. However, he failed to do so because of his health problems.

仁山去世后，逊之继承父志，开始建造振成楼。

原译：After his death, Xunzhi decided to continue his father's dream and started constructing Zhencheng Lou.

改译：After his father's death, Mr. Lin decided to continue his father's dream and started building Zhencheng Tulou.

实际上，振成楼的楼名是为纪念上代祖宗富成公、丕振公父子而命名的。林逊之取他们两人名字中的"振"与"成"二字命名振成楼。

原译：Actually, it was named by taking one character from each of the names of the family's ancestors, Pizhen and Fucheng.

改译：Actually, it was named by taking one character from each of the family ancestors' names, Pizhen and Fucheng.

振成楼的外观看起来就像古代中国的官帽。

原译：The building resembles a black gauze hat worn by officials in ancient China.

改译：The building looks like a black gauze hat worn by officials in ancient China.

平时楼内居民皆能从地门与人门出入，而天门则常年关闭，仅在逢年过节或婚丧嫁娶等重大日子开启。

原译：Usually only the Gate of Earth and the Gate of Human are used. The Gate of Heaven is closed except on festivals or important occasions like weddings or funerals.

改译：Usually only the Gate of Earth and the Gate of Human are open. The Gate of Heaven is only open on festivals or important occasions like weddings or funerals.

与一般的土楼不同的是，振成楼有两环：外环与内环。

原译：Different from other earthen buildings, Zhencheng Lou has two rings: an outer ring and an inner ring.

改译：Unlike other earthen buildings, Zhencheng Tulou has two rings: an outer ring and an inner ring.

外环楼是土木结构，而内环楼则是砖木结构。

原译：The outer ring was built in earth-wood structure while brick-wood structure was used in the building of the inner ring.

改译：The outer ring is of earth-wood structure and the inner ring is of brick-wood structure.

内外环的建筑都融合了中西方的建筑理念。

原译：Both rings embody Chinese architecture blended with western architecture.

改译：Both rings combine Chinese architecture and western architecture.

1931 年振成楼发生火灾后，二卦的隔墙有效阻止了火势蔓延。

原译：In 1931, a fire broke out in two of the sections, but was prevented from spreading to neighboring sections due to these fireproof walls.

改译：In 1931, a fire broke out in two of the sections, but didn't spread to neighboring sections due to these fireproof walls.

我们现在步入振成楼的中堂大厅，也称祖堂，祖堂的这四根石柱粗约 2 米，高近 7 米。

原译：This is the main hall, also the ancestral hall of the earthen building. These four stone columns are 7 meters high and 2 meters in circumference.

改译：This is the main hall, also the ancestral hall of the earthen building. These four stone columns are 7 meters high and 2 meters round.

祖堂是个多功能大厅，可以布置婚丧宴请，可以开会商讨族内事务，也可以当作舞台开展娱乐活动。

原译：It is a multifunctional hall, where dwellers held wedding ceremonies, funerals and meetings on family affairs. It's also a venue for recreational activities.

改译：It is a multifunctional hall. Here dwellers held wedding ceremonies, funerals and meetings on family affairs. It's also a place for recreational activities.

大家看，面对祖堂的二环楼上还设有小厅，是招待重要客人观看演出的地方。

原译：Now, please look at the hall upstairs in the inner ring. It is a vantage point reserved for important guests to enjoy the performances staged in the ancestral hall.

改译：Now, please look at the hall upstairs in the inner ring. It is a vantage point for important guests to enjoy the performances going on in the ancestral hall.

祖堂的墙上汇集众多名家墨宝。

原译：On the walls of the ancestral hall are valuable pieces of calligraphy done by many famous scholars.

改译：On the walls of the ancestral hall are valuable pieces of calligraphy by many famous scholars.

首先映入我们眼帘的是民国时期的黎元洪大总统赐给主人的五幅横批。

原译: Here are the five horizontal scrolls inscribed by the President of the Republic of China Li Yuanhong around the 1920s.

改译: Here are the five horizontal scrolls by the President of the Republic of China Li Yuanhong around the 1920s.

我们可以想象，以当时的那种交通条件，得花费多大的力气才能把这些栏杆从上海运到这偏僻的小山村啊！

原译: Given the poor transportation at that time, can you imagine the difficulty of shipping these railings to such a remote mountain village?

改译: The transportation was poor at that time. Can you imagine how difficult it is to ship these railings to such a remote mountain village?

这些栏杆非常精致，上面印有四朵百合花，百合花旁簇拥着代表高尚品德的花中四君子：梅、兰、竹、菊。

原译: These railings are exquisite and elegant with four lilies engraved on them. Clustering around the lilies are the so-called Four Gentlemen of Honor: the plum blossom, orchid, bamboo, and chrysanthemum; all representing noble human virtues.

改译: These railings are exquisite and elegant with four lilies engraved on them. Around the lilies are the so-called Four Gentlemen of Honor: the plum blossom, orchid, bamboo, and chrysanthemum. They all represent noble human virtues.

先生们、女士们，接下来，我将带领大家参观规模宏大，素有"土楼之王"美名的承启楼。

原译: Ladies and gentlemen! Next, I will show you around Chengqi Lou, which is known as "the King of Tulou" owing to its large scale.

改译: Ladies and gentlemen! Next, I will show you around Chengqi Tulou. We call it "the King of Tulou" because of its size.

1986 年，中国邮电部就曾发行一套包括承启楼在内的中国民居邮票。

原译: Its picture was included in the set of stamps issued by China's Ministry of Posts and Telecommunications in 1986 featuring Chinese vernacular dwellings.

改译: China's Ministry of Posts and Telecommunications issued a set of stamps in 1986, featuring Chinese vernacular dwellings. One of them is Chengqi Tulou.

大家或许有个疑问：为什么这土制的房子能够经受几百年的风吹雨打而屹立不倒呢？

原译：You might wonder how this earthen building can still stand intact after hundreds of years of weathering.

改译：You might wonder how this Tulou can still stand intact after hundreds of years.

第一、二层外墙不开窗，只在内墙开一小窗。通过小窗，居民可以呼吸外面的新鲜空气，并且享受从屋顶射下来的阳光。

原译：For those rooms on the first and second floor in the outer ring, no windows were built on the exterior wall. Instead, small windows were built on the interior wall to let in fresh air and sunlight.

改译：For those rooms on the first and second floor in the outer ring, there are no windows on the exterior wall. Instead, there are small windows on the interior wall to let in fresh air and sunlight.

一层是灶房，二层是禾仓，三、四层都是卧室。走进楼内，我们会看到第二环，楼高2层，每层有40个房间。

原译：The first floor was used for cooking and dining, the second floor is the granary, and rooms on the third and fourth floors are bedrooms. Please come with me. We are now at the second ring, a two-story building with 40 rooms on each floor.

改译：The first floor was for cooking and dining, the second floor is the granary, and rooms on the third and fourth floors are bedrooms. Please come with me. We are now at the second ring. It's a two-story building with 40 rooms on each floor.

祖堂位于中央的内环，是楼内居民举行重大仪式的场所。

原译：The ancestral hall is housed in the middle ring. It is where the dwellers hold important ceremonies.

改译：The ancestral hall is in the middle ring. The dwellers hold important ceremonies here.

祖堂内随处可见名家政客的题匾，其中包括20世纪30年代国民政府主席林森的题匾。

原译：The ancestral hall houses many horizontal scrolls inscribed by famous politicians and calligraphers including Lin Sen, Chairman of the National Government of the Republic of China in the 1930s.

改译：The ancestral hall houses many horizontal scrolls by famous politicians and calligraphers including Lin Sen, Chairman of the National Government of the Republic of China in the 1930s.

最吸引人眼球的是清代朝中大官送给承启楼建造者之子江建镛的寿屏。

原译: This wooden screen was a birthday gift from a governmental official in the Qing Dynasty to this building's designer's son Lin Jianyong.

改译: This wooden screen was a birthday gift from a governmental official in the Qing Dynasty to Lin Jianyong, son of the building's designer.

素有"最大方形土楼"之称的遗经楼也是我们不能错过的土楼。

原译: Yijing Lou, reputed as the largest square Tulou, is another earthen building we shall not miss.

改译: Yijing Tulou is the largest square Tulou, another Tulou we shall not miss.

与圆形土楼相比，方形土楼在福建的农村地区较为常见。

原译: Square Tulou is actually more common than circular ones in the rural areas of Fujian Province.

改译: Square Tulou are actually more common than circular ones in the rural areas of Fujian Province.

然而，遗经楼规模宏大，别具一格，值得一游。

原译: Yijing Lou is worth a visit because of its great size and ingenious style.

改译: Yijing Tulou is worth a visit because of its size and style.

遗经楼中央有一天井，也是祖堂所在地与整栋楼的中心点。

原译: Right in the middle of the building is a court. It is where the ancestral hall is located.

改译: Right in the middle of the building is a court. The ancestral hall is here.

土楼的后面有个很漂亮的花园，大家可以在这里欣赏一下盛开的花朵。

原译: Well, at the back of the building lies a beautiful garden where we could appreciate the booming flowers.

改译: Well, at the back of the building lies a beautiful garden. Here we could appreciate the blooming flowers.

福裕楼是一座府第式的建筑，而奎聚楼则是宫殿式的建筑。奎聚楼建于 1834 年，外观呈方形状，里面是宫殿式的建筑，被人称为土楼中的"布达拉宫"。

原译: Kuiju Lou is a rectangular structure built in 1834. While Fuyu Lou is a mansion-style architecture, Kuiju Lou is a palace-like one. It is nicknamed "the Potala Palace" among Tulous.

改译：Kuiju Tulou is a rectangular structure built in 1834. While Fuyu Tulou is a mansion-style architecture, Kuiju Tulou is a palace-like one. We call it "the Potala Palace of Tulou".

从高处看，奎聚楼与背后的山脊连成一体，就像猛虎下山。

原译：If you look at it from a lofty point, you will see that Kuiju Lou blends in well with the ridge behind it, with the imposing air of a tiger charging down a mountain.

改译：If you look at it from a high place, you will see Kuiju Tulou blends in well with the ridge behind it, like a tiger charging down a mountain.

福裕楼坐落在洪坑村的一条河边，是典型的府第式建筑，也称五凤楼，突出的屋檐就像欲飞的凤凰。

原译：Fuyu Lou is located near a river in Hongkeng Village, a typical example of mansion style building. It is also called Five Phoenixes Building or Wufeng Lou, with protruding eaves like phoenixes ready to take flight.

改译：Fuyu Lou is near a river in Hongkeng Village. It is a typical mansion style Tulou. It is also called Five Phoenixes Tulou or Wufeng Tulou. It has protruding eaves like phoenixes ready to take flight.

各位朋友，你们或许在想福裕楼的设计是不是有什么说道。

原译：You may wonder why Fuyu Lou was designed with this particular layout.

改译：You may wonder why Fuyu Tulou has such a particular layout.

其实，这个建筑理念来源于福裕楼三位主人的名字：林仲山、林仁山、林德山，都包含一个"山"字。

原译：Well, the idea came from the names of the building's three owners: Lin Zhongshan, Lin Renshan and Lin Deshan, all with the character "shan" in them, which means "hills" or "mountains".

改译：Well, the idea came from the names of the building's three owners. They all have the character "shan" in the name, meaning "hills" or "mountains".

从外面看，主楼与横屋连成一体，然而，走进一看，则分为三大单元。

原译：If you look at it from the outside, the building is an integrated whole. Once inside, you will see that it can be divided into three independent sections.

改译: If you look at it from the outside, the building is an integrated whole. Once inside, you will see that there are three independent sections.

由于客家人多居住在野兽出没、盗匪四起的山区，他们建成的这种群居住房具有良好的防御功能。

原译: As most Hakka resided in mountains, these communal houses were built to provide protection against bandits and wild animals.

改译: As most Hakka resided in mountains, these communal houses provided protection against bandits and wild animals.

土楼是漳州本土建筑的代表，漳州土楼的总数多达 800 多座。

原译: Tulou represents a vernacular architecture specific to Zhangzhou, where there are more than eight hundred of these Earth Buildings in total.

改译: Tulou represents a vernacular architecture specific to Zhangzhou. In Zhangzhou there are more than eight hundred Tulou in total.

高大的土楼内部，厅堂、储藏室、水井、卧室等应有尽有，俨然一座小小的卫城。

原译: With all the halls, storehouses, wells, bedrooms and other necessary living facilities inside, the huge earthen building functions almost as a small fortified city.

改译: The huge earthen building has halls, storehouses, wells, bedrooms and other necessary living facilities inside. It is like a small fortified city.

各位团友大家好！今天我们游览的第一站是田螺坑土楼群，俗称"四菜一汤"。这片由五栋土楼组成的土楼群被誉为最美的土楼群。

原译: Ladies and gentlemen, our first stop of the Tulou trip today is the Tianluo keng Earth Building Cluster. Figuratively nicknamed as "Four Dishes and One Soup", the quintet cluster is honored as the most attractive Earth Buildings in the country.

改译: Ladies and gentlemen, our first stop of the Tulou trip today is the Tianluo keng Tulou Cluster. We call it "Four Dishes and One Soup". This quintet cluster is honored as the most attractive Tulou in the country.

有一种说法是当地山路都是一圈又一圈的，就像田螺壳一样。

原译: Some people say it is because of the local winding mountain roads that look like the shell of a river snail.

改译: Some people say the local winding mountain roads look like the shell of a river snail.

据说，美丽的田螺姑娘有一次被一个青年搭救，后嫁给他为妻。

原译：She was said to be saved by a young man and then married him.

改译：It is said a young man saved her and she married him.

现在我们到了可以俯瞰"四菜一汤"的上观景台。

原译：Now we are on the viewing platform overlooking the cluster situated halfway up the mountain.

改译：Now we are on the viewing platform overlooking the cluster halfway up the mountain.

大家看，这个土楼群坐落在半山坡上，共有 5 座楼，一座方形楼位于当中，四座圆形楼围绕方楼，形成"四菜一汤"的格局。中间的这座方形楼叫作步云楼。

原译：It consists of five Tulou buildings with one square building in the center and 4 round ones around it, forming a pattern of "Four Dishes and One Soup". The square building sitting at the center of the cluster is Buyun Lou, literally translated as Reach-the-Cloud Building.

改译：It consists of five Tulou with a square one in the center and 4 round ones around it. It forms a pattern of "Four Dishes and One Soup". The square Tulou at the center of the cluster is Buyun Tulou. Literally it means Reach-the-Cloud Building.

4.8 小结

从本章对申遗文本、景区文本、酒店介绍、导游词翻译质量的评估来看，福建世界遗产翻译的很多质量问题，如术语不统一、与类比文本相比语言特征差距较大等，都可以通过 CCAT 平台下的翻译模式解决，即利用 CCAT 平台的 CAT 术语库保证术语统一，利用 CCAT 平台的类比语料库为缩小语言差距提供借鉴。具体操作见第 6 章。

第 5 章 福建世界遗产网站本地化研究

5.1 引言

网站本地化是指网站为目标访客提供以其本国语言显示的网页，如美国旅游网站为中国客户提供中文网页，就是针对中国客户的本地化，而中国旅游网站为国外客户提供英文网页，则是针对国外客户的本地化体现（王朝晖，余军：2016）。

网站本地化需将一个网站的指定部分或全部改编成面向特定目标用户的一种或多种语言，包括文字、图片、动画以及网站工程的处理等。不同于简单的网站翻译，在进行网站本地化时，不仅仅要考虑到文字翻译方面的精确，还要兼顾到客户群体的语言习惯、色彩好恶、言辞忌讳、文化习俗等一系列的问题。

网站本地化是对外宣传、交流或商贸往来的必要手段，其作用极其重要。主要分为两种类型。

第一种类型是本地化网站栏目与原网站存在不同，即定制型。其中又分为两种情况。一种是原网站与本地化网站分属地址完全不同的网页，如美国Amazon 的本土网页为 www.amazon.com，而其中国网站的网址为 www.amazon.cn。两个网站的栏目有所差别，所售商品也不相同，这种情况一般是由于该公司在美国和中国分别运营，两个区域的产品和服务不相同。另一种情况是原网站和本地化网站在同一域名内，如携程旅行网，其中文网页的网址为 http://www.ctrip.com/，在中文网页上有英文网页的链接，点开即进入英文页面，网址为 http://english.ctrip.com/，属同一网站，但栏目和页面与中文网站不完全相同（王朝晖，余军：2016）。

第二种类型是本地化网站与原网站在栏目设置及内容等方面完全一样，即同一型（王朝晖，余军：2016），如著名的酒店预订网站缤客网（www.booking.com）。其网站以英语为主，同时提供了四十余种语言的选择，包括中文。缤客网的本地化是此类网站中的佼佼者。虽然该网站首页、网站栏目及多数酒店页面都已本地化，但仍可能有部分页面，即使选择中文，显示的也大部分是英文。原因可能是有的酒店加入不久，未及完全本地化。

对于世界遗产的对外宣传而言，网站本地化是其走向世界的桥梁，也是国

福建世界遗产网站 第 5 章 本地化研究

87

际化的必由之路，因而至关重要。

　　本章根据福建世界遗产双语语料库中的网站本地化类比语料库，对福建世界遗产网站的本地化现状做出基于实证的客观评估，在比较中、英、韩三国世界遗产网站及分析语料库数据的基础上，探讨世界遗产网站本地化的策略和模式，以促进世界遗产网站本地化研究的发展以及世界遗产网站本地化水平的提高。

5.2　网站本地化研究现状

　　国外对于网站本地化的研究始于 20 世纪 90 年代，主要随着电子商务的出现而逐渐兴起。Singh 和 Pereira（2005）以及 Cyr 和 Trevor-Smith（2004）的研究发现，企业要在跨境电子商务中取得成功，必须从语言和文化两个方面进行网站本地化。成功的本地化可以使企业的跨境电子商务销售额增长 200%（Tixier，2005）。著名的全球化研究机构 Byte Level Research 在其"全球化年度报告"中将网站本地化作为评估企业全球化水平的 4 个标准之一（Brandel，2007）。Singh 等（2009）提出了网站本地化的动态评估框架，包括内容本地化、网站入口、文化顺应、翻译质量等几个方面，翻译只是其中的考察因素之一。此外，Amant（2005）从原型理论（prototype theory）的视角，Ahmed 等（2009）从权利距离和高语境文化的视角，Cyr 等（2010）等从文化内及文化间的颜色差异的视角，Singh 和 Pereira（2005）从文化顺应的视角，分别探讨了网站本地化。

　　除理论研究外，国外学者对网站本地化还展开了较多的应用研究，如译者培训（Austermühl，2006），翻译策略（Sandrini，2005 ；Nauert，2007），面向亚洲用户的网站本地化评估（Rau and Liang，2003），文化、地域及基础设施对欧洲航空公司网站本地化决策的影响（Shneor，2012），等等。总体而言，国外网站本地化的研究不论在理论还是应用方面都取得了较多成果，并处于迅猛发展之中，但其研究对象主要为西方跨国公司，研究内容主要是英语向其他语言的本地化，尚未涉及中国的网站由中文向其他语言的本地化。

　　国内的相关研究相比国外而言则滞后很多。以"网站本地化"为关键词在 CNKI 中检索，仅《译员在网站本地化过程中的角色定位》（刘雯，2011）、《旅游网站本地化质量评估探讨》（王韵，2008）及《网站本地化过程研究》（谢姆西努尔·阿力木，张太红，2015）等 3 篇论文。而有关网站翻译的论文则相对较多，约 50 篇，可见国内学界对网站本地化了解不够深入，研究范围较为狭窄，仅限于传统的翻译视角。其中有关旅游网站翻译的文章共 16 篇，所涉领域包括本地化视角（李丹，2012 ；周红，2015）、目的论（王丽丽，2010 ；彭金玲，

2013）、生态翻译学（韩笑，2012；林菲，2014）、变译理论（顾伟，2010）、目的地认知行为模式（黄琼英，2014a）、跨文化视角（韩军利，2009；张珺莹，2014）、文本类型理论（李赛男，2012）、传播学（郑周林，2011）以及区域性旅游网站翻译调查（万永坤，2012；杨嫚，2014；马会峰，2014；黄琼英，2014b），等等，专门考察世界遗产网站本地化的则尚付阙如。

5.3　福建世界遗产网站建设现状

据调查，福建土楼、武夷山和泰宁等 3 处世界遗产均建有官方旅游网站，相关网站列具如下：

（1）武夷山官网：http://www.wuyishan.gov.cn/wbj/ly/（中文、英文）

（2）南靖土楼官网：http://www.fjtlw.gov.cn/（中文、英文）

（3）永定土楼官网：http://www.yoding.cn/tulou/（中文）http://amazing fujian tulou.com/（英文）

（4）泰宁旅游官网：http://www.tnly.net/（中文）

以上网站中，泰宁旅游官网仅有中文版，无其他语言版本，本地化程度为零；南靖土楼官网的中文页面上提供了英文入口，但点开为有道翻译引擎，实际并无英文页面；武夷山官网主页提供了中文、英文、日文、韩文、电子商务等入口，其网站本地化属同一域名的定制型；永定土楼官网的网站本地化也属定制型，但英文版与中文版域名不同。

据以上初步调查结果，福建世界遗产的本地化网站数量较少，对已建成的武夷山及永定土楼本地化网站进行质量评估，促进福建世界遗产网站本地化的建设，有助于福建世界遗产的对外传播和相关文化产业的发展。

5.4　福建世界遗产网站本地化质量评估——武夷山及永定土楼

由于泰宁和南靖土楼尚无本地化网站，下面以武夷山和永定土楼官网为例，对福建世界遗产网站本地化进行质量评估。

根据 Singh 等（2009）的动态评估框架模型，本节在网站入口、内容本地化、文化顺应、翻译质量等 4 个评估维度的基础上，确定网站入口、网站设计、网站内容、语言特点、文本翻译等 5 个世界遗产网站本地化质量评估的观测点，与世界遗产网站本地化类比语料库中的英国世界遗产 New Lanark（新拉纳克）官网（http://www.newlanark.org/）及韩国世界遗产 Suwon Hwaseong Fortress（水原华城）英文官网（http://english.swcf.or.kr/?p=31）进行比较，考察武夷山和土楼官网的本地化质量，以期在此基础上，构建符合目标客户语言、文化及心理预期的网站本地化策略和模式。

5.4.1 网站入口

对于网站入口的考察，主要看其是否易于通过 Google 等主流搜索引擎检索到，检索结果出现的排名越前，易达性越好，本地化的效果也越好。

分别以"tulou"和"Mount Wuyi"为关键词，在 Google、Bing、Yahoo 等国外 3 个主流搜索引擎中进行检索（检索结果的语言选择英文），排名前 10 位的网站／网页如表 5-1、表 5-2 所示：

表 5-1　在 Google、Bing、Yahoo 中检索"tulou"排名前 10 的网站

搜索引擎	检索词：tulou
Google	1. https://en.wikipedia.org/wiki/Tulou
	2. https://en.wikipedia.org/wiki/Fujian_Tulou
	3. http://whc.unesco.org/en/list/1113
	4. http://english.cntv.cn/program/journeysintime/special/tulou/
	5. http://amazingfujiantulou.com/
	6. https://www.youtube.com/watch?v=wNl_WbeFyiU
	7. https://www.youtube.com/watch?v=ZZ_Z58r3mIs
	8. http://news.nationalgeographic.com/news/2015/01/150102-hakka-china-tulou-fujian-world-heritage-culture-housing/
	9. www.chinabackpacker.info/dest/d70.html
	10. http://www.chinahighlights.com/xiamen/attraction/tulou.htm
Bing	1. https://en.wikipedia.org/wiki/Fujian_Tulou
	2. https://en.wikipedia.org/wiki/Tulou
	3. http://travel.cnn.com/China-travel-tulou-unesco-919371/
	4. http://www.chinadwelling.dk/hovedsider/clan_homes-tekst.ht
	5. www.chinadwelling.dk/hovedsider/clan_homes-tekst.htm
	6. whc.unesco.org/fr/list/1113
	7. http://tulou.org/（与福建土楼无关）
	8. www.chinatourguide.com/fujian/fujian_tulou.html
	9. www.chinadiscovery.com/fujian-tulou/yongding-tulou.html
	10. http://www.healthgrades.com/physician/dr-nicolas-tulou-3fmd5（与福建土楼无关）

续表

搜索引擎	检索词：tulou
Yahoo	1. www.LifeScript.com/MD（与福建土楼无关） 2. https://en.wikipedia.org/wiki/Fujian_Tulou 3. htttps://en.wikipedia.org/wiki/Tulou **4. http://amazingfujiantulou.com/** 5. www.chinadwelling.dk/hovedsider/clan_homes-tekst.htm 6. www.tulou.org（与福建土楼无关） 7. http://travel.cnn.com/China-travel-tulou-unesco-919371/ 8. http://whc.unesco.org/fr/list/1113 9. www.chinatourguide.com/fujian/fujian_tulou.html 10. www.chinadiscovery.com/fujian-tulou/yongding-tulou.html

表 5-2　在 Google、Bing、Yahoo 中检索"Mount Wuyi"排名前 10 的网站

搜索引擎	检索词：Mount Wuyi
Google	1. https://en.wikipedia.org/wiki/Wuyi_Mountains 2. http://whc.unesco.org/en/list/911 3. https://wikitravel.org/en/Mount_Wuyi 4. https://www.travelchinaguide.com/attraction/fujian/wu-yi-shan.htm 5. www.chinahighlights.com/xiamen/attraction/mount-wuyi.htm 6. http://www.tour-beijing.com/blog/china-travel/china-top-10/top-10-wuyis-han-attractions-top-10-things-to-do-in-wuyi-mountain 7. http://www.tour-beijing.com/fujian_tour/wuyishan_tour/ 8. ttps://www.tripadvisor.com/Attraction_Review-g424920-d319629-Reviews-Wuyi_Mountain_Scenic_Resort-Wuyi_Shan_Fujian.html 9. https://en.wikivoyage.org/wiki/Mount_Wuyi 10. http://english.cntv.cn/program/documentary/wuyitea/
Bing	1. https://en.wikipedia.org/wiki/Mount_Wuyi 2. https://wikitravel.org/en/Mount_Wuyi 3. www.travelchinaguide.com/attraction/fujian/wu-yi-shan.htm 4. https://en.wikivoyage.org/wiki/Mount_Wuyi 5. www.mountwuyi.info 6. www.chinahighlights.com/xiamen/attraction/mount-wuyi.htm 7. www.eoearth.org/view/article/154713 8. www.chinatravel.com/xiamen-attraction/wuyi-mountain 9. www.chinahighlights.com/xiamen/attraction/mount-wuyi.htm 10. www.chinatravel.com/xiamen-attraction/wuyi-mountain

续表

搜索引擎	检索词：Mount Wuyi
Yahoo	1. https://en.wikipedia.org/wiki/Mount_Wuyi
	2. https://wikitravel.org/en/Mount_Wuyi
	3. www.travelchinaguide.com/attraction/fujian/wu-yi-shan.htm
	4. https://en.wikivoyage.org/wiki/Mount_Wuyi
	5. www.mountwuyi.info（与武夷山无关）
	6. http://www.eoearth.org/view/article/154713/
	7. www.chinahighlights.com/xiamen/attraction/mount-wuyi.htm
	8. www.chinatravel.com/xiamen-attraction/wuyi-mountain
	9. http://www.mountwuyi.info/?p=277
	10. https://www.tripadvisor.com/Attraction_Review-g424920-d319629-Reviews-Wuyi_Mountain_Scenic_Resort-Wuyi_Shan_Fujian.html

从以上检索结果来看，永定土楼官网的英文本地化（**http://amazing fujiantulou.com/**）在网站入口的易达性方面相对较为成功，分别在 Google 和 Yahoo 检索中排名第 5 和第 4；而武夷山官网的英文本地化（http://www.wuyishan.gov.cn/wbj/ly/）则未能进入 3 个搜索引擎中任何一个的前 10 名，网站入口在易达性方面较弱。

在 Google、Bing 和 Yahoo 搜索引擎中分别检索英国世界遗产"New Lanark"和韩国世界遗产"Suwon Hwaseong Fortress"，与永定土楼英文官网的排名比较（未进入前 10 则打 ×）：

表 5-3　3 个世界遗产网站检索排名比较

	New Lanark	Suwon Hwaseong Fortress	Tulou
Google	1	6	5
Bing	1	×	×
Yahoo	3	×	4

以上搜索结果中的网站／网页并无竞价排名，其排名主要是通过网站／网页的点击量和流量获得，而网站／网页的点击量和流量取决于网站／网页的性质、设计、内容及语言。

我们注意到 3 个搜索引擎中 Wiki 的相关网页和联合国教科文组织的世界遗产网页排名均较高，Wiki 作为著名开放式百科知识网站，其网页一贯质量颇高，而联合国教科文组织的武夷山及土楼页面则具有权威性，两者取得较高排名均在情理之中。英国 New Lanark 官网在三大搜索引擎中的排名很高，与其为英文原生网站有关，韩国 Suwon Hwaseong Fortress 英文官网的排名略差于永定土楼英文官网，与其为 http://english.swcf.or.kr/ 网站的子栏目，并非独立网站不无关系。

下面从网站设计、网站内容、语言特点、文本翻译等方面考察武夷山英文官网、永定土楼英文官网，并与韩国 Suwon Hwaseong Fortress 英文官网和英国 New Lanark 官网进行比较。

5.4.2　网站设计

网站设计，包括网站标志、导航栏、网页布局、色彩运用等。这些要素合理高效、恰到好处的组合运用，可令访客赏心悦目，在浏览时如鱼得水，心情愉悦，从而为网站带来好评和流量。

5.4.2.1　网站标志

表 5-4　4 个世界遗产网站标志调查

世界遗产网站	官网标志
Mount Wuyi	无
Tulou	
Suwon Hwaseong Fortress	
New Lanark	

以上标志中，韩国 Suwon Hwaseong Fortress 官网由于是 http://english.swcf.or.kr/ 网站的子栏目，因此只有水原文化财团的标志，未显示出其本身的名称，逊色于 Tulou 和 New Lanark 的标志。从标志所承载的信息量而言，永定土楼英文官网的标志包含"客家"、"Hakka"、"土楼"、"Tulou"等中英文信息，尤其是"Hakka"一词，较为国外访客所了解，减少了陌生感，标志中有一个象征圆形土楼的图形，但遗憾的是缺少世界遗产这一重要标记。英国 New Lanark 官网的标志包含 New Lanark 的名称、世界遗产标记以及当地典型建筑的图形，是 3 个标志设计中最全面、最成功的。

在文化的对外传播中，"文化符号"的构建是重要途径之一，世界遗产网站可以通过标志构造其独特的文化符号，加深国外访客的印象，促进世界遗产走向世界。

5.4.2.2 导航栏

表5-5　4个世界遗产网站导航栏比较

世界遗产网站	导航栏
Mount Wuyi	HOME PAGE；GENERAL INTRODUCTION TO WUYIS-HAN；TYPICAL SCENARY；CUTURE AND CUSTOM；VIDEO GUIDE；TOURISM SERVICE；GUIDE SERVICE
Tulou	Home；About；See & Do；Plan your trip；Gallery；Customization
Suwon Hwaseong Fortress	TOUR；FESTIVAL；CUTURAL；SWCF NEWS；ABOUT SWCF
New Lanark	VISITOR CENTRE；WORLD HERITAGE SITE；WHAT'S ON；ACCOMMODATION；WOOL & TEXTILES；LEARN-ING；CONTACT

以上为一级导航，武夷山英文官网的导航栏目设置显得杂乱，缺乏分类依据，"TOURISM SERVICE"和"GUIDE SERVICE"栏目重叠。

永定土楼英文官网的导航栏目设计从信息传递的角度来看，缺乏效率，如访客想要了解土楼的历史文化，就无法立即判断应点击哪个栏目。其"About"栏目下包括"Introduction"和"Travel Guide"两个子栏目，"See & Do"下包括"Best spots"、"Architecture"、"Culture"、"Customs"、"Cuisine"、"Tea Ceremony"、"Rice Wine Workshop"、"Hot Springs"等子栏目，"Plan your trip"下包含"Tours"和"Accommodation"两个子栏目，子栏目归类较为杂乱，"Gallery"下面没有子栏目，"Customization"是定制旅游线路，应归在"Plan your trip"栏目下。

韩国 Suwon Hwaseong Fortress 英文官网导航栏的分类则更为清晰，"TOUR"（观光指南）下面包括与旅游有关的信息；"Festival"则介绍水原华城的戏剧节、国际音乐节和文化节；此外还有一个"SWCF NEWS"（财团消息）栏目，起到动态宣传的作用。

英国 New Lanark 官网的导航栏最为全面，也最具逻辑。"VISITOR CENTRE"聚集有关旅游观光的咨询，如景点、交通线路等等；"WORLD HERITAGE SITE"聚集了该世界遗产的历史文化信息；"WHAT'S ON"介绍当地举办的各种活动，也起到动态宣传的作用；"WOOL & TEXTILES"突出该地的特色产业；"Learning"介绍当地的教育，如图5-1所示：

图 5-1　英国 New Lanark 官网"Learning"栏目

此外,"CONTACT"栏目在醒目位置提供咨询服务,为访客提供了联系和沟通渠道,较为人性化。

从以上简要分析来看,英国 New Lanark 官网的导航栏设置全面,分类合理,信息齐全,值得我们学习、借鉴。

另外,就语言文字的正确使用而言,永定土楼英文官网的"See & Do"栏目不符合目标读者的语言使用习惯,改为"What to See & Do"或"Things to See & Do"为宜,韩国 Suwon Hwaseong Fortress 英文官网的"Cultural"则应改为"Culture"。

5.4.2.3　网站布局

访客在浏览网页的时候,都希望能够便捷地通过点击链接转向其需要获取的页面,页面布局是否方便、合理,对访客的浏览体验至关重要。4 个网站的网页布局如表 5-6 所示。

表5-6　4个世界遗产网站按照网页布局比较

	Mount Wuyi	Tulou	Suwon Hwaseong Fortress	New Lanark
左侧快捷栏	√	×	√	√
右侧快捷栏	×	×	√	×
顶部二级栏目	×	√	√	√
底部快捷链接	×	√	×	√
网页文本超链接	×	×	×	√

武夷山英文官网仅包含左侧快捷栏（见图5-2），用户体验可能是4个网站中最差的。

图5-2　武夷山英文官网左侧快捷栏

永定土楼英文官网略好一些，包含了顶部二级栏目和底部快捷链接，如图5-3：

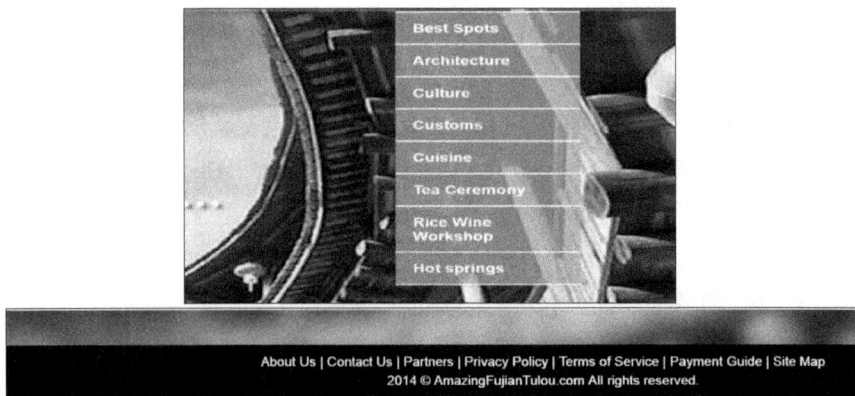

图5-3　永定土楼英文官网快捷栏

韩国 Suwon Hwaseong Fortress 英文官网除提供左侧快捷栏和顶部二级栏目外，还包括右侧快捷栏，如图 5-4：

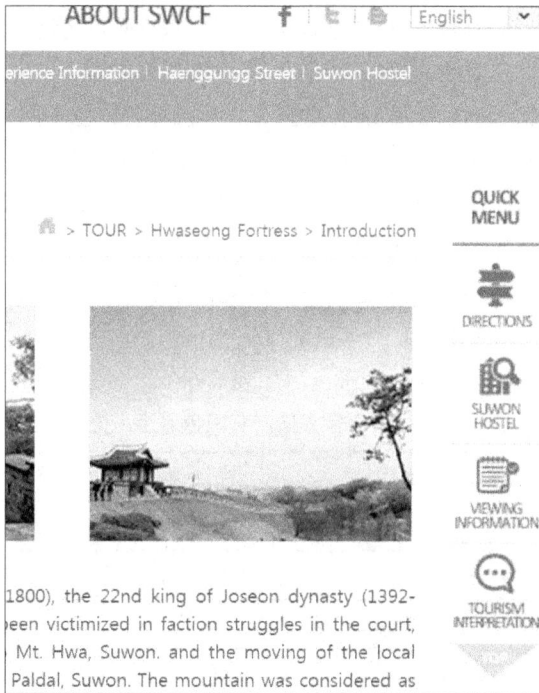

图 5-4　Suwon Hwaseong Fortress 英文官网右侧快捷栏

英国 New Lanark 官网除包含左侧快捷栏、顶部二级栏目、底部快捷链接之外，还在网页文本中提供了超链接，如图 5-5：

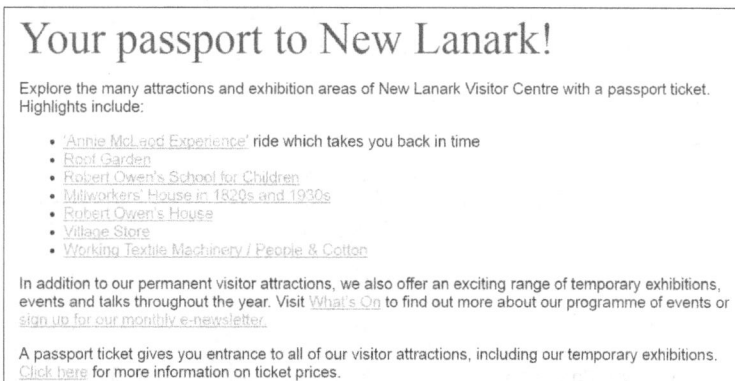

图 5-5　New Lanark 官网网页文本超链接

从以上比较可以看出，4 个网站页面布局设置的优劣排名为：

New Lanark > Suwon Hwaseong Fortress > Tulou > Mount Wuyi

5.4.2.4 色彩运用

有关色彩运用对网站吸引力的影响，国内外研究较少。Cyr 等（2010）在一项调查中考察了来自加拿大、德国和日本等 3 个不同文化的试验者对于网站色彩运用的反应，证明和推翻了一些假设。该研究发现，3 个文化的试验者都对网站使用黄色表示强烈反感，推翻了日本人会喜欢该色彩网站的假设；另外，还证明了德国人喜欢网站使用蓝色，而加拿大人则喜欢灰色的假设。该研究认为，色彩运用得当的话，可以增加访客对网站的信任以及忠诚度，反之亦然。

以上实验对于网站本地化中色彩的运用具有启发意义，网站本地化在色彩的运用上应该避免黄色，红色由于在西方文化中易引起与暴力相关的联想，也应尽量避免，而灰色（黑色）和蓝色则可适当使用。

4 个世界遗产官网的网站色彩运用如表 5-7：

表 5-7　4 个世界遗产官网色彩运用比较

世界遗产网站	栏目颜色	网页底色
Mount Wuyi	蓝色	白色
Tulou	橙色，灰色，红色	白色
Suwon Hwaseong Fortress	蓝色	白色
New Lanark	橙色，灰色	白色

永定土楼英文官网的色彩略多，显得杂乱，另外，红色运用不当。其他 3 个网站的色彩使用则没有问题。

5.4.3　网站内容

对网站内容的调查主要是通过网站语料的高频词比较 4 个世界遗产网站在主题及内容侧重点上的差异。

有关 4 个网站内容的基本信息如表 5-8：

表 5-8　4 个世界遗产网站内容基本信息

世界遗产网站	网页链接数量	网页总词数
Mount Wuyi	52	8200
Tulou	33	38000
Suwon Hwaseong Fortress	35	36000
New Lanark	214	90000

用雪人 CAT 分别加载 4 个网站的英文语料，统计词频，"最少出现频率"

设为 10，统计界面如图 5-6：

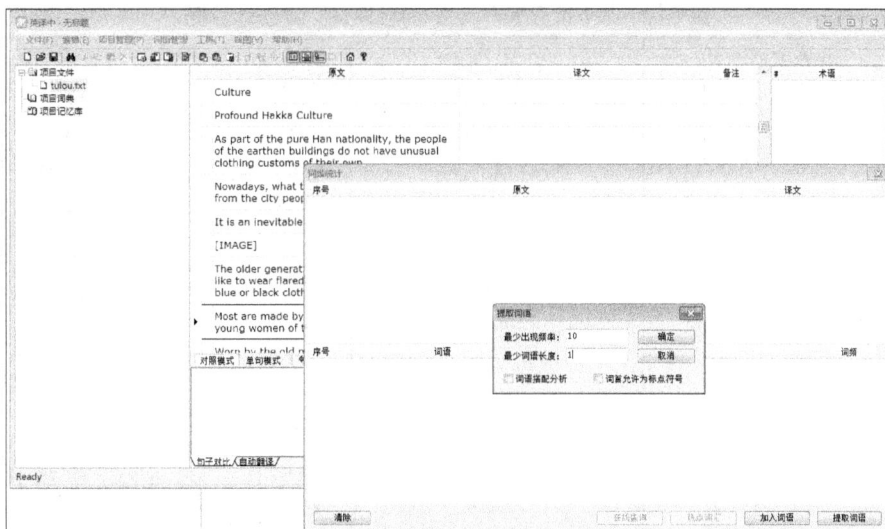

图 5-6　雪人 CAT 词频统计界面

统计结果如图 5-7：

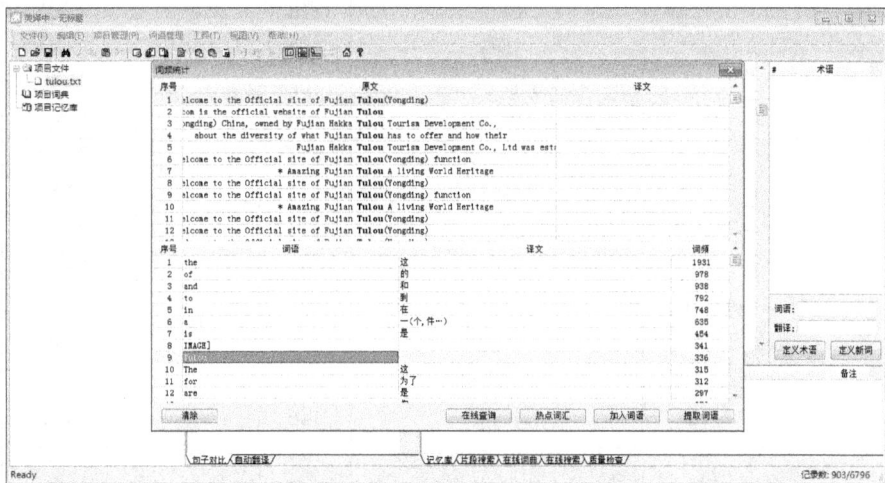

图 5-7　雪人 CAT 词频统计结果

导出统计结果，人工删除虚词，词频排名前 10 位的统计数据如下：

表 5-9　4 个世界遗产网站词频排名前 10 统计数据

世界遗产名称	前 10 词表	词频	总词数	每万字词频
Mount Wuyi	Wuyi	98	8200	119.51
	Tourism	74		90.23
	Wuyi Mountain	58		70.73
	Fujian	54		65.85
	Wuyishan	52		63.41
	Culture	51		62.19
	Wuyi Mountain City	46		56.09
	Scenery	37		45.12
	tea	31		37.80
	Service	30		36.58
Tulou	Tulou	336	38000	88.42
	Hakka	245		64.47
	Fujian	192		50.52
	Yongding	143		37.63
	tulou	137		36.05
	Xiamen	136		35.78
	China	118		31.05
	trip	110		28.94
	Fujian Tulou	108		28.42
	Tour	99		26.05
Suwon Hwaseong Fortress	Suwon	653	36000	181.38
	Hwaseong	513		142.5
	Information	343		95.27
	Cultural	282		78.33
	Haenggung	224		62.22
	Suwon Hwaseong	173		48.05
	Festival	162		45
	King	146		40.55
	Hwaseong Haenggung	145		40.27
	fortress	143		39.72

续表

世界遗产名称	前10词表	词频	总词数	每万字词频
New Lanark	New Lanark	2114	90000	234.88
	World Heritage	606		67.33
	Trust	425		47.22
	Scotland	345		38.33
	New Lanark World Heritage	324		36
	World Heritage Site	299		33.22
	Mill	292		32.44
	Visitor Centre	265		29.44
	Owen	260		28.88
	Tourist	257		28.55

对表5-9分析如下：

（1）武夷山英文官网：在武夷山申遗文本中，武夷山的英文名为"Mount Wuyi"，该英文名未在前10词表中出现，"Wuyi Mountain"却出现在前10词表中，频率比"Mount Wuyi"还高，说明术语表达不统一的情况比较严重；武夷山市的译名也不统一，既有"Wuyishan"，也有"Wuyi Moutain City"，较为混乱；武夷山以茶文化著称，但前10词表中未出现大红袍的英文，也未见"Zhu Xi"、"World Heritage"等词。前10词表中包含了"scenery"、"tourism"、"service"等词，说明旅游主题意识较强。总体而言，关键词较分散，文化传播意识较弱。

（2）永定土楼英文官网：前10词表中出现了"Yongding"、"Fujian"、"Xiamen"等词汇，具有一定的外宣意识，"Tulou"和"tulou"都出现在词表中，后者不规范，术语不统一。前10词表中出现了"trip"、"tour"等词，说明旅游主题意识较强，但未出现"World Heritage"，说明利用世界遗产这一国际级称号进行宣传的意识仍不足。

（3）Suwon Hwaseong Fortress英文官网：前10词表中包含了"Suwon"、"Hwaseong"、"fortress"等词，具有一定的外宣意识，未出现土楼英文官网的术语不一致问题。与之类似的是，前10词表中也未出现"World Heritage"，说明利用世界遗产这一国际级称号进行宣传的意识仍显不足。前10词表中未见旅游相关的主题词汇。

（4）New Lanark官网：前10词表中既有该遗产所在地的"New Lanark"、"Scotland"等地名，又有与旅游有关的"tourist"、"visitor center"等主题词汇，以及可资宣传的"World Heritage"，还有与传统纺织产业相关的"Mill"，说明关键词极为集中，主题突出，文化意识很强。

5.4.4　语言特点

除网站设计和网站内容外，本地化网站的语言运用对于提高网络吸引力和流量也非常重要。成功的本地化网站往往句式丰富，简洁易读，层次分明，内容充实。

本小节从第一人称及第二人称使用频率、平均句长、句式特征等方面检索4个世界遗产网站语料，考察4个世界遗产网站的语言特点，最后用 Readability Studio 2015 软件验证其易读指数。

5.4.4.1　第一人称及第二人称使用频率

据李丹（2012：121）研究，国外旅游网站的景点介绍文字，如澳大利亚官方网站，使用第二人称和第一人称较多，这种方式会拉近和预期游客的距离，使读者倍感亲切。另据康宁（2012：108）研究，中国网站英语文本在人称代词（we、us、our、you、your）的使用上明显少于英语本民族旅游文本。因此，世界遗产本地化网站的第一人称及第二人称代词的使用频率，可以作为判断其本地化质量的一个依据。

4个世界遗产网站语料中第一人称"we"和第二人称"you"的使用频率统计如表5-10：

表 5-10　4 个遗产网站"we"和"you"词频统计

世界遗产网站	"We"词频（‰）	"you"词频（‰）
Mount Wuyi	0.731	1.097
Tulou	2.263	7.500
Suwon Hwaseong Fortress	0.361	0.361
New Lanark	2.100	3.655

表 5-10 显示，武夷山英文官方网站和 Suwon Hwaseong Fortress 英文官方网站第一人称和第二人称使用的频率相比英国 New Lanark 官网明显偏低，而永定土楼英文官网则与 New Lanark 官网相近（"we"频率）甚至超过（"you"频率）。

5.4.4.2　平均句长

在平均句长方面，武夷山英文官网文本为 25.15 词，永定土楼英文官网为22.125 词，Suwon Hwaseong Fortress 官网为 28.59 词，New Lanark 官网为 18.27词。结果并不出人意料，康宁的研究（2012：107）曾发现中国网站文本平均句长为 19.23 词，而英语国家网站平均句长为 15.44 词。

究其原因，在于西方的简洁英语运动（Plain English Movement）使得当代英文越来越追求简短明了。随机从 New Lanark 网站抽取数句为例。

福建世界遗产

双语语料库构建与应用

Explore the many attractions and exhibition areas of New Lanark Visitor Centre with a passport ticket. In addition to our permanent visitor attractions, we also offer an exciting range of temporary exhibitions, events and talks throughout the year. Visit What's On to find out more about our programme of events or sign up for our monthly e-newsletter. A passport ticket gives you entrance to all of our visitor attractions, including our temporary exhibitions. Click here for more information on ticket prices. (81 词，平均句长 16.2 词)

5 句中没有从句，没有连词，故而简洁。

如果是中国网站的本地化版本，上面这段英文可能写成：

If you have a passport ticket, you can explore many attractions and exhibition areas in the New Lanark Visitor Centre. Besides our permanent visitor attractions, we can also offer a lot of temporary exhibitions, events and talks, *which* are very exciting throughout the year. Please visit What's On to find out more about our programme of events or you can sign up for our monthly e-newsletter. *If* you have a passport ticket, you will be able to enter all of our visitor attractions, including our temporary exhibitions. *If* you want to know about the ticket prices, please click here for more information. (102 词，平均句长 20.4 词)

Suwon Hwaseong Fortress 官网较多下面这类句子（历史文化的介绍增添了很多背景信息），故而平均句长是最冗长的。

Suwon Hwaseong Fortress was constructed by king Jeongjo (reigning 1777-1800), the 22nd king of Joseon dynasty (1392-1910) after moving the tomb of his father Sadoseja, Crown Prince, who had been victimized in faction struggles in the court, and put inside a rice chest and had died in it, from Mt. Baebong, Yangju, to Mt. Hwa, Suwon, and the moving of the local government headquarters from near Mt. Hwa to the current location under Mt. Paldal, Suwon. The mountain was considered as the best place to build tombs according to the theory of geomancy in those days. (92 词，平均句长 46 词)

平均句长超过英语国家网站，是世界遗产网站本地化中存在的一个问题，因为在快节奏和数据爆炸的当代社会，依国外读者的阅读习惯，恐怕越来越不能容忍冗长累赘的句子。文之愈简，行之愈远。

5.4.4.3　句式特征

句式特征的考察包括祈使句的使用情况、关系代词（which）和关系副词（where）、从属连词（if、when）的使用情况。

（1）祈使句的使用情况

李丹对澳洲旅游网站的调查发现，为提高读者的阅读快感，网站在进行旅游文本写作时，强调其口语化，句式多样简短，尤其青睐于祈使句（2012：121）。对祈使句使用情况的考查，有助于评估世界遗产网站本地化在句式运用方面是是否与国外原生英文网站的习惯一致。

下表是四个世界遗产网站语料中祈使句的频率统计（每千词）：

表 5-11　4 个世界遗产网站祈使句频率统计

	Mount Wuyi	Tulou	Suwon Hwaseong Fortress	New Lanark
祈使句频率（‰）	0.12	1.131	0.191	4.200

表 5-11 显示，在祈使句的使用上，前 3 个世界遗产本地化网站与英国世界遗产 New Lanark 原生英文网站存在较大差距。据语料库检索数据显示，这些祈使句中出现频率较高的词为：visit、see、enter、book、contact、purchase、send、use、join、find、bring、follow、make、begin、explore、click、talk、travel、look、dress、take、let，等等。

（2）关系代词、关系副词和从属连词的使用情况

关系代词、关系副词和从属连词的使用在一定程度上反映了句式的复杂程度，其大量使用可能造成冗长累赘的文体风格，对其进行考察，可以了解世界遗产本地化网站的语言风格是否与国外原生英文网站接轨。

下表是对关系代词（which）、关系副词（where）和从属连词（if、when）在 4 个世界遗产网站语料中每千词的频率统计：

表 5-12　4 个世界遗产网站"which"、"where"、"if"、"when"频率统计

世界遗产网站	"if"频率（‰）	"When"频率（‰）	"Which"频率（‰）	"Where"频率（‰）	合计
Mount Wuyi	6.304	1.697	4.364	1.454	13.819
Tulou	5.657	1.447	1.763	1.315	10.155
Suwon Hwaseong Fortress	3.388	1.416	1.694	1.25	7.748
New Lanark	3.500	0.432	1.227	0.432	5.591

从表 5-12 可以看出，使用从句的频率由低到高依次为：New Lanark ＜ Suwon Hwaseong Fortress ＜ Tulou ＜ Mount Wuyi。

使用 Readability Studio 检测 4 个网站网页文本的难度，结果如图 5-8：

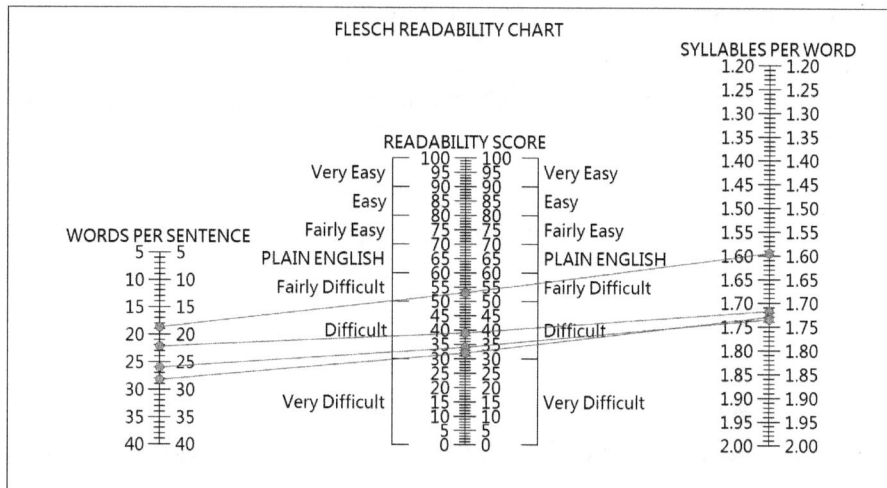

图 5-8　4 个世界遗产网站的 Readability Studio 易读性检测

该图显示，4 个网站的文本易读性指数从高到低分别为：New Lanark（53）＞永定土楼（39）＞武夷山（34）＞ Suwon Hwaseong Fortress（32）。与上面的各项分析一致。

可见 3 个世界遗产本地化网站在文体简洁与易读性方面与 New Lanark 这样的世界遗产原生英文网站仍存在差距。

5.4.5　文本翻译

鉴于武夷山英文官网和永定土楼英文官网都未提供中文原文，本小节仅以其英文文本为依据，评估其网页文本翻译质量。

评估采用人工分析、语料库统计以及英文写作辅助软件自动检测三者结合的方式进行。人工分析选取两个网站的"Introduction"部分为考察对象；语料库统计批量考察术语不统一的情况；英文写作辅助软件则自动检测各种错误。

5.4.5.1　人工分析

（1）武夷山英文官网的"Introduction"

该篇介绍共 260 词，11 句，平均句长 23.64 词。

（http://www.wuyishan.gov.cn/Articles/20130503/20130503145229250.html）

① The serene beauty of the dramatic gorges of the ***Nine Bend River***, with its numerous temples and monasteries, many now in ruins, provided the setting for the development and spread of neo-Confucianism, which has been influential in the cultures of East Asia since the 11th century.

说明："Nine Bend River"改为"Nine-bend Stream"为宜，后者在国外的接受度更高；"its"指代不清，可删除。

② Its massive walls enclose an archaeological site of great ***significance***

说明：后缺句号。

③ Mount Wuyi was first a center of Taoism, when many temples and study centers were established, but Buddhism also developed alongside, and by the 17th century had largely superseded Taoism.***and inscriptions*** in this area.

说明：文字有缺漏。

从以上分析可以看出，武夷山英文官网译文在文字的校对方面存在较大问题，缺漏较多。

（2）土楼英文官网的"Introduction"

（http://amazingfujiantulou.com/About-tulou/tulou-presentation-overview.html）

该篇介绍共 1065 词，48 句，平均句长 22.19 词。

① Fujian's "earthen buildings" (Hakka houses) were among the twenty-seven that were ultimately ***selected***.

说明：改为"inscribed"。

② Since the 1980s, the Fujian Tulou has been variously called "Hakka ***tulou***", "earth dwelling", "round stronghouse" or simply "***tulou***".

说明："tulou"改为"Tulou"为宜。

③ Fujian ***Tulous's*** literal translation is "Fujian earthen structures", ***and*** scholars of Chinese architecture have recently standardized the term Fujian Tulou.

说明："Tulous's" 应为 "Tulou's"；"and" 改为 "but"。

④ However, this would not be a useful definition, since, as the scholar of China's traditional architecture Huang Hanmin notes, rammed-earth ***building*** of one kind or another can be found in virtually all parts of China.

说明："building" 改为 "buildings"。

⑤ The earliest extant earthen building was constructed in 769 during ***the Tang dynasties***; There are more than 20,000 ***tulous*** in Fujian, while there are only around three thousand "Fujian Tulou" located in ***southwestern region*** of Fujian province, mostly in the mountainous regions of Yongding County of Longyan City and Nanjing County of Zhangzhou City.

说明："the Tang dynasties" 改为 "the Tang Dynasty"；"tulous" 改为 "Tulou"；"southwestern region" 前加 "the"。

⑥ The top ***level*** of these earth buildings has gun holes for defensive purposes.

说明："level" 改为 "storey" 或 "floor"。

⑦ Among them, the "six ***complexes*** and four buildings" comprising forty-six earthen buildings chosen for World Cultural Heritage status are doubtless the best.

说明："complexes" 改为 "clusters"。

⑧ Public duties such as organization of festivals, cleaning of public areas, opening and closing of the main gate, etc., ***was*** also assigned to a family branch on a rotational basis.

说明："was"改为"were"。

从以上分析可以看出，土楼英文官网存在较多语法错误及用词不当之处。

5.4.5.2 术语译名的批量检测

通过雪人软件批量提取术语，筛选后比较，找出译名不统一的术语。

批量检测发现，武夷山英文官网和土楼英文官网均存在较严重的术语不统一现象。武夷山有 5 个术语存在不同译名，其中最严重的情况是同一术语多达 5 个译名，如下：

① Wuyi Mountains, Mount Wuyi, Wuyi Mountain, Wu Yi Shan

② Dahongpao, Da Hong Pao

③ Dawang peak, Great King peak

④ Nine-bend River, Nine Bend River, Nine Bend Stream

⑤ Wu Yi Rock Wulong Tea, Wu Yi Yan Cha, Rock Wulong, Wu Yi Shan's wulong tea, Rock Tea

永定土楼英文官网有多个术语存在不同译名，尤其各个土楼的译名极其混乱，列举数例如下：

① Rusheng Tulou, Rushenglou

② Fuyulou, FuYu Lou, Fuyulou Building, Fuyunlou Earth Building, Fuyunlou

③ Kuijulou tulou building, Kuijulou, Kuijulou Building, KuiJuLou

④ Jiqinglou Hakka building, Jiqing Tulou Building, Jiqinglou, jiqing lou

⑤ Zhenchenglou, Zhengcheng Lou, Zhengchenglou, Zhencfulou, ZhenChengLou

⑥ Chengqi Lou, Chengqilou, ChengQiLou

⑦ HongKhengCun, Hukeng township

⑧ Chuxi complex, Chuxi Tulou Cluster

从以上术语译名统计的情况来看，福建世界遗产本地化网站存在严重的术语不统一问题，亟须引起重视。

5.4.5.3 英文写作语法检测 / 润色软件自动检测错误

Whitesmoke（http://www.whitesmoke.com/）和 Grammarly（https://www.grammarly.

com/）是国外开发的功能较为强大的英文写作语法检测／润色软件，除能够自动检测各种类型的语法错误外，还提供了写作润色、同义词提示等特色功能。

两款软件的检测都存在误报的情况，但一般均能发现文本中诸如拼写错误、标点错误、漏用冠词、用词重复等问题，功能比 Word 的语法检查强很多。

使用两款软件分别检测武夷山英文官网和永定土楼英文官网各 1000 词的网页文本，检测结果分别简要介绍如下。

（1）武夷山英文官网

Whitesmoke 的检测界面如图 5-9：

图 5-9　Whitesmoke 检测界面

Whitesmoke 共指出 19 处问题，经人工审核，其中 5 处需要修改，如下：

① The ***highest*** peak in the area is Mount Huanggang at 2,158 metres (7,080 ft) on the border of Fujian and Jiangxi, making it the ***highest*** point of both provinces; the lowest altitudes are around 200 metres.

说明："highest"重复。

② He reached the city just in time to sit for the entrance examination which he *passed with flying colors*. He later graduated from the university and became a renowned scholar.

说明：陈词滥调。

③ As he was also a handsome young man, the daughter of the Emperor fell in love with *him* and subsequently they got married and he became a nobleman.

说明："him"后面应加逗号。

④ The leaves of these three plants had good therapeutic *values* which had helped to cure his illness and that of the Empress.

说明："values"后面应加逗号。

⑤ *the* One Line Sky-Huxiao Rock Scenic Area

说明："the"应首字母大写。

此外，虽然 Whitesmoke 提出的修改建议中有两处并不正确，但原文的确存在问题，相当于间接指出了错误，如下：

⑥ wuyi Geology
⑦ wuyi Climate

说明："wuyi"应首字母大写。

Grammarly 的检测界面如图 5-10：

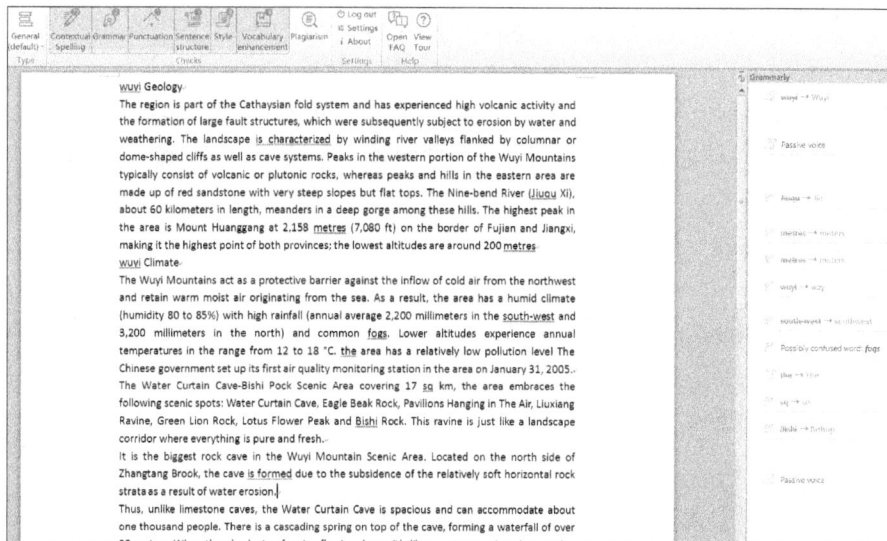

图 5-10　Grammarly 检测界面

Grammarly 共提出 27 个修改建议，经人工审核，其中 6 处可以采纳：

① ***the*** area has a relatively low pollution level The Chinese government set up its first air quality monitoring station in the area on January 31, 2005.

说明："the"应首字母大写。

② The area is the cradle of Neo-Confucianism, a current that became very influential beginning in ***11th century***.

说明："11th century"前加定冠词。

③ As he was also a handsome young man, the daughter of the Emperor fell in love with him and subsequently they got ***married*** and he became a nobleman.

说明："married"后加逗号。

此外，Grammarly 检测也发现了 Whitesmoke 例⑤、⑥、⑦等 3 处错误。

（2）永定土楼英文官网

Whitesmoke 共提出 30 处修改建议，经人工审核，其中 7 处可以采纳：

① There are two temples: Fayun Temple **_built_** in the late Song Dynasty, and Lingzhi Temple mainly offers sacrifice to Kwan-yin, the mercy Buddha.

说明："built"前加"is"。

② Almost all **_of_** the circular buildings have only one main entrance.

说明：删除"of"。

③、④ After you walk through **_hall_**, there are two verandas—one along either side, as if they are two long arms gathering all **_of_** the rooms, which are of the same size and shape, into a circle.

说明："hall"前加定冠词；删除"of"。

⑤ Children stand at the sides of the door and often exert all their **_strength_** and yet they cannot budge the door.

说明："strength"后加逗号。

⑥ This is the passageway for going in and out of the whole **_building_** and it is also a public lounge.

说明："building"后加逗号。

⑦ Stand upon its **_flat topped_** summit, you will see a panoramic vista of villages among green field toward the west.

说明："flat ropped"间加连字符。

福建世界遗产　双语语料库构建与应用

Grammarly 共提出 54 处修改建议，经人工审核，其中 15 处可以采纳：

① Each building is besprinkled with marvelous basso-relievoes, couplets, plaques and stone sculptures, all are exquisite in workmanship.

说明：逗号改为分号。

② Peitian folk house building mass, a _**xanadu**_ with marvelous architectures, has become a must see place of interest in Fujian.

说明："xanadu" 应首字母大写。

③ Lingzhi Peak, shaped like _**a**_ fungi, is the main peak, measuring 2,168 feet in height.

说明：删除 "a"，"fungi" 为复数。

④、⑤ _**Stand**_ upon its flat _**topped**_ summit, you will see a panoramic vista of villages amongst green field toward the west.

说明："Stand" 改为 "Standing"；"flat topped" 之间增加连字符。

⑥ To the east, high cliffs _**stand**_ majestically, stacked one upon another.

说明：与上文重复，换用其他词。

⑦ Situated in Xiayang Town, this _**village**_ has a population of two to three thousand, but about 3,000 overseas Chinese trace their ancestry to this _**village**_, which makes it one of the leading ancestral homes for Chinese from other countries.

说明：与上文重复。

⑧ In ancient times, a family produced five third-degree scholars in the imperial examinations and another family ***produced*** four ministers over three generations.

说明：与上文重复。

⑨ In modern times, ***a number of*** prominent people have emerged from this village.

说明：冗长，改为 some。

⑩ As soon as the main door is closed, the interior becomes a world of its ***own*** and everything outside is kept at bay.

说明："own"后加逗号。
另外 5 例为：

① The two shutters of the entrance are thick and high, and are ***generally*** also covered with sheet iron:***it***'s almost as if two armored warriors are guarding the entrance.

说明：删除"generally"；"it"前加空格。

②、③ And so there is also this kind of scene:***women*** pounding rice or milling flour, and making sound rich in rhythm, while the men chat about all ***kinds*** of subjects.

说明："women"前加空格；"kinds"使用过多，改为"sorts"。

④、⑤ In quite a few halls, you'll see hullers for rice and other grains, stone ***mils***, and mortars for pounding cooked glutinous rice into ***paste***.

说明："mils"改为"mills"；"paste"前加限定词。

双语语料库构建与应用
福建世界遗产

5.5　福建世界遗产网站本地化对策

从以上评估来看，武夷山英文官网和永定土楼英文官网均存在各种问题。福建世界遗产网站本地化的质量尚需提高，途径如下。

5.5.1　网站设计优化

世界遗产网站的本地化可在以下几个方面进行设计优化：

（1）按功能分类的导航栏目设计

以永定土楼英文官网为例，从网站访客角度出发的话，应将导航栏目按4种功能分类：首先是"Orientation"功能，让访客了解土楼的历史、文化等，栏目可取名"World Heritage Site"，该栏目起到吸引访客进一步了解的作用；第二种功能是"Persuasion"，即劝导访客来土楼旅游，栏目可取名"What to do & see"，具体介绍可做的事情、可看的景点；第三种功能是"One-Click"，即一键下单，订购或者定制旅游产品／服务，可与旅游企业合作，实现无缝对接，该栏目可取名"Tour"，下设各种旅游产品／服务，如景点门票购买、旅游线路下单／定制，等等；第四种功能是"Communication"，即双向交流，该栏目可取名"Contact us"，为访客／顾客提供一个咨询、反馈及评价的交流平台。

（2）独具特色的标志设计

在文化"走出去"的大形势下，旅游网站应积极设计符合各地文化底蕴的标志，使游客在不知不觉中感受中国文化的影响，接受中国特有的文化符号（李丹，2012：122）。标志以图文并茂、简洁明了、易于辨识、独具特色为设计原则。世界遗产官网的标志应包含象征世界遗产的图标、遗产名称以及世界遗产标志，以武夷山为例，应包含"Mount Wuyi"（遗产名称）、"World Heritage Site"（世界遗产标志）及图标。

（3）便捷体贴的页面布局设计

世界遗产本地化网站的页面布局应便捷体贴，尽可能为网站访客提供便捷的浏览体验，应设计左侧快捷栏，右侧快捷栏，顶部二级菜单，以及底部快捷链接，以及网页文本中的超链接。

5.5.2　翻译质量优化

世界遗产网站本地化的翻译质量优化可从以下几个方面着手。

（1）术语一致

术语不一致容易导致网站访客的困惑，增加其辨识、理解上的难度，影响浏览体验。名称不统一也不利于文化"走出去"。如在武夷山官方英文网站中，"大红袍"的译名时而是"Dahongpao"，时而是"Da Hong Pao"，宜统一为"Da Hong Pao"，因为"Da Hong Pao"在国外的接受度更高。确保术语一致的途径是先从原文中提取出术语，制定需要统一译名的术语列表，然后拟出一个或数个译文，并通过网络检索验证无误后确定译名，制作为 CAT 软件的术语库，翻译时使用 CAT 软件加载术语库，一般就不会出现术语不一致的情况。

（2）简洁英语

译者在翻译过程中如果不加变通，机械地照汉语原文直译，就容易造成英文冗长或者松散。在翻译过程中应尽量避免重复，以简洁英语为指导原则，利用英语中的同位语结构、代词结构、介词结构、名词结构、形容词结构、过去分词、现代分词、前置定语、祈使句、省略结构等等，使英文简洁流畅，核心信息突出，而非冗长杂乱，缺乏重点。

试从武夷山英文官网摘录 2 例如下（网站无汉语原文，仅提供英文译文及修改译文）：

① On the 36 peaks, there are more than 700 places carved with inscriptions.

改：More than 700 places on the 36 peaks are carved with inscriptions.

说明：汉译英中应避免滥用"there be"结构，核心信息"More than 700 places"前置。

② Wuyi Academy is situated at the foot of screen peak, which was found by Zhu Xi, an important Song dynasty Confucian scholar, during the Song dynasty.

改：Wuyi Academy，situated at the screen peak foot，was founded in 1183 by Zhu Xi, the Song Dynasty Confucian scholar.

说明：删除"is"，将"is situated"由谓语结构改为过去分词作定语结构；删除"which"，减少一个从句，使"was founded"变成核心信息；"an important"改为"the"，即包含"著名、重要"之意；删除"during the Song dynasty"，前面已出现"the Song Dynasty Confucian scholar"，自然是在宋朝期间。

（3）编译策略

在世界遗产网站本地化过程中，由于语言文化、习俗及文体风格差异，部

福建世界遗产
双语语料库构建与应用

分中文写就的文本可能需要经过改编再译，以适合目的语读者的语言文化习惯，避免与其心理预期发生冲突。

本地化译员应了解目的语的语言文化，熟悉中文旅游文本及英文旅游文本各自的语言特色，掌握编译技巧，在把握好分寸的前提下，在本地化过程中充分运用编译策略。

（4）质量监控

整个本地化流程尽量依托语料库及 CAT 平台进行，以利于翻译质量的监控。如尚无条件依托语料库及 CAT 平台完成本地化工作，也应采取一定的措施进行质量监控，保证翻译质量，如译前聘请术语专家拟定术语表、译后聘请本地化专家审核译文等。

世界遗产网站的本地化可邀请申遗文本的译者负责或者参与。申遗成功之后的网站本地化建设或者维护也应以申遗中英文文本为重要参考，尽量借鉴利用，与其保持一致。

此外，还可利用 Grammarly 和 Whitesmoke 这两款英文写作语法检测 / 润色软件改进译文质量。上面的评测中两款软件都存在误报现象，但实际上很多误报是由于用于检测的译文中存在很多音译的名称，而软件词典未收入这些词语，对于标点、拼写、常见语法错误以及累赘、重复等问题，这两款软件纠错的准确率其实比较高。本地化译员在翻译过程中可以适当使用这两款软件，减少错误。

5.5.3　关键词优化

关键词优化（Search Engine Optimization，简称 SEO），是根据搜索引擎的收录和排名规则，对网站进行内容、版块、布局等的调整，使网站更容易被搜索引擎收录，在搜索引擎相关关键词的排名中居于前列。

在国外，SEO 的研究和发展比较成熟，而在国内还处于起步阶段。搜索引擎优化，可让网站在搜索引擎检索中排名靠前，从而获得更多的访客和流量，有利于网站影响力的提升以及网站内容的传播。

世界遗产网站的本地化属于跨学科的研究和应用，就网站文本翻译而言，不仅仅是原文意义的转换和传递，还需掌握关键词优化技巧，了解网络访客的搜索习惯、搜索用词，并据此确定译文——具有竞争力的关键词。

以土楼为例，国内外的译名五花八门，不胜枚举，有"earth building"、"earthen building"、"Tulou"、"round house"、"Fujian Tulou"、"Hakka earth building"、"Hakka round house"、"Hakka Tulou"、"earth castle"、"earthen castle"等等。

我们在 Google 中分别检索，并考察前 10 名的结果，看是否与土楼有关，检索结果列表如下：

表 5-13　Google 检索土楼不同译名的结果统计

检索词	Google 检索排名前 10 与土楼的相关度
earth building	0 条
earthen building	0 条
Tulou	10 条
round house	0 条
Fujian Tulou	10 条
Hakka earth building	10 条
Hakka round house	10 条
Hakka Tulou	10 条
earth castle	0 条
earthen castle	1 条

从表 5-13 可以看出，在这 10 个关键词中，具有竞争力的为"Tulou"、"Fujian Tulou"、"Hakka earth building"、"Hakka round house"和"Hakka Tulou"。据此，我们得出以下几点结论：

（1）部分图书，包括福建省出版的一些图书，将"土楼"译为"earth building"是不妥的。

（2）就土楼译名的关键词优化而言，具有强竞争力的关键词是"Tulou"和"Hakka"，这两个词处于核心地位。因此，在有关土楼的介绍文字、外宣文字中，应尽量使用"Tulou"和"Hakka"二词。

（3）关键词的不同带来巨大的检索排名差别，译者需要研究关键词优化技术，提高本地化网站的检索排名。

关键词优化较为复杂，涉及面较多，其中长尾关键词的发掘是本地化译员应该了解并掌握的利器。长尾关键词（long tail keyword）是指网站上非目标关键词，但也可以带来搜索流量的关键词。其特征是较长，往往由 2～3 个词组成，存在于内容页面。例如，目标关键词是"Tulou"，其长尾关键词可以是"Fujian Tulou"、"Tulou tour"、"tulou architecture"、"Tulou accommodation"等等。在网页文本的构建过程中，需要了解存在哪些长尾关键词，并设法将其加入文本之中。关键词优化领域已经开放了较多的长尾关键词发掘工具，下面以

KeyXtreme 为例说明其使用方法。

运行软件，点击软件菜单的"Research"按钮，在左边的"Seed Keywords"框输入目标关键词"Tulou"，下面的"Search Levels"可选择，选择的层级越多，挖掘的越深，获取的关键词越多，"Search Engines"可按需选择，此处选择"Google"，点击"Start"按钮运行软件，结果如图 5-11 右侧所示：

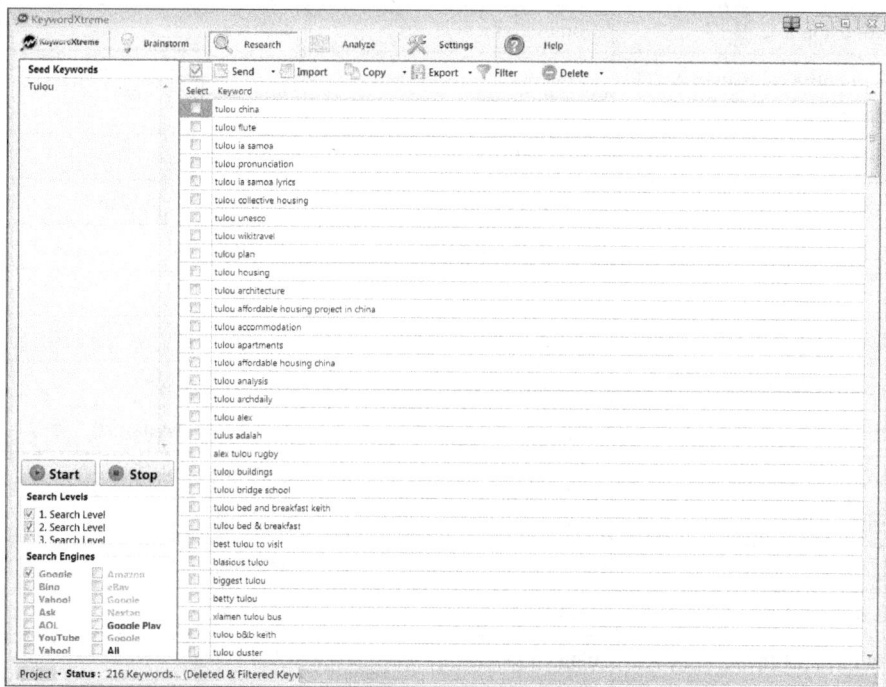

图 5-11 长尾关键词工具 KeyXtreme 界面

将发掘结果导出，如表 5-14：

表 5-14 KeyXtreme 挖掘的"tulou"长尾关键词列表

tulou china	pinghe tulou	pronounce tulou
tulou flute	tulou roundhouses	hakka tulou prince hotel
tulou pronunciation	gaobei tulou cluster	fujian tulou pdf
rectangular tulou	tulou house	tulou restaurant
tulou collective housing	tulou hotel	dali renjia
tulou unesco	tulou housing guangzhou	hakka tulou round earth buildings
tulou wikitravel	tulou history	tulou hakka houses
tulou plan	tulou hostel	tulou housing project

tulou housing	tulou hakka fujian	tulou singapore
tulou architecture	tulou affordable housing project in china	tulou sunshine international youth hostel
tulou accommodation	tulou hakka village	tulou shoes
tulou apartments	tulou in xiamen	tulou stay
tulou affordable housing china	tulou in fujian	tulou sunshine hostel
tulou analysis	tulou in china	tulou structure
tulou archdaily	tulou tours from xiamen	tulou souvenir anglais
tulou alex	tulou in fujian province	tulou tour
king tulou hotel	tulou tianluokeng	tulou travel
king tulou hotel yongding	tulou temple	tulou tourism
tulou buildings	tulou tea	tulou tripadvisor
tulou bridge school	jiangxi tulou	tulou bed & breakfast
tulou bed and breakfast keith	jiqing tulou	best tulou to visit
biggest tulou	xiamen tulou bus	kejia tulou
tulou cluster	tulou lonely planet	fujian tulou unesco
tulou china houses	tulou construction	urban tulou
tulou china map	tulou china tour	tulou village
tulou collective housing guangzhou china	tulou longyan	yuchanglou tulou
tulou chuxi	liulian tulou	yongding tulou map
tulou day trip	fujian tulou location	vanke tulou
tulou definition	fujian tulou lonely planet	visit tulou
tulou dwellings	chengqi lou tulou	xiamen tulou day trip
yongding tulou china	yongding tulou china	oldest tulou
tulou zhangzhou	tulou zhangzhou	nanjing tulou china
zhencheng tulou	zhencheng tulou	tulou weather
pronounce tulou	pronounce tulou	tulou wiki
daily tulou	yongding tulou	tulou wikipedia
yongding tulou tour	tulou meaning	tulou world heritage

dadi tulou cluster	tulou yongding	tulou wangzi hotel
tulou earth house	tulou map	fujian tulou wikitravel
tulou earth homes	tulou fujian province	hakka tulou walled villages
tulou earth buildings	fujian tulou xiamen	fujian tulou world heritage
tulou hakka earth building prince	modern tulou	tulou fujian china
tulou fujian	fujian tulou map	tulou xiamen
tulou from xiamen	tulou nanjing	tulou xiamen tour
tulou fujian tour	tulou near xiamen	tulou xiamen china
nanjing tulou cluster	tulou national geographic	tulou xiamen bus
nanxi tulou cluster	tulou open house	xiamen tulou hakka
tulou fujian hakka	friends of tulou	yuchang tulou
tulou guesthouse	king of tulou	yangchan tulou
pronunciation of tulou	tulou pdf	yongding tulou cluster

根据该词表，本地化译员可以在网页文本中加入相关的长尾关键词，如词表中有"pronounce tulou"，就可以在介绍土楼的网页文字中加上"Tulou（pronounced tŭlóu）"，查询"Tulou"发音的访客就可通过搜索引擎找到该网站。

长尾关键词的检索结果还可以帮助确定网页文本的内容选择，如"Tulou"长尾关键词词表中出现了"history"、"architecture"、"accommodation"、"oldest"、"biggest"、"tour"、"Xiamen"、"world heritage"等词，就可在网页文本中加入相关内容。

本书附录 1 列出了鼓浪屿、武夷山及土楼的一些目标关键词（如"Da Hong Pao"、"Zhu Xi"、"Mount Wuyi"、"Hakka"、"Minnan"等等）的长尾词，供本地化译员参考。

5.5.4 众包翻译

2006 年初，美国《连线》杂志记者 Jeff Howe 最早提出了"众包"概念，属分布式问题解决和生产模式，即将翻译任务以公开招标方式发布给解决方案提供者群体。该模式一经兴起，在语言服务行业的发展便如火如荼，其特点是把过去交由专职译员执行的任务外包给网络上的志愿译员完成（王华树，2015：13）。

众包翻译的译者具有多元化特点，包括职业译者、兼职译者、翻译爱好者等等，来自各行各业，各有所长，具有不同领域的知识储备。

著名的 TED 演讲视频字幕就是由志愿者通过众包翻译的方式完成的，目前这种众包式已经为 1000 多部演讲视频提供了多国语言的字幕翻译，TED 在全世界范围得到广泛传播，众包翻译功不可没。

在旅游行业，著名的 TripAdvisor（原中文名为到到网，现名猫途鹰）成功利用众包模式为其网站上来自全球旅客的 3 亿多条点评提供译文，如图 5-12 所示：

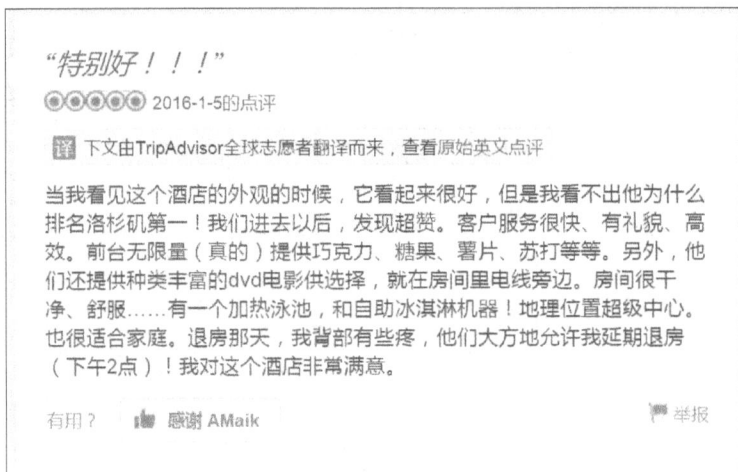

图 5-12　TripAdvisor 众包翻译

世界遗产网站的本地化也可以尝试众包翻译的模式，网站可先提供英文网站的机器译文（如南靖土楼官网英文版的有道机器翻译页面），然后邀请网络志愿者修改润饰译文，也可直接发布需翻译的中文文本，请网络志愿者翻译。网站需建立译文反馈系统，其他译员可以对众包翻译的质量进行修改及评价，报告质量较差的译文，以保障翻译质量。可通过赠送景点门票或者其他激励方式吸引网络志愿者参与。

5.5.5　Wiki 词条编辑及维护

维基百科（Wiki）是一个多语言、内容可编辑、任何人都能参与的协作计划，其目标是建立一个完整、准确的百科全书。该网站影响较大，其网页在各大搜索引擎的排名都较高。

福建世界遗产网站本地化的目的是对外文化交流、传播中国文化及地方文化，不一定要拘泥于形式。在目前世界遗产网站本地化建设滞后，且存在各种问题的情况下，尚无本地化官网的世界遗产，如泰宁和南靖土楼，可暂"借他山之石以攻玉"，组织人员在维基英文网站创建相关条目或者完善已有条目，待条件成熟之后，再启动官网的本地化。这样既可以节省网站建设的费用，还可以积累经验，利用 Wiki 网站的高排名提升知名度，促进旅游文化产业的发展。

Wiki 英文网站目前包括 3 个站点，即 https://en.wikipedia.org/，https://en.wikivoyage.org/wiki/Main_Page，http://wikitravel.org/en/Main_Page。第二个和第三个是专门收录旅游词条的站点。有关部门可采取课题立项或者其他形式，组织或者鼓励学界人士或译界人士参与 Wiki 英文网站上"Mount Wuyi"、"Nanjing Tulou"和"Taining Danxia"词条的编写或维护。

5.6　小结

世界遗产的申报、宣传、对外交流，对于实现中国文化和地方文化"走出去"的目标、提升软实力，具有重要意义。在"互联网 +"和大数据时代，这离不开本地化网站这个窗口。从福建武夷山和永定土楼世界遗产本地化网站的质量评估情况来看，目前世界遗产网站本地化还存在各种问题。希望学界对于网站本地化的研究，尤其是世界遗产网站的本地化研究予以更多重视，进行更全面、深入的探讨，促进世遗网站本地化的发展，推动世遗文化的海外传播。

第 6 章 CCAT 平台下的世界遗产翻译模式

6.1 引言

第 4 章对于福建世界遗产翻译质量的评估发现了种种问题，其中最为严重、对福建世界遗产文化符号的传播影响最大的问题，是术语不统一，即译名混乱。福建申遗文本中的译名不统一，说明未能利用现代翻译技术，同时也意味着翻译效率的低下。福建申遗文本送审联合国教科文组织之前，必然经过了多番校对，但仍出现术语不统一的情况，只能说仅靠人力是无法完全做到术语统一的。但如果利用现代翻译技术，不但能做到术语统一，而且能极大提高翻译的准确性和效率。世界遗产翻译 CCAT 系统的构建目的之一便在于此。

本章以福建申遗文本翻译和酒店介绍翻译为应用个案，阐明 CCAT 平台下的世界遗产翻译模式。

6.2 CCAT 平台

此处所说的 CCAT 平台，包括福建世界遗产双语语料库及网络语料库、雪人 CAT 软件以及译员，属于单机平台。未来世界遗产翻译的 CCAT 系统建成在线平台、形成语联网之后，系统的每一个用户，如译员、译审、译评人、翻译研究者等，都属于系统的子平台，共享平台的公共语料库、术语库和记忆库。

6.3 世界遗产翻译模式

在 CCAT 平台下，世界遗产翻译模式分为机器辅助人工翻译和人工辅助机器翻译两种，视乎文本而定。

（1）机器辅助人工翻译

该模式以人工翻译为主，机器为辅，适用于需要精雕细琢的文本翻译，如申遗文本翻译。包括以下要素及流程：

①雪人 CAT：加载福建世界遗产双语语料库中的术语库，保持译文一致及术语一致；记忆库预翻译，与记忆库匹配的句子自动填充译文，提高翻译效率。

②机器翻译引擎：提供机器译文，如 Google 机器译文，译员自由决定是否使用。

③人工翻译：对于记忆库预翻译无匹配的句子，译员可选择机器译文＋译后编辑，或是直接人工翻译。

④福建世界遗产双语语料库及网络语料库：为译员提供译例查询、类比语料库比较，以及网络语料库查证。

（2）人工辅助机器翻译

该模式以机器翻译为主，人工为辅，适合于大批量的文本翻译，如酒店介绍翻译。包括以下要素及流程：

①雪人 CAT：加载福建世界遗产双语语料库中的术语库，保持译文一致及术语一致；记忆库预翻译。这一环节与机器辅助人工翻译相同。

②机器翻译＋译后编辑：对于记忆库预翻译无匹配的句子，采用机器译文，如 Google 机器译文，译员对机器译文进行译后编辑。

③福建世界遗产双语语料库及网络语料库：译员在译后编辑过程中可参考福建世界遗产双语语料库的对应语料库及类比语料库，以及网络语料库。

下面分别以申遗文本翻译和酒店介绍翻译为个案，介绍两种翻译模式的应用。

6.4 应用个案 I——申遗文本的机器辅助人工翻译

6.4.1 武夷山申遗文本翻译

本小节通过武夷山申遗文本中的几个译例，从术语统一以及原文解读两个方面说明机器辅助人工翻译模式在申遗文本翻译中的应用。

6.4.1.1 术语统一

武夷山申遗文本中，"九曲溪"出现了 43 次，其译名并不统一，见表 6-1：

表 6-1 武夷山"九曲溪"译文列表

译文	九曲溪	总计
译文 1	Nine-bent Stream	30
译文 2	Nine-bend Stream	6
译文 3	Nine Bend River	4
译文 4	Nine-bend River	2
译文 5	Stream of Nine Windings	1

从表 6-1 可见，本应统一译名的"九曲溪"，在申遗文本中出现了 5 个不同译名，是为术语不统一。对于申遗文本这种内容繁杂、原文经常修订的文本而言，译者如果不借助 CAT，译时很难做到术语统一，译后也很难发现术语不统一。而在翻译时使用 CAT 则较容易保持术语一致，具体操作如下。

（1）建立术语库（见本书2.6）。

（2）使用雪人CAT建立中译英项目，加载所建立的术语库，如图6-1：

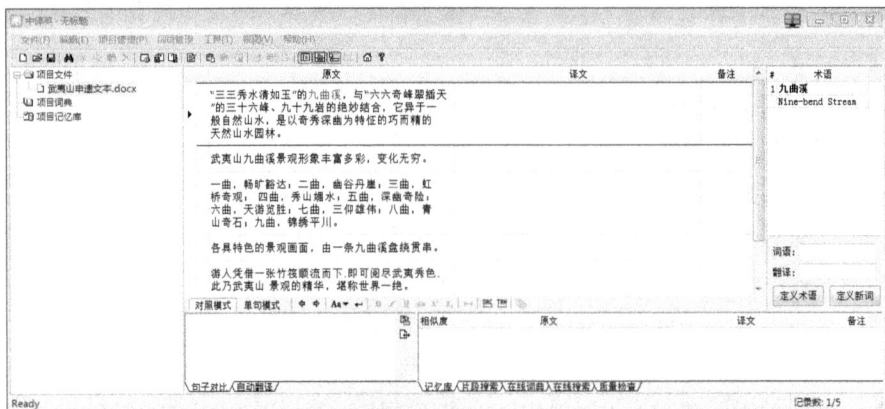

图6-1　加载术语库的武夷山申遗文本中译英项目

（3）鼠标置于译文框，右边显示术语"九曲溪"，译员只要点击一下，该术语便会显示在译文框，如图6-2：

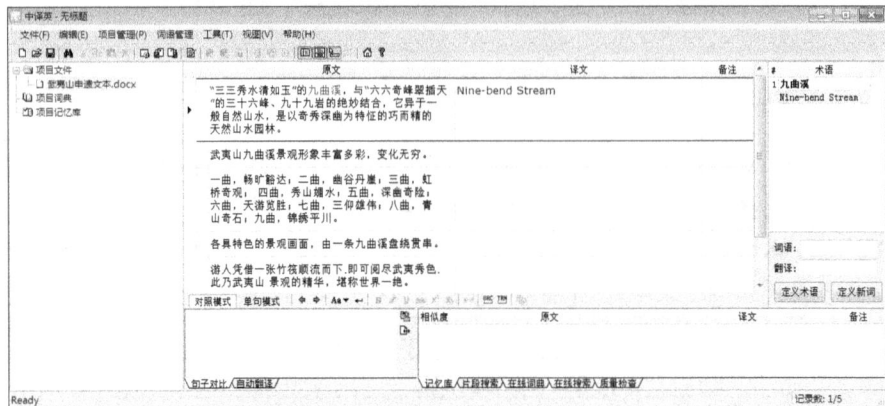

图6-2　将术语加至译文框

从图6-2中可以看出，第二句、第四句也出现了"九曲溪"，都可以通过术语库保持译文一致。

需要说明的是，武夷山申遗文本完成于90年代，那时CAT软件尚未在国内得到普遍运用，只能通过人工模式保持术语统一，虽然可以看出该译本已经仔细审校过，但结果仍不免译名混乱。

6.4.1.2　原文解读

在机器辅助人工翻译的过程中，福建世界遗产双语语料库及网络语料库起到了非常重要的作用。其中福建世界遗产双语语料库需要构建，而网络语料库则可以直接加以利用。下面以对申遗文本的原文解读为例说明网络语料库的作用。

申遗文本涉及面广，包括人文、地理等学科领域以及建筑（土楼）、植物（武夷山）等专业知识，因此申遗文本属于难度较大的文本。以武夷山为例，其申遗文本中就涉及朱子理学，稍有不慎，便可能出错。因此，申遗文本英译的第一关——原文理解便可能难倒译者，导致文本误读，此类例子不胜枚举。

纸质资料不易获取，且查证不易；一般网络搜索引擎，如 Google、Bing、百度之类，检索结果庞杂，来源杂乱，需要甄别，并非上选。而读秀收录了200 多万种中文电子图书以及数量不亚于中国知网的期刊论文，并且提供全文检索，是申遗文本理解的一大利器。

武夷山申遗文本中有一句话：

在中国文化史、传统思想史、教育史和礼教史上影响最大的，前推孔子、后推朱熹，因此，有些学者称朱熹为"三代下的孔子"。

The most influential figure in the histories of Chinese culture, traditional thought, education and feudal code of ethics is Confucius, and Zhu is the second most influential one. Some scholars called Zhu Xi "a Confucius three generations after Confucius."

将原文"三代"理解为"三代人"，并译为"three generations"，乍一看，似乎没有问题，但仔细一推敲，显然不合逻辑，因为据《美国传统词典》，"generation"的解释如下：

1. The people born and living about the same time, considered as a group: the baby-boom generation.

2. The average interval of time between the birth of parents and the birth of their offspring: a social change that took place over three generations.

3. All of the offspring that are at the same stage of descent from a common ancestor: Mother and daughters represent two generations.

依据上面的解释，"three generations"一般不会超过 100 年，但孔子和朱熹相距何止千年。

在百度中检索"三代下的孔子"，图 6-3 中第一个结果便是与此有关的解答：

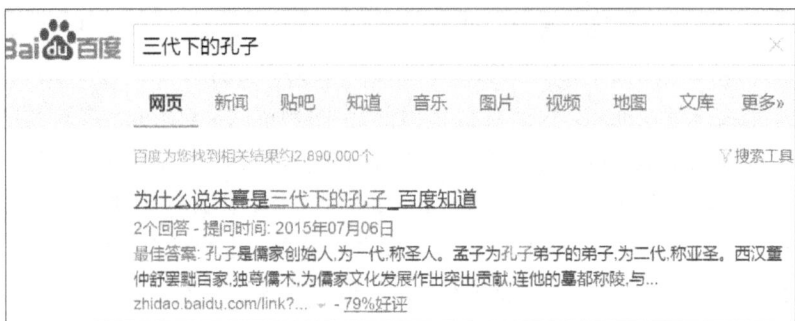

图 6-3 "三代下的孔子"百度检索结果

打开该链接，内容如下：

> 孔子是儒家创始人，为一代，称圣人。孟子为孔子弟子的弟子，为二代，称亚圣。西汉董仲舒罢黜百家，独尊儒术，为儒家文化发展作出突出贡献，连他的墓都称陵，与皇帝平级，他是董圣人，为三代。朱是南宋儒家代表人物，他为四书五经作注解，从此开创了一个新的时代。他是四代，即三代下。他也被称为圣人，即孔子。他的思想传播到了朝鲜，日本，东南亚。

问题似乎得到了解决，但据我们了解，在儒学体系中，朱熹的地位仅次于孔子，有"北孔南朱"之说，如果"三代下的孔子"是指孔子、孟子、董仲舒三代之后的孔子，与孟子、董仲舒同等，就降低了朱熹的地位，与实情不符。

究竟"三代下的孔子"该如何理解，在读秀中进行查证，便可知端倪。

登录读秀检索平台，点击"知识"，即可对读秀数据库的电子图书和期刊论文进行全文检索。输入关键词"三代下的孔子"，检索结果为 30 条，如图 6-4：

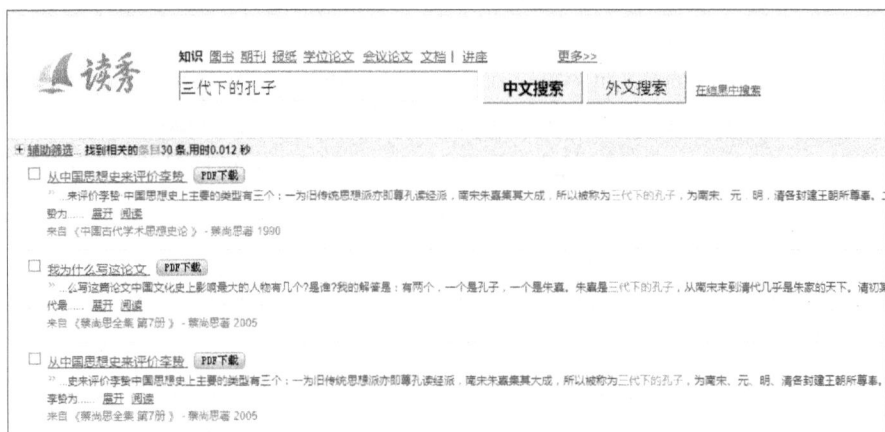

图 6-4 "三代下的孔子"读秀检索 1

其中第 28 条结果见图 6-5：

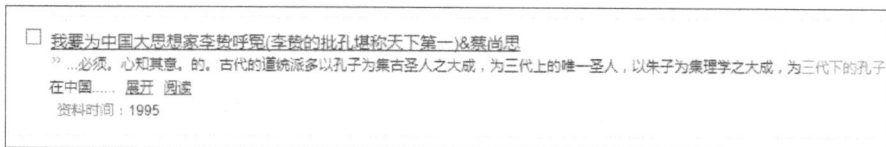

图 6-5　"三代下的孔子"读秀检索 2

图 6-5 中的句子为"古代的道统派多以孔子为集古圣人之大成，为三代上的唯一圣人，以朱子为集理学之大成，为三代下的孔子"（蔡尚思，1994：41）。可见"三代"是表时间的，不大可能指孔、孟、董这三代人。

继续在读秀检索"三代下孔子"，查到"三代下孔子"出自钱穆在《中国近三百年学术史》中所引清代考据家阎若璩的话："周元公（周敦颐）三代下伏羲，程纯公（程明道）三代下文王，朱文公（朱元晦）三代下孔子。"（1997：257）。

由此可确定"三代"并非指孔、孟、董这三代。经继续查找，确定"三代"指"夏商周"。例如，"文不读三代以下"，"三代以上有法，三代以下无法"，"三代专以天理行，汉唐专以人欲行"，等等。因此，申遗文本中"三代下的孔子"英译错误，应改为"a Confucius after the three dynasties of Xia, Shang and Zhou"。

申遗文本涉及领域广泛，译者应重视原文理解，勤于查证，以免望文生义；切忌顾此失彼，只顾推敲译文，忽略了原文解读。

6.4.2　土楼申遗文本翻译

下面以土楼申遗文本为例，说明机器辅助人工翻译的完整操作流程。

6.4.2.1　文本来源

所选文本为南阳楼的一段描述，来自土楼申遗文本的"2.a 遗产描述"部分，该部分与"3. 列入理由"部分是申遗文本中最重要的两个部分。

文本如下：

南阳楼

　　位于二宜楼东南侧，相距约 150 米。建于清嘉庆二十二年（1817 年），系二宜楼建造者蒋士熊之孙蒋经邦所建。双环圆形土楼，坐东南朝西北，占地 3100 平方米。楼高 13.25 米，直径 51.6 米，设 4 个单元，各有楼梯，每个单元均为 7 开间。包括门厅通道在内全楼共有 96 间。三层有内外通廊沟通全楼。斗拱雕花刻草，装饰精细。供案灵桌等都是清代遗物。南阳楼为福建省两大民系——客家民系、福佬民系之福佬民系地区的土楼中单元式与通廊式有机结合的经典之作。

6.4.2.2　机器辅助人工翻译操作流程

（1）在雪人 CAT 中建立中译英项目，加载术语库和记忆库[①]。

（2）加载待译文本，如图 6-6：

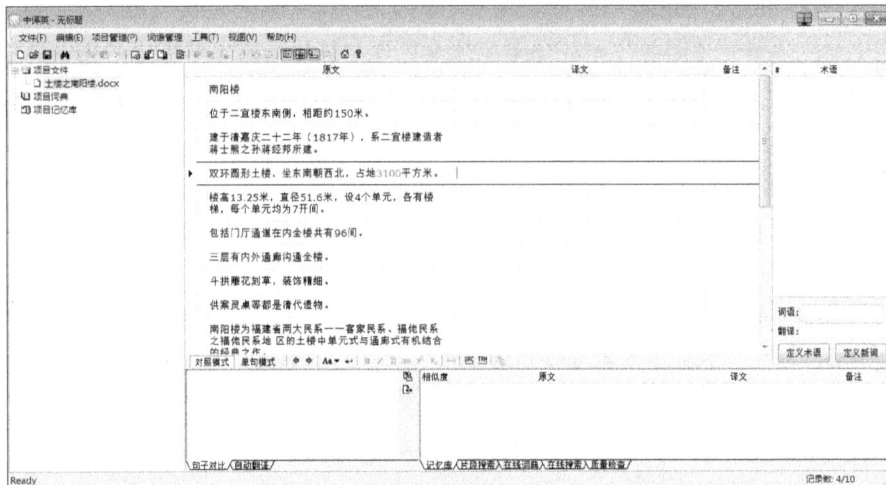

图 6-6　雪人 CAT 加载待译申遗文本

（3）首先使用预翻译功能，利用记忆库进行翻译，如图 6-7：

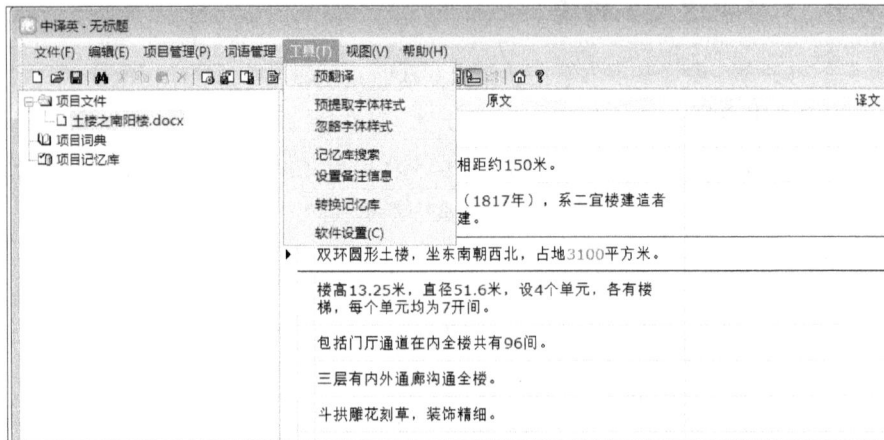

图 6-7　雪人 CAT 预翻译菜单

---

① 术语库和记忆库的构建见第 2 章。所加载的术语库和记忆库包括该部分文本之前的全部术语库和记忆库。

预翻译结果如图 6-8：

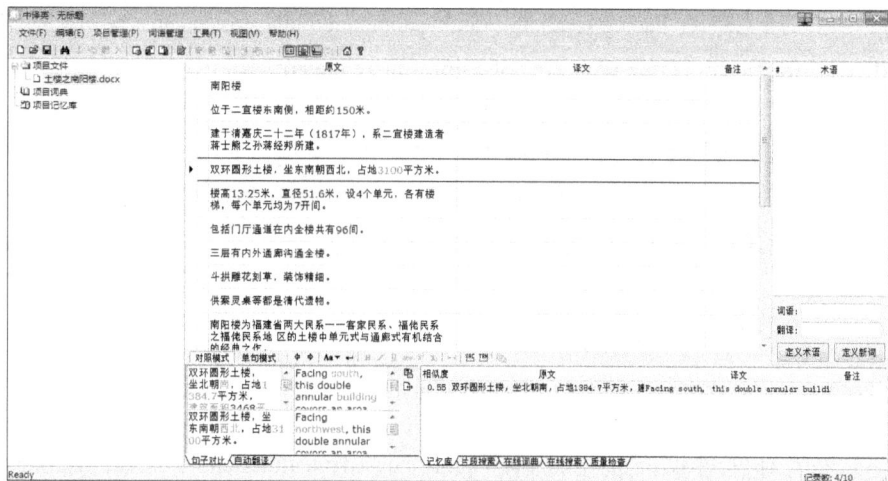

图 6-8　雪人 CAT 预翻译结果

图 6-8 显示，记忆库中有一句与待译文本的第四句匹配度为 55%，由于软件设置为匹配度最低为 50%，因此运行预翻译后便显示出来了。如果在"预翻译"菜单中设置匹配度大于 50% 时自动填充，则记忆库中的该句会自动填入译文框，如图 6-9：

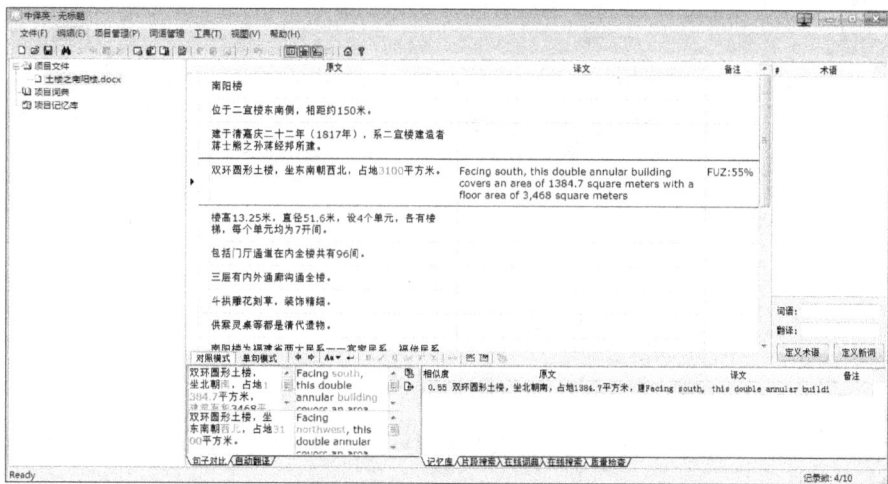

图 6-9　预翻译自动填充

下面比较一下该句原文、官方译文及自动填充的记忆库译文。

原文：双环圆形土楼，坐东南朝西北，占地 3100 平方米。

官方译文：The building covers an area of 3,100 square meters.

填充译文：Facing south, this double annular building covers an area of 1,384.7 square meters with a floor area of 3,468 square meters.

显然，官方译文漏译了"双环圆形"和"坐东南朝西北"，属于较为严重的错误。有无可能此类信息在英文译本中是一概略去不译的呢？填充译文给出了答案，该句译文来自南阳楼之前的文本，原文如下：

双环圆形土楼，坐北朝南，占地 1384.7 平方米，建筑面积 3468 平方米。

可见此类信息是要译出的。

填充译文可以轻易修改为：Facing northwest, this double annular building covers an area of 3,100 square meters.

以上为机器辅助人工翻译流程的第一步，即使用记忆库预翻译，这样一方面可以做到译文统一，另一方面，在相似译文的基础上修改，可以节省时间，减少失误（如官方译文的漏译）。

第二步操作是可选的，即使用机器译文，我们不妨一试。从第一句开始。

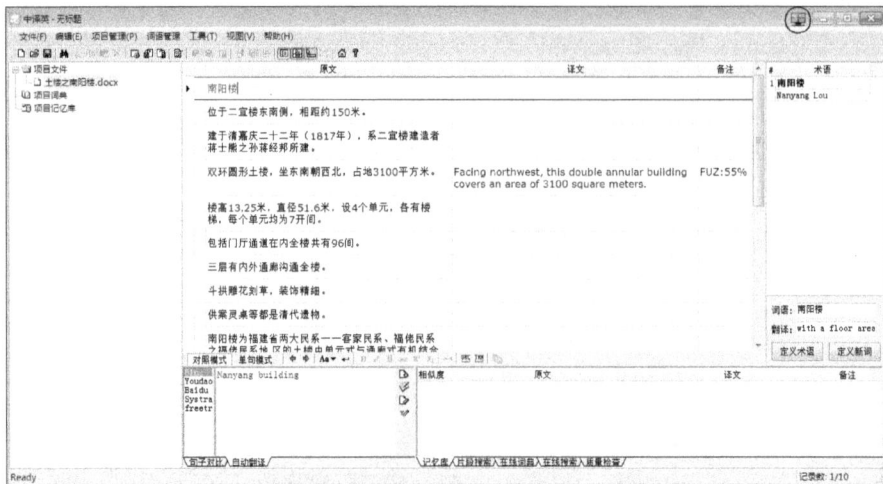

图 6-10　雪人 CAT 机器译文

如图 6-10 所示，软件下方显示了"南阳楼"的 Bing 机器翻译引擎的译文，即 Nanyang building，点击右侧含"+"的按钮，即可将该机器译文填充到译文框，如图 6-11。

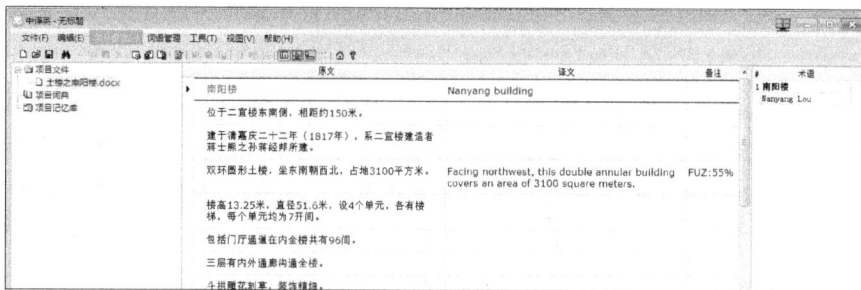

图 6-11　填充至译文框的机器译文

图 6-11 右侧显示，"南阳楼"已在术语库中，因此，只需点击该术语，就会填充至译文框，填充后删除机器译文即可，如图 6-12：

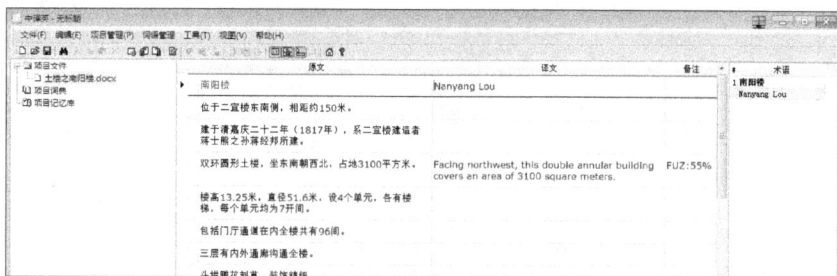

图 6-12　填充至译文框的术语

这个术语库是从土楼申遗文本及其译文中提取的，未作修订，但我们在第 4 章有关导游词翻译的讨论中认为"楼"应译为"Tulou"，因此将译文修改为"Nanyang Tulou"，如图 6-13：

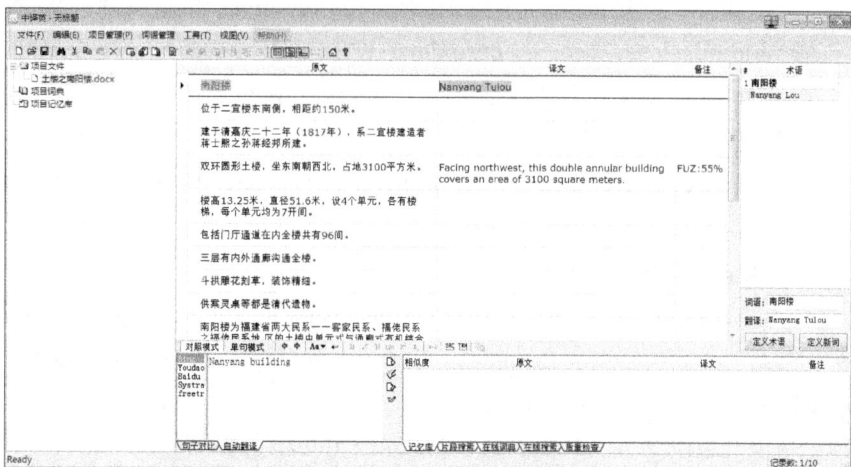

图 6-13　修改官方术语译文

修改后，划选"南阳楼"，在右下侧会显示"南阳楼"及其译文，点击"定义术语"，将修订后的术语译文加入术语库。

以上即为机器辅助人工翻译流程的第三步——人工翻译。在人工翻译过程中，除了利用术语库保持术语一致外，还可以查阅双语语料库、类比语料库，辅助做出翻译决策。例如，第二句为："位于二宜楼东侧，相距约150米。"我们查询土楼申遗中文文本，发现中文文本在描绘某座土楼时，用的都是"位于……"或者"坐落于……"，这说明申遗文本在介绍建筑物时，要遵循先表明位置的惯例，如图6-14：

581	田螺坑土楼群位于南靖县西部的书洋镇上坂村田螺坑自然村，距南靖县城60千 米
595	位于土楼群的中部，建于清代康熙年间（1662?1722年）。方形土楼，坐东北朝
597	位于步云楼的西侧，由黄氏族人于1930年合资共同建造。圆形土楼，坐东北朝西
599	位于步云楼的东南侧，由黄氏族人于1936年合资共同建造。圆形土楼，坐东北
602	位于步云楼的东侧，始建于元末明初(约1354年)，原为方楼，20世纪30年代被土
604	位于步云楼的西侧，由黄氏族人于1966年合资共同建造。椭圆形土楼，坐东北
606	河坑土楼群位于南靖县西部的书洋镇曲江村河坑自然村，距南靖县城58千米。 2
628	位于土楼群中部，始建于明代嘉靖年间(1549?1553年)，1923年失火后重修。方
630	位于朝水楼南侧，建于清代康熙年间（1662?1622年）。方形土楼，坐南朝北，占
636	位于绳庆楼东侧，建于清代乾隆年间(1736?1795年)，1954年重修。方形土楼，
638	位于绳庆楼西侧，建于清代道光年（1821?1850年）。五角形土楼，坐北朝南，
640	位于朝水楼的西侧，建于清代光绪元年（ 1875年）。方形土楼，坐西南朝东北，

图6-14 土楼申遗中文文本中的"位于"结构

在类比语料库中检索美国（San Antonio Missions）原生英文申遗文本的位置结构，发现如下句子：

① Mission Espada: Mission Espada is the most rural of the five San Antonio missions, located approximately 1.7 kilometers (1 mile) south of Mission San Juan and 12.4 kilometers (7.7 miles) south of Mission Valero / The Alamo (FIGURE 2.A.2).

② Rancho de las Cabras: This 40-hectare (98.8-acre) ranch, associated with Mission Espada, is located about 37 kilometers (23 miles) south of the mission (FIGURE 2.A.3).

③ Mission San Juan: Mission San Juan is located in a mostly rural section of San Antonio and retains much of its surrounding open land, including the labores as well as the original dam and acequia.

④ Late-Colonial Church Remnants: Located on the east wall of the complex, the stabilized remnants of this unfinished late eighteenth-century structure outline what was intended to be a vaulted, single-aisled church 21.6

福建世界遗产

双语语料库构建与应用

meters (71 feet) long by 8 meters (26 feet) wide, with an octagonal sacristy at the southeast corner and a square baptistery at the northwest (FIGURE 2.A.44).

　　再与土楼申遗英文译本比较，部分位置结构如图 6-15：

```
477  Shengqing Lou
478  It is situated beside the creek in the northwest of Chuxi Village. Built in 1799, the 4th year o
which is the inner building and the other is the outer building. The outer building is 39 meters in width,
480  Huaqing Lou
481  It is located in the central part of Chuxi Village, neighboring Fanqing Lou on the west and Fuqi
square meters. Two storeys in height, the Tulou is 19.5 meters in width, equaling to five bays, and 20.5 m
in the center of the inner yard. The whole Tulou is equipped with 4 staircases and 1 main gate (See 7.a-1
484  Xiqing Lou
485  It is in the central part of Chuxi Village, to the southeast of Jiqing Lou. Facing the north and
corridors, it is 3 storeys in height, 27 meters in width and 24 meters in depth. There are 20 rooms and 2
gates. The back hall serves as the ancestral hall (See 7.a-1 drawings 17, 18 and 19 as well as 7.a-2 photo
489  Fanqing Lou
490  It is in the central part of Chuxi Village, south of Jiqing Lou. Facing the north and covering a
or 10 bays in depth, the frontal part of roof being higher than the rear part. There are four staircases,
543  Rusheng Lou
544  It is situated in the northern part of Hongkeng Village, opposite to Fuyu Lou across the stream.
residence of the Lin family during the reign of Emperor Guangxu (1875-1908) of the Qing Dynasty. Facing th
floor without window is used for a kitchen and a dining room. The 2nd floor is used as a grain storage roo
hall) line along the central axis. There is a water well in the patio. Structurally, it is a combination o
545  Zhencheng Lou
546  It is commonly called Bagua Lou, and situated in the mid-south of Hongkeng Village. The building
for its grandeur and exquisitely versatile internal design. In terms of local architectural styles and the
Western architectural
774  2.a-9 Fujian Tulou-9: Hegui Lou
775  It is located in the center of Pushan Village of Meilin Town in Nanjing County, Fujian Province,
the Tulou in 2005, most of them engage in farming and tea planting.
815  Nanyang Lou
816  It is located in the southeast of Eryi Lou, with a distance of approx. 150m. This circular Tulou
building covers an area of 3,100 square meters. The Tulou measures 13.25 in height and 51.6 meters in diam
corridors on the third floor connect the whole building. The tiers of brackets inserted between the top of
corridor-style, the buidling is an outstanding example of Tulou for the Fulao people, who, together with t
822  Dongyang Lou
823  It is located in the west of Nanyang Lou. It was built in the 22nd year of Emperor Jiaqing's Rei
shaped Mountain, south to Eryi Lou, and is also named "foot print of baby lion". Facing southeast, Dongyan
the front and higher in the rear which features with a remarkable hierarchy. There are corridors connectin
99)
```

图6-15　土楼申遗英文文本的部分位置结构 1

　　英文原生文本与土楼译文比较得出的几点结果值得我们思考：

　　①英文原生文本位置结构比较灵活，有处于谓语位置的，如句②、句③，也有处于状语位置的，如句①、句④。状语有位于句首的，如句④，也有位于句中的，如句①。

　　②相比之下，土楼译文的位置结构都处于谓语位置，不够灵活。

　　③最重要的区别是，英文原生文本都是重复建筑物的名称，不用代词，这样有利于该文化符号信息传播的频率和力度（见本书 4.2 有关"信、达、效"原则的讨论）。相比之下，截图中的土楼译文文本则多使用代词。虽然也有重复建筑物名称的，但比用代词的少，如图 6-16。

```
603  2.a-4 Fujian Tulou-4: Yanxiang Lou
604  Yanxiang Lou stands in the Xinnan Village, Hukeng Town of the
2.a-5 Fujian Tulou-5: Zhenfu Lou
618  Zhenfu Lou is located in the Xipian Village of Hukeng Town, Yongding
County.
```

图 6-16　土楼申遗英文文本的部分位置结构 2

从以上类比语料库的比较可以看出，南阳楼简介文本中，第二句"位于"的主语应该用第一句的"南阳楼"，而不是代词，虽然一般的翻译规则建议使用代词，以避免重复。

参照英文原生文本(句①)，将第二句译为:Nanyang Tulou is located approximately 150 meters southeast of Eryi Tulou.

官方译文则为: It is located in the southeast of Eryi Lou, with a distance of approx. 150 m.

第二句的译法探讨说明了机器辅助人工翻译流程中语料库的重要作用，通过对原文文本的检索，我们注意到了"位于"这一结构，并借助类比语料库中的例证，得出了符合原生英文文本特征的译文。

剩下的句子中，有些术语，如"客家民系"、"福佬民系"、"二宜楼"等，都会在翻译过程中显示为术语，以保持术语一致，此处不再赘述。

综合以上探讨，我们认为，语料库及 CAT 平台下申遗文本的机器辅助人工翻译模式有助于提高申遗文本的翻译质量，值得提倡和推广。

6.5　应用个案 II——酒店介绍的人工辅助机器翻译

对于世界遗产网站的本地化、酒店介绍、酒店点评、旅游线路等，以及网站的动态更新，无论是机器翻译，还是人工翻译，都无法单独满足需要。机器翻译虽然速度快，但是无法达到 100% 的准确率，人工翻译虽然在一定程度上可以获得比机器翻译准确率更高的译文，但是无法高效应对大量或瞬时需要的翻译任务，而且没有 CAT 的辅助，无法确保术语的统一，也会造成同样内容的重复翻译，浪费资源。需要采用人工辅助机器翻译模式，既保证速度，又能保持一定的翻译质量。

6.5.1　机器翻译在旅游翻译中的应用——以 TripAdvisor 为例

在探讨人工辅助机器翻译模式之前，先以 TripAdvisor 网站为例，简要介绍一下机器翻译在旅游翻译中的应用情况。

TripAdvisor 是全球最大、最受欢迎的旅游社区，也是全球第一的旅游评论网站。月访问量达 3.4 亿人，同时拥有超过 800 万的注册会员以及超过 2 亿条的旅游点评和评论，并且数量还在不断增加中。旅行者的真实评论是 TripAdvisor 最大的特点。目前 TripAdvisor 已成为一个大型的在线"数据库"，它拥有大量关于旅游目的地的信息，包括酒店、景点、餐厅等。其点评页面如图 6-17：

图 6-17　TripAdvisor 点评页面

由于点评数量众多，并且不断更新，TripAdvisor 并没有提供其官方译文，而是双管齐下，一方面要求网络志愿者翻译，即第 5 章提到的众包翻译，如图 6-18：

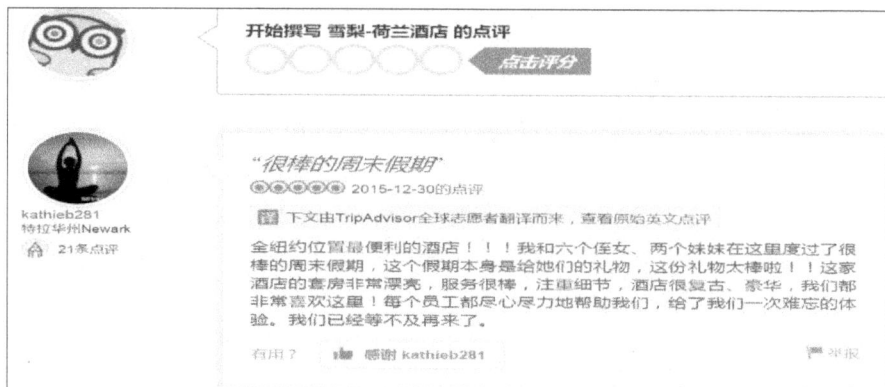

图 6-18　TripAdvisor 上由志愿者提供的酒店点评译文

一方面为尚未经过人工翻译的点评提供 Google 机器译文，如图 6-19：

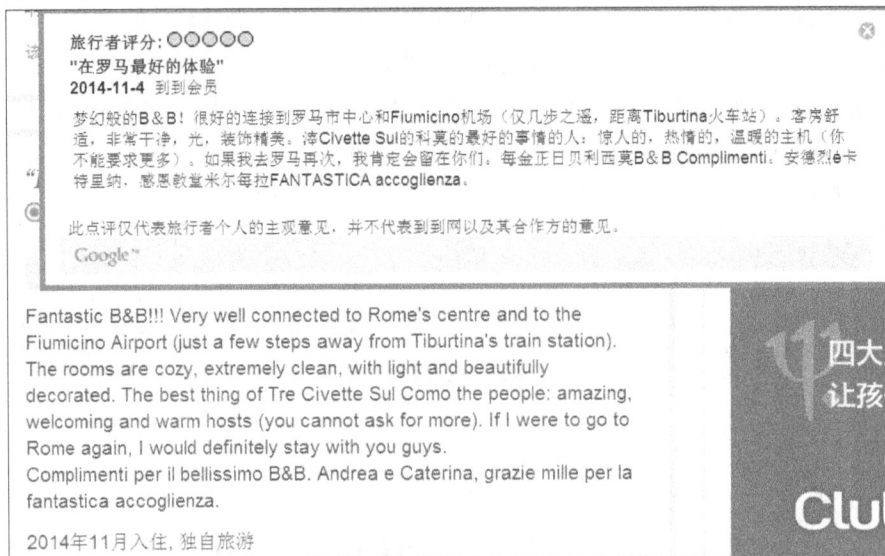

图 6-19　TripAdvisor 上客人点评的 Google 译文

除 Google 译文外，还提供 Asia Online Language Studio 的机器译文，如图 6-20：

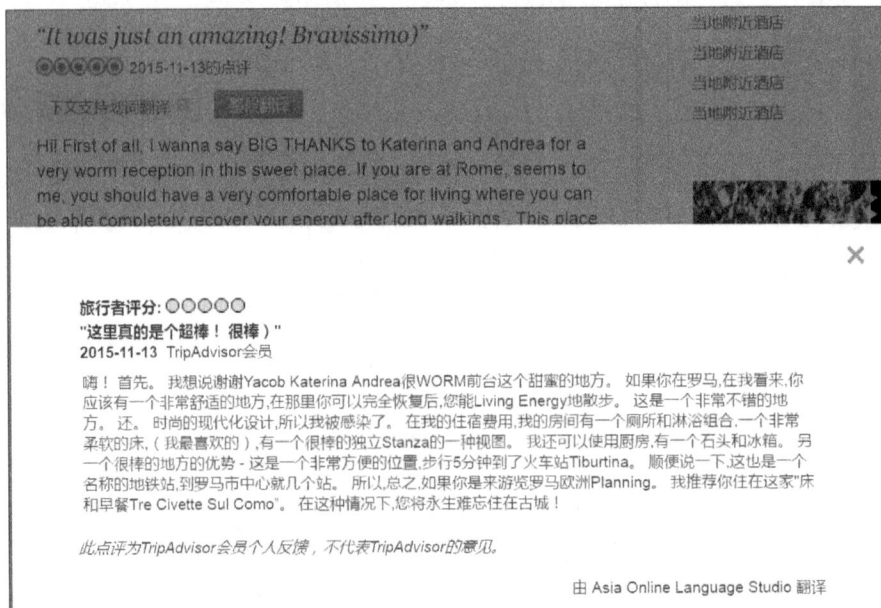

图 6-20　TripAdvisor 上客人点评的 Asia Online Language Studio 译文

通过机器译文，访客可以对酒店有一个大体了解，如 Google 译文中的"仅几步之遥"、"客房舒适，非常干净"、"装饰精美"，这些译文单独看的话，不像机器译文。

就 TripAdvisor 这类网站的经营模式而言，点评太多，且变化更新快，网站不可能为所有点评提供经专业译者翻译或者人工审核的译文，所以只能选择志愿者众包翻译或机器翻译。"互联网＋"时代，信息的海量及快速传播需要机器翻译技术的提高。而各个行业经审核的正确的双语对应语料，对于机器翻译技术的改善而言，非常重要。

下面以缤客网南靖酒店介绍为例，说明人工辅助机器翻译的操作流程。

6.5.2　酒店介绍文本来源

所选文本为土楼情客栈的中文介绍，来自缤客网。

文本如下：

土楼情客栈位于南靖县塔下村，设有实惠的客房和免费 WiFi，可应要求提供位于附近的免费停车位。

土楼情客栈距离南靖塔下土楼景区仅有几分钟步行路程，距离沭阳长途汽车客运站有 30 分钟车程，距离南靖县有 80 分钟车程。

客房均设有干净被褥和平板电视。私人浴室配有淋浴、拖鞋、免费洗浴用品和吹风机。

前台提供行李寄存处、自行车和汽车租赁服务、订票服务和旅游服务。

客人可在客栈租用设施，举办欢乐的晚间烧烤派对，还可在公共休息室与他人聊天，放松身心。客人可以在内部餐厅享用餐点，也可步行前往其他众多餐馆享用美食。

6.5.3　人工辅助机器翻译的操作流程

（1）使用网络矿工从缤客网批量采集南靖酒店介绍的中英文文本。共采集中英文介绍约 8000 字／词；将土楼情客栈的中英文介绍删除。

（2）使用雪人 CAT 软件将上述酒店介绍中英文文本自动对齐，人工校对后导出为记忆库。

（3）从该记忆库中提取术语，制作为术语库。

（4）在雪人 CAT 软件中建立一个中译英项目，加载制作的术语库和记忆库，加载土楼情客栈中文介绍，在软件中共分割为 7 句，如图 6-21。

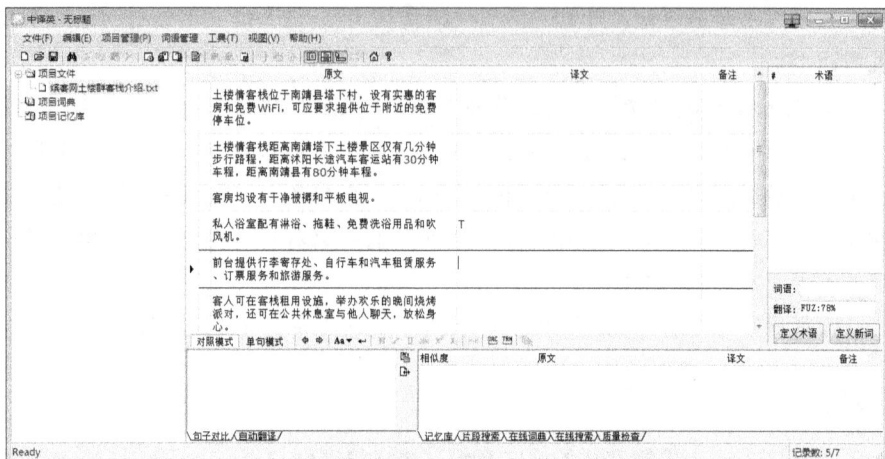

图 6-21 雪人 CAT 加载待译酒店介绍文本

（5）人工辅助机器翻译的操作顺序为 CAT 记忆库＋机器翻译＋译后编辑＋语料库查证。先运行记忆库预翻译，自动填充译文，如图 6-22：

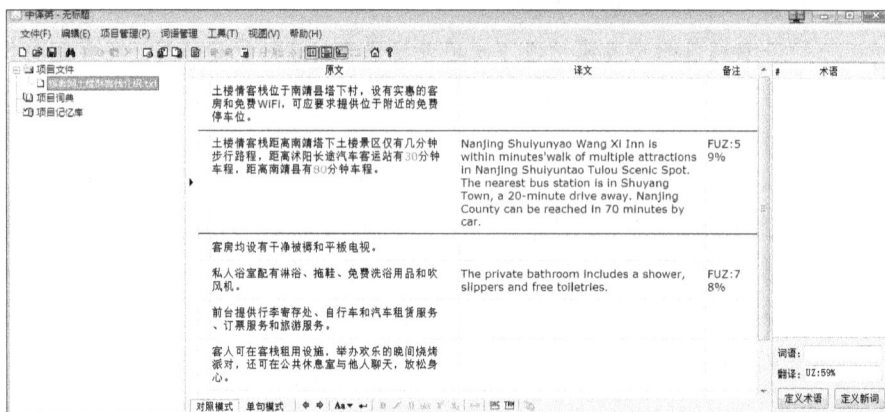

图 6-22 预翻译填充

预翻译通过记忆库填充的两句如下：

①土楼情客栈距离南靖塔下土楼景区仅有几分钟步行路程，距离沭阳长途汽车客运站有 30 分钟车程，距离南靖县有 80 分钟车程。

记忆库译文：Nanjing Shuiyunyao Wang Xi Inn is within minutes' walk of multiple attractions in Nanjing Shuiyuntao Tulou Scenic Spot. The nearest bus station is in Shuyang Town, a 20-minute drive away. Nanjing County can be reached in 70 minutes by car.

说明：修改 4 处即可，改译如下：

Nanjing **_Tulou Qing_** Inn is within minutes' walk of multiple attractions in
Nanjing **_Taxia_** Tulou Scenic Spot. The nearest bus station is in Shuyang Town, a
_30_-minute drive away. Nanjing County can be reached in **_80_** minutes by car.

②私人浴室配有淋浴、拖鞋、免费洗浴用品和吹风机。
The private bathroom includes a shower, slippers and free toiletries.

说明：增加"吹风机"即可，改译如下：

The private bathroom includes a shower, slippers, free toiletries and a
hairdryer.

（6）使用机器翻译（此处为 Bing）自动翻译剩下 5 句，如图 6-23：

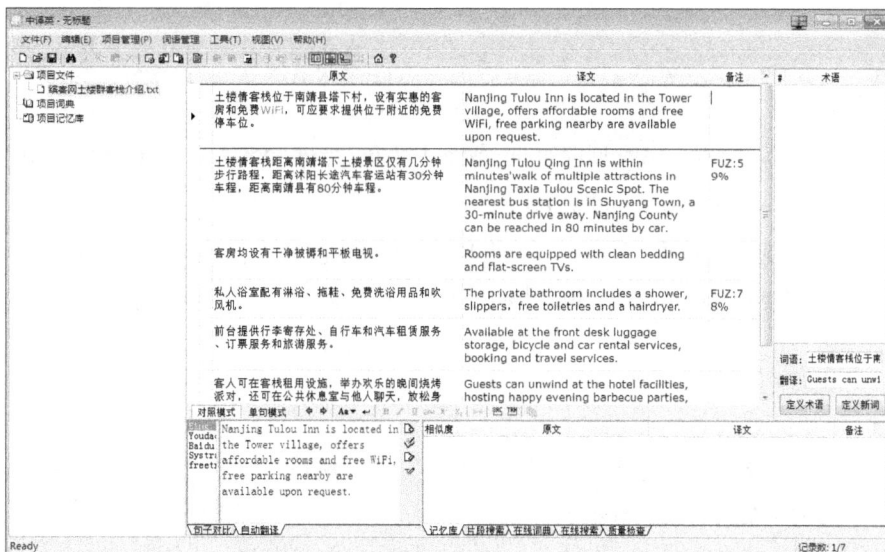

图 6-23　机器填充译文

（7）译后编辑（PE），修订机器译文。

①土楼情客栈位于南靖县塔下村，设有实惠的客房和免费 WiFi，可应要求提供位于附近的免费停车位。

机器译文：***Nanjing Tulou Inn*** is located in ***the Tower*** village, ***offers*** affordable rooms and free WiFi, free parking nearby ***are*** available upon request.

修订：Nanjing Tulou Qing Inn is located in Taxia village, offering affordable rooms and free WiFi, with free parking nearby available upon request.

说明：机器译文的译后编辑以高效以准则，采取顺序驱动方式，即尽量在原文顺序上增、删、改。上句修订中，增词 2 处（"Qing"及"with"），删词 2 处（"the"及"are"），改词一处（"offers"改为"offering"）。

②客房均设有干净被褥和平板电视。

机器译文：Rooms are equipped with clean bedding and flat-screen TVs.

说明：该句无须修订（"flat-screen TVs"改为"a flat-screen TV"较好，但对于 PE 而言，不改也无妨）。

③前台提供行李寄存处、自行车和汽车租赁服务、订票服务和旅游服务。

机器译文：Available at the front ***desk luggage*** storage, bicycle and car rental services, booking and travel services.

修订：Available at the front desk ***are*** luggage storage, bicycle and car rental services, booking and travel services.

说明：增词 1 处（"are"）。

④客人可在客栈租用设施，举办欢乐的晚间烧烤派对，还可在公共休息室与他人聊天，放松身心。

机器译文：Guests can ***unwind at*** the hotel facilities, hosting happy evening barbecue parties, ***you can*** chat with others in a ***public restroom, relax***.

修订：Guests can rent the hotel facilities, hosting happy evening barbecue parties, and chat with others in a shared lounge.

说明：删一处（"relax"），改 3 处（"rent" "and" 以及 "shared lounge"）。

④客人可以在内部餐厅享用餐点，也可步行前往其他众多餐馆享用美食。

机器译文：Guests can enjoy meals at the ***restaurant***, ***also*** within walking distance ***to*** many other ***restaurant food***.

修订：Guests can enjoy meals at the on-site restaurant, and within walking distance are many other restaurants.

说明：增 1 处（"on-site"），删 1 处（"food"），改 3 处（"and"、"are" 及 "restaurants"）。

附官方英文文本：

Featuring free WiFi, Tulouqing Inn offers affordable accommodation in Taxia Village, Nanjing. Free parking spaces are available around the site on request.

Tulouqing Inn is within minutes' walk of Nanjing Taxia Tulou Scenic Spot. Shuyang Coach Terminal is a 30-minute drive away. Nanjing County can be reached in 80 minutes by car.

All rooms are equipped with clean bedding and a flat-screen TV.

Slippers, free toiletries and a hairdryer are provided in the private bathroom with a shower.

Staff at the front desk can assist with luggage storage, bicycle rental and car hire. Ticketing and tour services are also offered for guests' convenience.

Guests can organise a joyful barbecue party at night with the facilities borrowed from the property. There is also a shared lounge where guests can have a relaxing time chatting with each other.

Guests can enjoy meals at the on-site restaurant. Meanwhile many other restaurants can be found within walking distance.

从以上机器译文的修订情况来看，对于掌握译后编辑技巧的译者而言，人工辅助机器翻译模式会比人工翻译效率更高。另外，要说明的是，本则应用个案使用的是南靖酒店介绍的记忆库，库容小，仅 8000 字 / 词，如果记忆库更大，CAT 记忆库预翻译的句子会更多。

6.6　小结

CCAT 平台下的机器辅助人工翻译及人工辅助机器翻译融合了机器翻译与计算机辅助翻译技术，辅以语料库的检索及类比分析，在翻译的效率和准确性方面都优于传统的人工翻译模式、单纯的机器翻译或计算机辅助翻译模式。需要大力构建新型的世界遗产双语语料库，包括双语对应语料库、类比语料库、记忆库和术语库；另外，就创导 CCAT 平台下的世界遗产翻译模式而言，语料库翻译学界和语言服务行业应形成共识，充分重视语料库与 CAT 融合所带来的巨大价值。

第7章　福建世界遗产双语语料库的译文修订

7.1　引言

福建世界遗产双语语料库在构建过程中，对收入语料库的原文及译文进行了两类修订。

第一类修订是以译文最优化为目的的精细修订，根据本书所提出的"信、达、效"的翻译原则，选择部分语篇，如武夷山申遗文本中的某一小节、土楼申遗文本中关于某一土楼的全部介绍文字等，从语篇层次进行译文的审校修订，除校订各类错误外，在语言地道、语篇逻辑通顺、文字简洁流畅等方面亦着力追求，尽量符合"信、达、效"原则。审校修订过程中添加序号标注，并配上有关修订依据的说明文字。该类修订实例可用于翻译教学训练、较深层次的译本错误类型及成因分析，以及译文优化等方面的研究。从目前已完成的此类修订实例中选择两篇，作为样例收入本章。

第二类修订是以译文入库为目的的一般修订，是利用计算机辅助技术并辅以人工审校完成的译文修订，以句为单位，如遇术语不统一、语法错误等，则予以纠正，不对原译句式、选词等进行优化润饰，纠错后的句子收入翻译记忆库。该类修订实例可用于人工辅助机器翻译实战、译后编辑训练、译文审校训练、常见翻译错误类型及成因分析，以及译文批量审校的相关研究。亦从目前已完成的翻译记忆库中选择部分经修订的句子，作为样例收入本章。

限于作者水平，两类修订难免错误，敬请方家指正。

7.2　申遗文本译文的精细修订样例

7.2.1　武夷山申遗文本（原文及译文选自武夷山申遗官方文本）

（1）考古资料表明，武夷山早在四千多年前就有先民在此劳动生息，逐步形成偏居中国一隅的"古闽族"文化和其后的"闽越族"文化，在国内外是绝无仅有的。反映这一文化特征的是武夷山"架壑船棺"、"虹桥板"及占地4.8万平米的闽越王所居的汉城遗址，是消逝三千多年的古文明和古文化传统习俗的独特的实物见证。

原译：Archaeological materials show there were people living in Mount Wuyi as early as 4,000 years ago. They gradually developed ***the Gumin nationality culture*** [1] and the later Minyue nationality culture ***at the remote corner of China*** [2], which were unique both at home and abroad. The "Boat coffins hanging on cliffs" and "Hongqiao boards" as well as the 480,000 square-metre Han Dynasty city remains inhabited by the ancient king of Yue are the evidence of ***the ancient civilization and traditional custom which were vanished*** [3] more than 3,000 years ago.

改译：Human settlement on the slopes of Mount Wuyi can be traced back more than 4,000 years by archeological remains. In this remote corner of China gradually emerged the Ancient Min culture and the later Minyue culture, unique both at home and abroad. The "Boat coffins hanging on cliffs" and "Hongqiao boards" as well as the 480,000 square-metre remains of the Han Dynasty city inhabited by the ancient king of Minyue were typical evidence of the vanished ancient civilization and customs more than 3,000 years ago.

说明：

[1] "闽"音译为"Min"已成定译，如"Minnan（闽南）"，而"古闽"据查并无"Gumin"之音译，以"意译＋音译"为宜，"族"可不译，故"古闽族文化"改译为"the Ancient Min culture"，较原译"Gumin nationality culture"更清晰易懂。

[2] "at the remote corner of China"改为"in this remote corner of China"，"this"指代更清楚。

[3] 原译"the ancient civilization and traditional custom which were vanished"存在语法错误，改为"the vanished ancient civilization and customs"。

[4] 其他句式调整之处较原译更为紧凑简洁。

（2）程朱理学，始于"二程"（程颐、程颢），集大成于朱熹，构成中国宋代至清代一直处于统治地位的思想理论，代表具有普遍意义的传统民族精神，影响远及东亚、东南亚、欧美诸国。

原　译：***Neo-Confucianism*** [1] ***began from*** [2] ***Cheng Yi (1033-1107 AD) and Cheng Hao (1032-1085 AD)*** [3] and ***was pushed to its peak*** [4] by Zhu Xi (1130-1200 AD). ***This school of thought*** [5] became the dominant theoretical thought from Song to Qing dynasties. Representing the ***universal traditional national spirit*** [6], it ***exerted its influence to*** [7] East Asia, Southeast Asia, European and American countries.

改译：The Cheng-Zhu school, which began from the Cheng Brothers, Cheng Yi (1033-1107 AD) and Cheng Hao (1032-1085 AD), culminated in Zhu Xi's thought and became the dominant theoretical thought from Song to Qing dynasties. Representing the traditional Chinese spirit, it extended its influence to East Asia, Southeast Asia, European and American countries.

说明：

[1]"程朱理学"为理学（Neo-Confucianism）之一派，译为 Cheng-Zhu School 是学界惯例，原译有误。详细可考察 Google Books 数据库检索结果，如图 7-1：

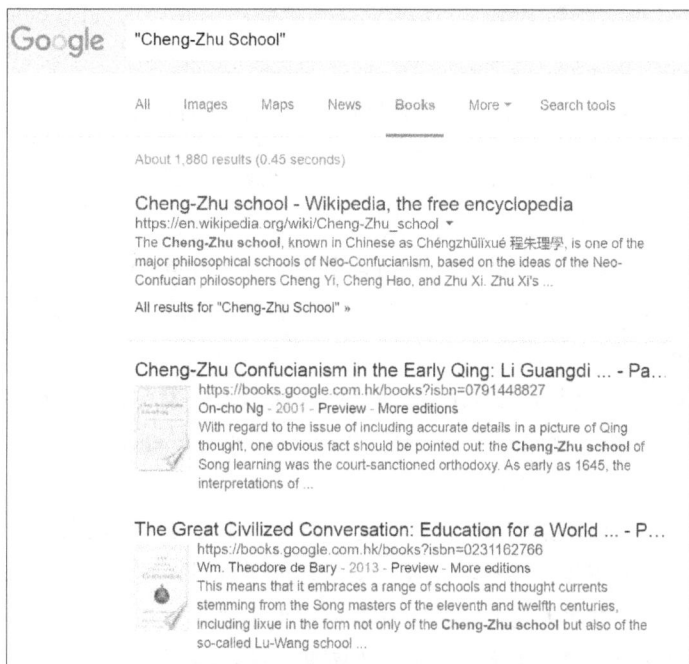

图 7-1 Google Books 数据库检索"Cheng–Zhu School"

[2] 使用定语从句合句译法。

[3]"二程"宜译出其内涵，即"程氏兄弟"，改译为"the Cheng Brothers"，并以二人姓名为同位语，增补相关背景信息。

[4]"集大成于"译为"was pushed to its peak"不妥，查 Google Books 数

据库并无此类表达，如图 7-2。

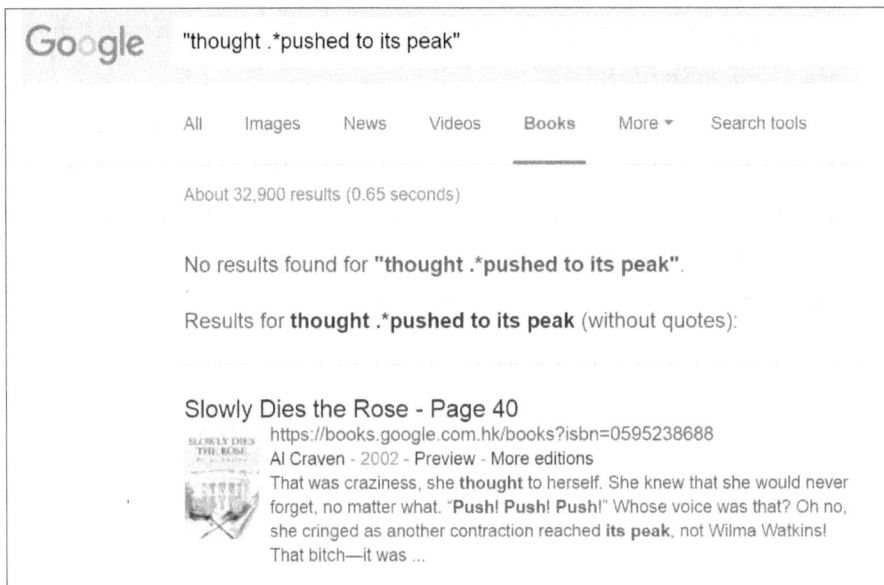

图 7-2 Goole Books 数据库检索"thought.*pushed to its peak"

改译为"culminated in Zhu Xi's thought"准确且地道。

[5] 使用定语从句合句译法。

[6] "universal"与"traditional"词义重复，译为"traditional"即可；"national"宜改为 Chinese，更为明确，符合对外宣传惯例，如习近平在国外演讲时，"我国"多译为"China"。

[7] 原译搭配有误，"exert"后应使用介词"on"，但此处"exert its influence on"有"施以影响"之意，不妥。改为"extended its influence to"。

（3）孔子集前古思想之大成，开创中国文化传统之主干的儒学。朱熹集孔子以下学术思想之大成，使程朱理学达到顶峰，为儒学注入新的生机，形成儒学思想文化的杰出代表——朱子理学，至今仍吸引着世界上几十个国家的专家、学者致力于理学思想的研究。

原译：Confucius, epitomizing the thoughts of his forefathers, created Confucianism, which constituted ***the main body of*** [1] the traditional Chinese culture. Zhu Xi, ***agglomerating*** [2] academic thoughts after Confucius, ***pushed the Cheng-Zhu Neo-Confucianism to its summit*** [3], ***rejecting*** [4]new vitality into Confucianism by establishing Zhuzi Neo-Confucianism, an outstanding representative of

福建世界遗产

双语语料库构建与应用

Confucianist [5] culture. Today, experts and scholars from dozens of countries *of the world* [6] are still dedicated to the study of *this school of thought* [7].

改译：Confucius, epitomizing the thoughts of his forefathers, created Confucianism, which constituted the core of the traditional Chinese culture. Zhu Xi, drawing on the academic thoughts after Confucius, pushed the Cheng-Zhu Neo-Confucianism to its greatest development, injecting new vitality into Confucianism by establishing Zhuzi Neo-Confucianism, an outstanding representative of the Confucian culture. Today, experts and scholars from dozens of countries are still dedicated to the study of Neo-Confucianism.

说明：

[1] "the main body" 与 "culture" 搭配较罕见，改为 "the core"。

[2] "agglomerate" 与 "thought" 搭配不妥，改为 "draw on"。

[3] 原译在 Google Books 数据库中未见检索结果，改译之英文表达则有例可查。

[4] 显为 "inject" 之误。

[5] "Confucianist culture" 这一表达较罕见，改为 "Confucian culture"。

[6] "of the world" 多余，不妨删除。

[7] 原译累赘，据上下文，原译指的是朱子理学，朱子理学仅为理学之一派，原文为 "理学思想"，宜尊重原文，译为 Neo-Confucianism。

（4）朱熹（公元 1130—1200）是中国文化史上最有地位的人物之一。在中国文化史、传统思想史、教育史和礼教史上影响最大的，前推孔子、后推朱熹。因此，有些学者称朱熹为 "三代下的孔子"。

原译：Zhu Xi is one of the most influential figures in China's cultural history. *The most influential figure* [1] in the histories of *Chinese culture* [2], traditional thought, education and feudal code of ethics is Confucius, and *Zhu is the second most influential one* [3]. Some scholars called Zhu Xi "*a Confucius three generations after Confucius.*"[4]

改译：Zhu Xi is one of the most influential figures in China's cultural history, only second to Confucius in the histories of traditional thought, education and feudal code of ethics. So some scholars called Zhu Xi "the Confucius after the three dynasties of Xia, Shang and Zhou."

说明：

[1]、[3] 原译两句之中出现 3 次 "most influential"，累赘之极，利用 "only second to" 这一短语将两句合译。

[2] 与第一句意思重复，可删除。

[4] "三代下的孔子" 指的是 "夏商周之后的孔子"，而非 "三代人之后的孔子"，孔子与朱子在年代上相差何止千年，故原译颇不合情理，改为 "the Confucius after the three dynasties of Xia, Shang and Zhou"。

（5）朱熹在武夷山生活达 50 余年，著述教学，使武夷山成为理学名山。山间溪畔留下众多的理学文化遗迹，对研究朱子理学和儒教思想的兴衰演变以及中国哲学思想史都是非常珍贵的，是中国传统文化的瑰宝，素有"东周出孔丘，南宋有朱熹。中国古文化，泰山与武夷"之说。

原译：Zhu Xi lived, wrote and lectured in Mount Wuyi for more than 50 years, making it a mountain known for the _**Neo-Confucianist**_ [1] study. Many sites of _**Neo-Confucianist**_ [2] culture _**remained in the mountain and stream side, which are very valuable to the study of Neo-Confucianism and Confucianism as well as the history of Chinese philosophy. They are the gems of traditional Chinese culture**_ [3]. There is a saying that "Confucius was born in Eastern Zhou Dynasty while Zhu Xi was born in Southern Song Dynasty; Chinese ancient culture originates in Mount Tai and Mount Wuyi."

改　译：Zhu Xi lived, wrote and lectured in Mount Wuyi for more than 50 years, making it a mountain known for the Neo-Confucian study. The rich remains of Neo-Confucian culture in the mountain and by the stream are the gems of traditional Chinese culture, invaluable to the studies of Neo-Confucianism and Confucianism as well as the Chinese philosophy history. There is a saying that "Confucius was born in Eastern Zhou Dynasty while Zhu Xi was born in Southern Song Dynasty; Chinese ancient culture originates in Mount Tai and Mount Wuyi."

说明：

[1]、[2] Neo-Confucian 即可，原译较罕用。

[3] 将 "Many sites" 改为 "The rich remains"，构成头韵修辞格，删除 "remained"、"which" 和 "they"，将 "are the gems of traditional Chinese culture" 提前，将 "valuable..." 改为 "invaluable..." 置后。改译利用了译文修订的"删"

字法和"移"位法，较原译简练流畅。

7.2.2 土楼申遗文本（原文及译文选自土楼申遗官方文本）

（1）二宜楼

坐落于大地村中部。建于清乾隆五年（1740年）。2005年住有39户，196人。

原译：

Eryi Lou

It is located [1] in the center of Dadi village. ***It was built*** [2] in the 5th year of Emperor Qianlong's Reign in the Qing Dynasty (1740). In 2005, ***there were*** 196 persons of 39 households ***inhabiting*** here [3].

改译：

Eryi Tulou

Eryi Tulou, located in the center of Dadi village, was built in the 5th reigning year of Emperor Qianlong, Qing Dynasty (1740). In 2005 it had 196 residents of 39 households.

说明：

[1]、[2] 原译句式单调重复，第一句改为过去分词做定语的结构，与第二句合并。第一句的代词"It"改为"Eryi Tulou"，利用重复凸显该文化符号，有利于受众留下更深印象。

[3] 原译使用"there be"句型，句中含有动词结构"inhabiting"，简练不足，将"people … inhabiting"改为"residents"。原文动词"住"、"有"和译文"residents"体现了汉语多用动词而英语名词结构占优的语言差异。

（2）双环圆形土楼，坐东南朝西北，占地9300平方米。外环高4层，内环单层。外径73.4米。整座楼分成16单元，共有房间224间。其中4个单元是作为共用的门、梯道及厅堂，余下的12个单元为住户，每个单元均有独自的楼梯上下，是福建省两大民系——客家民系、福佬民系之福佬民系地区单元式土楼的代表。

原译：***It faces the northwest and covers an area of 9,300 square meters. The Tulou consists of two annular constructions. The outer one has four floors and the inner has one floor. The diameter of the Tulou is 73.4 meters*** [1].

The whole building is divided into 16 units [2]. Four units serve as gateways and lobbies for public use. *There are totally 224 rooms in the remaining 12 units for private use and each unit is equipped with a separate staircase* [3]. It is a typical example of *unit-type* [4] Tulou *for Fulao people* [5] *who together with the Hakka people* [6] constitute two important branches of the Han nationality in Fujian Province.

改译：Facing the northwest with an area of 9,300 square meters, it is of a double annular construction with a 4-storey outer ring 73.4 meters in diameter and a one-storey inner ring. The whole building is divided into 16 units with 224 rooms. Four units serve as gates, stairways and lobbies for public use. The other units are for residents, each equipped with a separate staircase. It is a typical example of the unit-type Tulou of the Fulao people, who, together with the Hakka people, constitute the two important branches of the Han nationality in Fujian Province.

说明：

[1] 原译句式太散，单句过多，杂乱无章。将第一句改为现在分词形式的从属结构，将第一句的动词"cover"及第三句的动词"has"改为介词"with"，将第四句改为"73.4 meters in diameter"，从而将原译由 4 句改为 1 句，句式紧凑简练，信息层次分明，逻辑关系清楚。

[2] 原译将"共有房间 224 间"挪到了后面，无此必要，改译将其出现顺序复原，译为"with 224 rooms"。

[3] "for private use"意思含糊，改为"for residents"；"and each unit is equipped with …"改为独立主格结构"each equipped with …"。改译较原译更简练。

[4]、[5] 增加定冠词"the"，使译文合乎语法。

[6] 在"who"前加逗号，将限制性定语从句改为非限制性定语从句，"together with the Hakka people"前后加逗号，使句子结构更为清晰。

（3）每个单元都从公共内院入口，单元内部设有户内私用的小庭院，这是一个较有私密性的空间。从圆楼外走进中心内院、再进入各单元内的小庭院，这种室外空间私密性层次的变化，是对人们聚族而居生活中不同要求的满足。

原译：Each unit *has their doors located in the public inner court, and has a personal courtyard, which is a space of privacy* [1]. Walking into the Tulou and then the courtyard of each unit, one can witness the variation of *private outdoor space* [2] by which different requirements are satisfied when *the whole family* [3] live together.

改译：Each unit, though only accessible from the public inner court, has a private courtyard of its own. Walking into the Tulou and then the courtyard of each unit, one can witness the variation of outdoor space privacy by which different requirements are satisfied when families live together.

说明：

[1] 原译逻辑层次不太清晰，使用定语从句表达原文"较有私密性的空间"较为累赘，将第一句改为"though only accessible from the public inner court"，较原译更好地传达了各单元的出入均需经由公共内院这一信息，与后面的"has a private courtyard of its own"逻辑关系清晰，层次分明。使用"private"一词做前置定语，修饰"courtyard"，便可表达原文"较有私密性的空间"之意。

[2] "室外空间私密性"应为"outdoor space privacy"。

[3] "the whole family"改为"families"，从上下文来看，2005 年该土楼有 39 户人家，所以"聚族而居"是指多个家庭生活在同一个土楼，而非一个家庭。

（4）二宜楼的室内空间布局也独具一格，进入单元内是位于内环的入口门厅，其两侧分别是厨房、库房，内外环楼之间连以过廊，围合出单元内的小庭院，过廊与小庭院之间以透空的木隔扇分隔。外环楼的室内空间布局也与内通廊式土楼不同，底层不是用作厨房、餐厅，而是用作客厅，二、三层均作卧房。四层中间是大空间的祖堂，由各户单独设置，两侧为粮仓。

原译：The indoor layout is also unique. The entrance hall *comes first* [1], *with kitchen and storeroom beside* [2]. Corridors *linking* [3] the inner and outer ring *create* [4] *courtyards* [5]. Between the courtyard and the corridor are the wooden partition boards. The layout of *rooms and space in* [6] the outer ring is different from *those* [7] of the inner one which has corridors: the ground storey *is not kitchens and dinning halls but* [8] guest rooms and bedrooms; the second and third storeys are all bedrooms. In the middle of the fourth storey is a large ancestral hall which can be arranged by each family itself. A barn is provided at two sides.

改译：The indoor layout is also unique，the entrance hall flanked by the kitchen and storeroom, and courtyards enclosed with corridors between the inner and outer ring. Between the courtyard and the corridor are the wooden partition boards. The layout of the outer ring is different from that of the inner one which has corridors: the ground storey is not used as kitchens and dining halls but as guest rooms and bedrooms; the second and third storeys are all bedrooms. In the middle of the fourth storey is a large ancestral hall which can be arranged by each family itself. A barn is provided at two sides.

说明：

[1] "entrance hall" 已暗含 "comes first" 之意，可删除 "comes first"。

[2] "with kitchen and storeroom beside" 中 "kitchen" 和 "storeroom" 前应有限定词，可改为 "flanked by the kitchen and storeroom"，与 "the entrance hall" 合为一个独立主格结构。

[3] "linking" 改为 "between"，减少一个动词。

[4] 删除 "create"，使该句降为从属结构。

[5] 将 "courtyards" 提前，后加 "enclosed by"，成为独立主格结构。经上述步骤的修订润饰，原译 3 句改为 1 句，更为简练。

[6] "rooms and space" 与 "layout" 语义重复，删除。

[7] "those" 指代错误，改为 "that"。

[8] "is not" 突兀，后加 "used as"；"dinning" 拼写错误，更正为 "dining"；"guest rooms" 前加 "as"。改译修正了原译的语法错误和拼写错误。

（5）在结构上，二宜楼也与众不同。外环楼房的外围是土墙到顶，内围也是承重土墙直抵三层。各个单元之间完全以承重的土墙隔开，每个单元内部 1—3 层的纵墙也是用承重的土墙分隔。

原译：Eryi Lou also differs from others **_due to_** [1] its structure. The outer ring is enclosed by a wall of the same height, while the inner ring **_is also enclose_** [2] by a main wall as **_top_** [3] as its third floor. Each unit, as well as **_the interior walls from the first to the third floor of each unit_** [4], is separated by the main wall.

改译：Eryi Lou also differs from others in its structure. The outer ring is enclosed by a wall of the same height, while the inner ring by a main wall as high as its third floor. Each unit, as well as its interior walls from the first to the third floor, is separated by the main wall.

说明：

[1] "differ" 与 "in" 搭配，意为 "在某方面不同"，故 "due to" 改为 "in"。

[2] 原译 "is also enclose by" 存在明显的语法错误。根据承前省略规则，"is also enclose by" 可删除。

[3] "as top as" 有误，改为 "as high as"。

[4] 将 "the interior walls" 改为 "its interior walls"，之后可删除语义重复的 "of each unit"。

（6）更为别致的是其二、三层内圈土墙上又伸出窄窄的木挑廊，形成廊道外的又一个檐廊，方便衣物等晾晒。

原译：More exquisitely, ***upon the wall of inner ring are narrow verandas on the second and third floor out of the inner corridor for clothes airing*** [1].

改译：More exquisitely, narrow verandas like the inner corridor are built on the wall of the inner ring's second and third floor for clothes airing.

说明：原文 "廊道外的又一个檐廊" 意思似为 "除廊道外，还有一个像廊道一样的檐廊"，原译意思含糊，改译意思清楚，忠实于原文。

7.3 入库译文的修订样例

本小节选录部分录入翻译记忆库的译文修订作为样例，无修订依据说明。

7.3.1 武夷山申遗文本（原文及译文选自武夷山申遗官方文本）

（1）武夷山有着悠久的历史文化和丰富的历史文化遗存及理学文物，符合文化遗产标准的第三项和第五项条款以及文化景观标准的第三项。

原译：With ***long history*** and rich cultural remains as well as relics of Neo-Confucianism, Mount Wuyi meets Criteria (iii) and (v) for natural heritage as well as Criterion (iii) for cultural landscape as stipulated in the World Heritage Convention.

改译：With a long history and rich cultural remains as well as relics of Neo-Confucianism, Mount Wuyi meets Criteria (iii) and (v) for natural heritage as well as Criterion (iii) for cultural landscape as stipulated in the World Heritage Convention.

（2）1990 年中国佛教协会会长赵朴初题写寺名。寺前有弥勒佛岩雕像 1 尊，高 12 m，宽 13 m，厚 12 m。

原译：In 1990, Zhao Puchu, chairman of China Buddhism Association wrote the name of ***temple***. In front of the temple is a Hall of Meitreya, 12 m tall, 13 m wide and 12 m thick.

改译：In 1990, Zhao Puchu, chairman of China Buddhism Association wrote the temple name. In front of the temple is a Hall of Meitreya, 12 m tall, 13 m wide and 12 m thick.

（3）"三三秀水清如玉"的九曲溪，与"六六奇峰翠插天"的三十六峰、九十九岩的绝妙结合，它异于一般自然山水，是以奇秀深幽为特征的巧而精的天然山水园林。

原译：The "pure, crystal-clear" ***Nine-bent Stream***, the "green, supernatural" 36 peaks and 99 ghostly rocks make a perfect combination. Differing from ***ordinary mountain*** and waters, they constitute an extraordinary garden of natural mountains and waters characterized by its incomparable beauty and endless tranquility.

改译：The "pure, crystal-clear" Nine-bend Stream, the "green, supernatural" 36 peaks and 99 ghostly rocks make a perfect combination. Differing from ordinary mountains and waters, they constitute an extraordinary garden of natural mountains and waters characterized by its incomparable beauty and endless tranquility.

（4）一曲，畅旷豁达；二曲，幽谷丹崖；三曲，虹桥奇观；四曲，秀山媚水；五曲，深幽奇险；六曲，天游览胜；七曲，三仰雄伟；八曲，青山奇石；九曲，锦绣平川。

原译：***Bent 1***: wide and open; ***Bent 2***: ***Deep*** valley and red cliff; ***Bent 3***: ghostly "rainbow-bridge-like boards" ("Hongqiao board")；***Bent 4***: beautiful mountain and water; ***Bent 5***: deep and dangerous; ***Bent 6***: the picturesque Tianyou scenic area; ***Bent 7***: magnificent Sanyang Peak; ***Bent 8***: green mountain and eccentric rocks; ***Bent 9***: gorgeous plains.

改译：Bend 1: wide and open; Bend 2: deep valley and red cliff; Bend 3: ghostly "rainbow-bridge-like boards" ("Hongqiao board") ; Bend 4: beautiful mountains and water; Bend 5: deep and dangerous; Bend 6: the picturesque Tianyou scenic area; Bend 7: magnificent Sanyang Peak; Bend 8: green mountains and eccentric rocks; Bend 9: gorgeous plains.

（5）受当地居民传统的生产生活方式（武夷山及周边地区现有 14 个行政村，常住人口 22,710 人，主要从事茶叶、林农生产）和游人增长因素的影响，使植被水源、大气质量易受侵害，给监测和防止污染工作带来压力。

原译：Under the influence and impact of traditional production and living methods among the local residents (there are 14 administrative villages with a permanent population totaling 22,710 in Mount Wuyi and its surrounding areas, mainly engaging in the production of tea, agriculture and forestry) and under the influence of the factor of growing tourists, vegetation, water sources, ***air quality*** are vulnerable to damage, ***causing pressure to*** the monitoring and prevention of pollution.

改译：Under the influence and impact of traditional production and living methods among the local residents (there are 14 administrative villages with a permanent population totaling 22,710 in Mount Wuyi and its surrounding areas, mainly engaging in the production of tea, agriculture and forestry) and under the influence of the factor of growing tourists, vegetation, water sources, and air quality are vulnerable to damage, putting pressure on the monitoring and prevention of pollution.

（6）该图是英国植物采集家福菵（Robert Fortune, 1813—1880）于 1843 年 7 月在武夷山采集植物标本时，为九曲溪绮丽风光而作。

原译：This picture, which reflects the scenes on ***Nine-bent Stream***, was drawn by plant collector Robert Fortune (1813-1880) when he was collecting plant ***specimen*** in Mount Wuyi in July 1843.

改译：This picture, which reflects the scenes on Nine-bend Stream, was drawn by plant collector Robert Fortune (1813-1880) when he was collecting plant specimens in Mount Wuyi in July 1843.

（7）利用天然的悬崖裂隙洞穴，木构房舍，开"一夫当关，万夫莫开"之门于峭壁，整体布局结构独特，有"空中楼阁"之誉。

原译：The wood-structure dwellings were built by ***making use*** natural caves in the cliffs. The doors were opened in the cliffs. A hoister was used to transport articles and goods. With peculiar design, the dwellings are known as "buildings in the air."

改译：The wood-structure dwellings were built by making use of natural caves in the cliffs. The doors were opened in the cliffs. A hoister was used to transport articles and goods. With peculiar design, the dwellings are known as "buildings in the air."

（8）该书院建筑宏大，风格独具，毁于兵。

原译：The academy was _**grandiose**_ and _**beautifully**_ designed. It was destroyed in the war.

改译：The academy was constructed broadly in scale and uniquely designed. It was destroyed in the war.

（9）武夷茶文化有一千多年的悠久历史，元代始成为皇室贡品，并在武夷创办御茶园，茶文化遗址遍布武夷山中。

原译：Tea culture in Mount Wuyi has a history of more than 1,000 years. _**Starting from**_ Yuan Dynasty, tea produced here _**had been**_ presented to the imperial family. The imperial farm was also built in the mountain. Remains of tea culture can be seen everywhere in the mountain.

改译：Tea culture in Mount Wuyi has a history of more than 1,000 years. In the Yuan Dynasty, tea produced here began to be presented to the imperial family. The imperial farm was also built in the mountain. Remains of tea culture can be seen everywhere in the mountain.

（10）明代抗倭名将戚继光隆庆元年题，福建都司曹奎书，是戚继光即将离开镇守多年的福建前夕留下的遗迹，表达了他保家卫国、抗击强虏的必胜信念和对武夷山水的眷恋之情。

原译：It was written by anti-Wo (today's Japan) hero Qi Jiguang in Ming Dynasty, and the calligraphy was done by Cao Kui, an official of Fujian Province. Qi wrote the inscription before leaving Fujian where he _**stationed**_ for many years, expressing his desire to defend the country and fight against the intruders and _**love**_ for the landscape in Mount Wuyi.

改译：It was written by anti-Wo (today's Japan) hero Qi Jiguang in Ming Dynasty, and the calligraphy was done by Cao Kui, an official of Fujian Province. Qi wrote the inscription before leaving Fujian where he had been stationed

福建世界遗产

双语语料库构建与应用

for many years, expressing his desire to defend the country and fight against the intruders and his love for the landscape in Mount Wuyi.

7.3.2 土楼申遗文本（原文及译文选自土楼申遗官方文本）

（1）福建土楼分布范围以福建西南地区尤为集中，总数达 3000 多座。

原译：Fujian Tulou ***concentrates*** in the southwestern region of Fujian Province and a total of three ***thousands*** Tulou ***Buildings*** have been found across this province.

改译：Fujian Tulou are concentrated in the southwestern region of Fujian Province and a total of three thousand Tulou buildings have been found across this province.

（2）福建土楼以"天圆地方"作为建筑主体造型的设计理念，以满足家族聚落群居和良好的防御功能需要来安排建筑的规模，采用夯土墙与穿斗式木构架共同承重的两层以上封闭式围合型大型民居建筑，坐落于山地间，依偎于溪流畔，耸立在田园间，宛如翠绿的原野上长出的朵朵蘑菇，巧似天外的来客留下的神奇飞碟。

原译：Fujian Tulou is mainly built according to the concept of "round heaven and square earth" and in a certain scale to meet the needs of the whole clan living together and a sound defensive function. As an enclosed communal house with two or more storeys in ***double load-bearing design***, i.e. ***rammed earth wall plus column and tie construction***, it is mostly located in the mountainous regions, neighboring with streams, fields and gardens. Visitors may easily fall into a reverie and associate its delicate shape with mushrooms on the emerald plain or a fantastic UFO from the outer space.

改译：Fujian Tulou is mainly built according to the concept of "round heaven and square earth" and in a certain scale to meet the needs of the whole clan living together and a sound defensive function. As an enclosed communal house with two or more storeys in a double load-bearing design, i.e. the rammed earth wall plus the column and tie construction, it is mostly located in the mountainous regions, neighboring with streams, fields and gardens. Visitors may easily fall into a reverie and associate its delicate shape with mushrooms on the emerald plain or a fantastic UFO from the outer space.

（3）位于土楼群中部，始建于明代嘉靖年间 (1549—1553 年)，1923 年失火后重修。

原译：At the center of ***the Tulou***, this square construction was first built during Emperor Jiajing's Reign in the Ming Dynasty (1549-1553). It was rebuilt after a fire in 1923.

改译：At the center of the Tulou cluster, this square construction was first built during Emperor Jiajing's Reign in the Ming Dynasty (1549-1553). It was rebuilt after a fire in 1923.

（4）楼内按中国传统《易经》八卦原理布局，以青砖防火墙分隔成 8 个单元，楼房呈辐射状 8 等分，寓意乾、兑、坤、离、巽、震、艮、坎八卦，每等分 6 间起脚为一卦。每卦关起门户自成院落。

原译：The internal layout is made according to the principle of the Eight Tri-grams from the Chinese classic *Book of Changes*. The internal space is circularly divided into eight equal units by grey-brick firewalls, each of which represents one of the Eight ***Diagrams***, that is, the sky, the swamp, the earth, the fire, the wind, the thunder, the mountain and the water. Each portion is a unit having six rooms and forming an independent living environment when the door is closed.

改译：The internal layout is made according to the principle of the Eight Tri-grams from the Chinese classic *Book of Changes*. The internal space is circularly divided into eight equal units by grey-brick firewalls, each of which represents one of the Eight Trigrams, that is, the sky, the swamp, the earth, the fire, the wind, the thunder, the mountain and the water. Each portion is a unit having six rooms and forming an independent living environment when the door is closed.

（5）1985 年，该楼模型作为中国建筑模型之一，在美国洛杉矶国际建筑模型展览会上展出。

原译：In 1985, the model of the building was selected as one of ***Chinese architectural models*** and displayed on the ***Unite*** States (L.A.) International Architectural Model Exhibition.

改译：In 1985, the model of the building was selected as one of the Chinese architectural models and displayed on the United States (L.A.) International Architectural Model Exhibition.

（6）该楼具有突出的防火功能。以砖墙隔成的 8 个单元，如果某一单元发生火灾，火势被砖砌防火墙所隔，不会殃及邻近的单元；外环的二、

三、四层和内环的二层包括通廊在内全部楼板都铺设青砖，一旦发生火灾，楼板被烧毁后青砖会自然往下压，起着灭火作用。

原译：The **_hall_** possesses outstanding fireproofing function, comprising 8 units separated by brick- made **_wall_**. If one **_certain_** unit be on fire, the fire flame would be separated by the fireproofing walls, thus protecting the surrounding units from catching fire. The second, third and fourth floors of the outer ring and the second floor of the inner ring, including the corridors, are covered by blue bricks. Once the building is on fire, the blue bricks will spontaneously fall to put out the fire after the floor slabs are **_burn down_**.

改译：The Tulou possesses outstanding fireproofing function, comprising 8 units separated by brick-made walls. If one unit was on fire, the fire flame would be separated by the fireproofing walls, thus protecting the surrounding units from catching fire. The second, third and fourth floors of the outer ring and the second floor of the inner ring, including the corridors, are covered by blue bricks. Once the building is on fire, the blue bricks will spontaneously fall to put out the fire after the floor slabs are burnt down.

（7）内环南面的厅堂约占 2 个房间位置，又称中堂或中厅，位于中轴线上。

原译：The hall on the South of the inner ring, which is also called middle lobby or middle hall, is located on the central axis, covering an area **_equaling_** to two houses.

改译：The hall on the South of the inner ring, which is also called middle lobby or middle hall, is located on the central axis, covering an area equal to two houses.

（8）对楼主来说，该围屏在重大节庆时反复向族人展示，既是让大家分享艺术珍品，更是对全体族人进行传统美德的再教育。

原译：The building owner considers that to display this screen in major festivals **_not only can_** delight people's eyes **_but also can_** conduct education again on traditional **_virtue_** among the whole clan.

改译：The building owner considers that to display this screen in major festivals can not only delight people's eyes but also conduct education again on traditional virtues among the whole clan.

（9）每逢重大节日，祖堂摆设的巨型围屏，即 16 世祖江馨轩 71 寿辰时的祝寿屏风，由 12 块组成，高 2.72 米，中间 8 块每块宽 0.46 米，两边每块宽 0.47 米，精雕细刻，金碧辉煌，古事人物栩栩如生，其中最引人注目的是千古流传的"二十四孝图"。

原译：When important festivals come, the jumbo enclosed screen, once served as the present for the 71st birthday of Jiang Xinxuan, the 16th generation of the clan, will be put in the ancestral hall. The screen consists of 12 plates, 2.72 meters in heigh, *__of which__* the 8 plates in the middle are 0.46 meters wide for each and the plates at two sides are 0.47 meters wide for each. Some time-honored *__storeys__* are inscribed on the delicately carved screen, *__particular__* the long-lasting "pictures of 24 filial persons".

改译：When important festivals come, the jumbo enclosed screen, once served as the present for the 71st birthday of Jiang Xinxuan, the 16th generation of the clan, will be put in the ancestral hall. The screen consists of 12 plates, 2.72 meters in height. The 8 plates in the middle are 0.46 meters wide for each and the plates at two sides are 0.47 meters wide for each. Some time-honored stories are inscribed on the delicately carved screen, particularly the long-lasting "pictures of 24 filial persons".

（10）厅堂后向上方和前向屋檐下悬挂清代至 20 世纪 80 年代一些名人赠送给该楼的题匾；两侧两对石柱上镌刻警示子孙后代的楹联："一本所生，亲疏无多，何必太分你我？共楼居住，出入相见，最宜重法人伦。"

原译：Some boards bearing inscriptions of famous figures of *__Qing Dynasty__* and the 1980s still highly hang on the back-oriented place of the hall and under the front-oriented eaves; *__Couplets__* on the stone columns of two sides read: "Originating from the same root, we regard least the distance in relationship as we love each other; Living in the same building, we cherish most the importance of kinship as we meet every day."

改译：Some boards bearing inscriptions of famous figures of the Qing Dynasty and the 1980s still highly hang on the back-oriented place of the hall and under the front-oriented eaves; couplets on the stone columns of two sides read: "Originating from the same root, we regard least the distance in relationship as we love each other; Living in the same building, we cherish most the importance of kinship as we meet every day."

（11）田螺坑土楼群位于南靖县西部的书洋镇上坂村田螺坑自然村，

双语语料库构建与应用
福建世界遗产

距南靖县城60千米，坐落在海拔787.8米的湖岽山半坡上，由方形的步云楼和圆形的振昌楼、瑞云楼、和昌楼、文昌楼组成，均保存完好。

原译：60 kilometers from Nanjing County, it sits on the slope of the Hudong Mountain, 787.8 meters above the sea level. The building cluster consists of one square Tulou, three circular Tulou buildings ***and one oval Tulou***, namely ***Buyun Lou***, ***Zhenchang Lou***, ***Ruiyun Lou***, ***Hechang Lou*** and ***Wenchang Lou***, all standing intact.

改译：60 kilometers from Nanjing County, it sits on the slope of the Hudong Mountain, 787.8 meters above the sea level. The building cluster consists of one square Tulou, namely Buyun Tulou, and four circular Tulou, namely Zhenchang Tulou, Ruiyun Tulou, Hechang Tulou and Wenchang Tulou, all standing intact.

（12）上述进入福建东南部漳州、泉州等地区的中原人民，在与当地人民的相互融合、发展过程中，形成了以闽南话为代表的福佬民系，并通过随后的不断向海外迁徙，形成了主要分布东南亚各国数以千万计的闽南华侨群体。

原译：Those who settled in southeast Fujian, such as Zhangzhou and Quangzhou, became the Fulao people speaking Minnan (south Fujian) dialect during the course of merging with local people. Some of their descendants went even further to overseas countries. In Southeast Asian countries now, there are ***tens millions*** of overseas Chinese with an origin in south Fujian.

改译：Those who settled in southeast Fujian, such as Zhangzhou and Quangzhou, became the Fulao people speaking Minnan (south Fujian) dialect during the course of merging with local people. Some of their descendants went even further to overseas countries. In Southeast Asian countries now, there are tens of millions of overseas Chinese with an origin in south Fujian.

（13）战国晚期至西汉初期，福建的生土夯筑技术已相当成熟，福州新店战国晚期至汉代古城遗址（公元前2世纪—前1世纪）、武夷山城村闽越王城遗址（公元前1世纪）等所遗留的城墙，均为生土夯筑而成。

原译：From the late Warring States period to the early Western Han period, the technology of rammed earth for construction became relatively mature in Fujian. Some cultural heritages are built by walls of rammed earth, for example the ancient city relic in the Xindian of Fuzhou from the late Warring States period to the Han dynasty (the 2nd century B.C.-the 1st century B.C.) and **_King Yue_** city relic (the 1st century B.C.) in the Cheng village of Mount Wuyi.

改译：From the late Warring States period to the early Western Han period, the technology of rammed earth for construction became relatively mature in Fujian. Some cultural heritages are built by walls of rammed earth, for example the ancient city relic in the Xindian of Fuzhou from the late Warring States period to the Han dynasty (the 2nd century B.C.-the 1st century B.C.) and the Minyue Han Dynasty city relic (the 1st century B.C.) in the Cheng village of Mount Wuyi.

（14）19世纪晚期起，海外文化影响在部分土楼建造中得到了一定的反映，一些土楼内出现了中西融合的建筑形式与装饰。

原译：From late 19th century on, the traces of overseas culture could be found in some of these buildings, **_the_** architectural types and decorations integrated with Western style **_had occurred_** in some Tulou.

改译：From late 19th century on, the traces of overseas culture could be found in some of these buildings, and the architectural types and decorations integrated with Western style occurred in some Tulou.

（15）初溪土楼群从建成至今，除了正常检修中极少量对屋顶瓦面进行必要的修补外，土楼墙体、结构、内外空间一直维持原状，没有任何改变。

原译：Since the Chuxi Tulou Cluster was **_construction_**, except the necessary repair to the roof tiles during normal maintenance, all wall bodies, structures and inside/outside space of **_Tulou_** have kept their original state without any changes.

改译：Since the Chuxi Tulou Cluster was constructed, except the necessary repair to the roof tiles during normal maintenance, all wall bodies, structures and inside/outside space of it have kept their original state without any changes.

7.4 小结

有关世界遗产翻译译文修订的实例及分析目前并不多见。本章通过分析福建世界遗产翻译中质量最高的申遗文本译文，发现了一些申遗文本中具有的普遍性的问题，如缺少定冠词这种语法上的瑕疵，拼写错误这种粗心导致的问题，术语不一致这种利用计算机辅助技术才可能避免的老大难问题，等等。要解决这些问题，需要严格的翻译流程质量监控和计算机辅助技术的有效运用。希望所提供的这些译文修订样例能引发学界对世界遗产翻译的重视，提高世界遗产翻译的质量，促进世遗文化的对外传播。

参考文献

Ahmed, T., Mouratidis, H. and Preston, D. Website design guidelines: High power distance and high context culture[J]. *International Journal of Cyber Society and Education*, 2009, 2(1): 47-60.

Amant, K.S. A prototype theory approach to international website analysis and design[J]. *Technical Communication Quarterly*, 2005, 14(1): 73-91.

Austermühl, F. Training translators to localize[A].In Pym, A., Perekrestenko, A. and Starink, B.(eds.)*Translation Technology and its Teaching*[C]. Tarragona: Intercultural Studies Group, 2006.

Brandel, M. The global/local web site: Why you need it; how to build it[J].*Computerworld*, 2007(19): 29-32.

Cyr, D. and Trevor-Smith, H. Localization of web design: An empirical comparison of German, Japanese, and United States web site characteristics[J]. *Journal of the American Society for Information Science and Technology*, 2004, 55(13): 1199-1208.

Cyr, D., Head, M. and Larios, H. Colour appeal in website design within and across cultures: A multi-method evaluation[J]. *International Journal of Human-Computer Studies*, 2010, 68(1-2): 1-21.

House, J. *Translation Quality Assessment: A Model Revisited*[M]. Tubingen: Gunter Narr, 1997.

House, J. *Translation Quality Assessment: Past and Present*[M]. London and New York: Routledge, 2014.

Leech, G. Introducing corpus annotation[A]. In Garside, R., Leech, G. N. and McEnery, T. (eds.) *Corpus Annotation: Linguistic Information from Computer Text Corpora*[C]. London: Longman, 1997.

Nauert, S. Translating Websites[A]. In *Proceedings of the Marie Curie Euroconferences MuTra: LSP translation*[C]. 2007.

Rau, P. L. P. and Liang, S. F. M. Internationalization and localization: evaluating and testing a website for Asian users[J]. *Ergonomics*, 2003, 46(1-3): 255-270.

Reiss, K. *Translation Criticism: The Potential and Limitations*[M]. Manchester: St. Jerome, 2000.

Sandrini, P. Website localization and translation[A]. In *EU-High-Level Scientific Conference*

Series MuTra[C]. 2005.

Shneor, R. Influences of culture, geography and infrastructure on website localization decisions[J]. *Cross Cultural Management: An International Journal*, 2012, 19(3): 352-374.

Singh, N. and Pereira, A. *The Culturally Customized Web Site*[M]. Burlington: Elsevier, 2005.

Singh, N., Toy, D. R. and Wright, L. K. A diagnostic framework for measuring Web-site localization[J]. *Thunderbird International Business Review*, 2009, 51(3): 281-295.

Tixier, M. Globalization and localization of contents: Evolution of major internet sites across sectors of industry[J].*Thunderbird International Business Review*, 2005, 47(1): 15-48.

Williams, M. *Translation Quality Assessment:An Argumentation-Centered Approach* [M].Ottawa: University of Ottawa Press, 2004.

蔡尚思 . 我要为中国大思想家李贽呼冤——李贽的批孔堪称天下第一 [J]. 首都师范大学学报 (社会科学版), 1994(5): 41-42.

陈刚 . 涉外导游词翻译的特点及策略 [J]. 浙江大学学报 (人文社会科学版), 2002(2): 68-74.

陈洪福 . 福建省主要旅游景区景点英语导游词 [M]. 厦门 : 厦门大学出版社 , 2014.

陈静 . 英汉酒店介绍语篇的语用对比与翻译 [J]. 辽宁工程技术大学学报 (社会科学版), 2012(5): 516-520.

陈淑霞 . 目的性原则与涉外导游词的英译 [J]. 青岛大学师范学院学报 , 2008(4): 56-59.

陈先元 . 作为媒介的世界遗产 [J]. 上海交通大学学报 (哲学社会科学版), 2004(3): 65-69.

陈孝静 , 唐有胜 . 景点名翻译试析——以武夷山风景区为例 [J]. 福建工程学院学报 , 2011(2): 167-171.

陈孝静 . 武夷山风景区标识用语翻译评析 [J]. 福建工程学院学报 , 2008(2):153-159.

丁小月 . 景点导游词的英译研究——以河南旅游景点为例 [J]. 漯河职业技术学院学报 , 2011(3): 82-83.

杜金榜 . 法律交流原则与法律翻译 [J]. 广东外语外贸大学学报 , 2005(4): 11-14.

方梦之 . 达旨·循规·喻人——应用翻译三原则 [Z]. 首届全国旅游暨文化创意产业翻译研讨会上的主题发言 , 2007-10-20.

顾伟 . 变译理论指导下的旅游网站汉英翻译 [J]. 语文学刊 (外语教育与教学), 2010(10): 73-75, 101.

郭艳 . 格莱斯的会话合作原则与导游词的英语翻译 [J]. 四川职业技术学院学报 , 2006(3): 32-34.

韩军利 . 从跨文化角度分析河南旅游网的英文网站 [J]. 商业文化 (学术版), 2009(2):102.

韩笑 . 生态翻译视角下河南省旅游景区英文网站翻译研究 [J]. 科教文汇 (中旬刊),

2012(9): 143, 148.

何兰芳, 张美君, 张素芳, 林丽端. 武夷山市公示语英译现状及规范性探析 [J]. 武夷学院学报, 2016(4): 61-65.

何兰芳. 留学生对武夷山市公示语英译满意度调查分析 [J]. 武夷学院学报, 2018(1): 55-58.

何三宁. "关联理论" 视角下的翻译质量评估 [J]. 南京师大学报 (社会科学版), 2010(1): 155-160.

恒齐, 隋云. 商务应用文的英译应与国际接轨 [J]. 中国翻译, 2003(3): 74-77.

胡佳炜, 姜诚. 目的论视角下的机器翻译稿译后编辑探析——以 Asiarooms500 酒店资料机器翻译译后编辑项目为例 [J]. 安徽文学 (下半月), 2015(1): 127-129.

黄琼英. 云南入境游客旅游目的地认知行为模式与旅游网站翻译策略研究 [J]. 海外英语, 2014a(2): 1-4.

黄琼英. 云南省旅游网站翻译现状调查与分析 [J]. 曲靖师范学院学报, 2014b(4): 88-93.

贾文波. 历届全国应用翻译研讨会综述 [J]. 上海翻译, 2014(3): 86-90.

姜荷梅. 商务英语的汉译原则 [J]. 上海翻译, 2011(1): 29-32.

康宁. 基于类比语料库的中国网站英语旅游文本语言分析 [J]. 青岛科技大学学报 (社会科学版), 2012(4): 105-109.

赖德富. 生态翻译学视阈下应用翻译底线标准的构建 [J]. 钦州学院学报, 2015a(4): 25-30.

赖德富. 生态翻译学视域下论酒店外宣翻译的译有所为 [J]. 哈尔滨学院学报, 2015b(12): 68-72.

李丹. "文化走出去" 战略背景下的中国官方旅游网站英译 [J]. 曲靖师范学院学报, 2012(5): 120-122.

李德超, 王克非. 平行文本比较模式与旅游文本的英译 [J]. 中国翻译, 2009(4): 54-58+95.

李德超, 王克非. 新型双语旅游语料库的研制和应用 [J]. 现代外语, 2010(1): 46-54.

李克兴. 论法律文本的静态对等翻译 [J]. 外语教学与研究, 2010 (1): 59-65, 81.

李静雯. 功能加忠诚视角下土楼旅游文本汉英翻译 [J]. 黄山学院学报, 2017(6): 48-50.

李良辰. 基于目的论的景点现场导游词英译 [J]. 中国科技翻译, 2013(2): 51-54.

李明清. 基于 "变通" 原则的商务英语翻译 [J]. 外语学刊, 2009(1): 120-122.

李楠. 英汉法律翻译基本原则探析 [J]. 漯河职业技术学院学报, 2012 (5): 93-95.

李赛男. 文本类型理论指导下的政府门户网站翻译策略——以上海市政府门户网站旅游文本翻译为例 [J]. 湖北函授大学学报, 2014(1):174-176.

栗长江. 涉外公证书汉译英 [J]. 中国科技翻译, 2005(4): 3-6.

廖为群. 从奈达 "功能对等" 理论浅谈导游词的翻译方法 [J]. 上饶师范学院学报, 2010 (4): 71-74, 86.

林菲.福建旅游网站翻译现状的生态翻译学审视 [J]. 北京航空航天大学学报 (社会科学版), 2014(6):88-91.

刘法公 . 商贸汉英翻译的原则探索 [J]. 中国翻译 , 2002(1): 44-48.

刘红新 . 应用文本翻译原则探究 [J]. 语文学刊 (外语教育教学), 2014(9): 45-48.

刘红婴 , 王健民 . 世界遗产概论 [M] . 北京 : 中国旅游出版社 , 2003.

刘金水 , 吴婧 . 武夷山景区门票英译误区与对策分析 [J]. 黑龙江教育学院学报 , 2013(9): 158-160.

刘迎春 , 王海燕 . 论 " 译名同一律 " 原则在中国古代法律英译中的应用——兼评约翰逊《唐律》英译本 [J]. 外语与外语教学 , 2008(12): 60-62, 65.

刘雯 . 译员在网站本地化过程中的角色定位 [J]. 商丘职业技术学院学报 , 2011(1): 75-76.

吕万英 . 法律法规汉译英中一致性原则的遵循——以《劳动合同法》三个译本为例 [J]. 中南民族大学学报 (人文社会科学版), 2018(2):172-176.

马会峰 . 海南岛旅游网站汉英翻译研究 [J]. 湖北广播电视大学学报 , 2014(8): 84-85.

毛菁 , 邱天河 .WordSmith 在翻译批评中的应用——借助 WordSmith 工具分析《匆匆》译文的风格 [J]. 科技信息 (学术研究), 2007(34): 14-16.

莫红利 . 功能翻译理论视阈下的酒店对外推介的英译 [J]. 韶关学院学报 , 2009(5): 99-103.

莫红利 . 酒店文宣英译文本质量评估模式研究 [J]. 安徽工业大学学报 (社会科学版), 2011(4): 62-65.

牛新生 . 关于旅游景点名称翻译的文化反思——兼论旅游景点翻译的规范化研究 [J]. 中国翻译 , 2013(3): 99-104.

潘涓涓 . 漫谈福建土楼旅游文本的汉译英翻译策略 [J]. 怀化学院学报 , 2010(7): 93-95.

彭金玲 . 功能翻译理论视角下的旅游景点网站英译探析——兼评桂林某英文旅游网站 [J]. 海外英语 , 2013(6): 143-145.

钱穆 . 中国近三百年学术史 [M]. 北京：商务印书馆 , 1997.

邱贵溪 . 论法律文件翻译的若干原则 [J]. 中国科技翻译 , 2000(2): 14-17.

尚琼 .WordSmith 软件界面下的《石油勘探英语》词汇检索 [J]. 江汉石油职工大学学报 , 2011(3): 91-93.

司显柱 . 论功能语言学视角的翻译质量评估模式研究 [J]. 外语教学 , 2004(4): 45-50.

司显柱 . 系统功能语言学路向翻译研究述评 [J]. 外语研究 , 2007(4): 85-89.

谭美云 . 从德国目的论看商务语篇 [J]. 湖南社会科学 , 2011(4): 184-186.

屠国元 , 王飞虹 . 跨文化交际与翻译评估——J.House《翻译质量评估 (修正) 模式》述介 [J]. 中国翻译 , 2003(1): 60-62.

万永坤 . 玉溪市旅游网站翻译的 " 全球本土化 " 研究 [J]. 海外英语 , 2012(1): 13-14.

王冬梅.导游词的文本功能与翻译 [J].黔南民族师范学院学报,2008(2): 79-83.

王华树.信息化时代背景下的翻译技术教学实践 [J].中国翻译,2012(3): 57-62.

王华树.计算机辅助翻译实践 [M].北京:国防工业出版社,2015.

王克非.中国英汉平行语料库的设计与研制 [J].中国外语,2012(6): 23-27.

王立非,梁茂成.WordSmith 方法在外语教学研究中的应用 [J].外语电化教学,2007(3): 3-7, 12.

王丽丽.目的论视角下的旅游网站翻译 [J].齐齐哈尔大学学报 (哲学社会科学版),2010(5): 118-120.

王连义.导游翻译二十讲 [M].北京:旅游教育出版社,1990.

王艳红,徐桂艳.近十年导游词翻译研究述评 [J].科技信息,2012(12): 450.

汪懿婷.鼓浪屿旅游文本翻译现状研究 [J].文学教育 (下),2014(4): 58-60.

王韵.旅游网站本地化质量评估探讨 [J].中原工学院学报,2008(1): 59-62.

王朝晖,余军.基于 CAT 及语料库技术的电子商务翻译研究 [M].厦门:厦门大学出版社,2016.

韦忠生.对外宣传翻译策略的"接受美学"阐释——基于福建土楼世遗申报报告 [J].长春大学学报,2011(11): 50-55.

文军,齐荣乐,赖甜.试论博物馆解说词适度摘译的基本模式 [J].外语与外语教学,2007(12): 48-50, 54.

乌永志.文化遗产旅游解说与翻译:评述与启示 [J].地域研究与开发,2012(3): 93-97.

肖晓玲.框架理论对客家土楼摄影文本误译的阐释 [J].嘉应学院学报,2015(6): 16-20.

谢爱玲."多维转换"原则下的旅游外宣英译——以福建土楼为例 [J].闽南师范大学学报 (哲学社会科学版),2016(3): 114-118.

谢姆西努尔·阿力木,张太红.网站本地化过程研究 [J].无线互联科技,2015(20): 44-45.

谢天振.新时代语境期待中国翻译研究的新突破 [J].中国翻译,2012(1): 13-15.

夏远利.从语言模糊性角度探索法律语言翻译原则 [J].徐州建筑职业技术学院学报,2007(2): 62-65.

熊德米,熊姝丹.法律翻译的特殊原则 [J].西南政法大学学报,2011(2): 128-135.

徐珊,杨铭.功能翻译理论在导游词翻译中的应用——以武当山景区导游词为例 [J].淮海工学院学报 (人文社会科学版),2013(2): 89-91.

许家金,贾云龙.基于 R-gram 的语料库分析软件 PowerConc 的设计与开发 [J].外语电化教学,2013(1): 57-62.

许家金,吴良平.基于网络的第四代语料库分析工具 CQPweb 及应用实例 [J].外语电化教学,2014(5): 10-15, 56.

杨嫚.旅游网站英文文本翻译探究——以青岛旅游官方网站英文文本为例 [J]. 郑州航空工业管理学院学报 (社会科学版), 2014(3): 109-112, 118.

杨清平.应用翻译的规律与原则应当如何表述——评林克难教授 " 看易写 " 原则 [J]. 上海翻译 , 2007(3): 9-12.

杨荣广, 黄忠廉.应用翻译研究 : 进展与前瞻——基于《上海翻译》卅年办刊宗旨之嬗变 [J]. 上海翻译 , 2016(2): 18-23, 94.

叶玉龙 , 等.商务英语汉译教程 [M]. 天津 : 南开大学出版社 , 1998.

余婷.法律英语的语言特点与翻译技巧 [J]. 湖南大众传媒职业技术学院学报 , 2007(3): 95-98.

袁琼.导游词英译策略 : 功能翻译理论视角 [J]. 湖南商学院学报 , 2007(6): 126-128.

袁式亮.合作原则在旅游文本翻译中的应用 [J]. 东北师大学报 (哲学社会科学版), 2011(4): 164-166.

张慧.旅游景点名称翻译的模糊对等原则研析 [J]. 商业时代 ,2010(26):144-145.

张建英 , 闵西鸿.目的翻译理论下的昭通红色旅游导游词分析——以《昭通旅游导游词》英译文本为例 [J]. 昭通师范高等专科学校学报 , 2011(2): 52-55.

张珺莹.跨文化视角下旅游网站文本英译研究 [J]. 经济研究导刊 , 2014(13): 267+283.

张新红 , 李明.商务英语翻译 [M]. 北京 : 高等教育出版社 , 2003.

曾丹.论导游词英译 [J]. 中国科技翻译 , 2006(2): 36-39.

曾利沙.论旅游指南翻译的主题信息突出策略原则 [J]. 上海翻译 , 2005(1): 19-23.

曾利沙, 李燕娜.从语境参数论看范畴概念 " 活动 " 英译的实与虚——兼论应用翻译研究的经验模块与理论模块的建构 [J]. 上海翻译 , 2011(2): 1-6.

曾咪.世界遗产特色词汇的文化隐喻及其异化翻译——基于福建土楼申报文本 [J]. 吉林农业科技学院学报 , 2014a(3): 89-92.

曾咪.中国世界遗产名称英译策略探析 [J]. 闽南师范大学学报 (哲学社会科学版), 2014b(3): 105-109.

郑周林.旅游网站文本翻译 : 传播学诠释——兼评长沙市岳麓山风景名胜区网站汉英翻译 [J]. 湖南商学院学报 , 2011(5): 125-128.

周红.本地化视角下的旅游网站英译标准刍议 [J]. 绥化学院学报 , 2015(11): 60-63.

周学恒.功能翻译观下的翻译质量评估模式的构建——以 Harry Potter and the Deathly Hallows 汉译本为例 [J]. 盐城工学院学报 (社会科学版), 2011(1): 72-77.

福建世界遗产网站本地化长尾关键词样例

Da Hong Pao

da hong pao amazon

da hong pao auction

da hong pao australia

da hong pao aliexpress

da hong pao tea australia

aged da hong pao

authentic da hong pao

da hong pao oolong tea

da hong pao taste

da hong pao tea

da hong pao tea benefits

da hong pao price

da hong pao benefits

da hong pao charcoal taste

da hong pao brewing

da hong pao buy

da hong pao big red robe

da hong pao bushes

da hong pao buy online

da hong pao big red robe wuyi oolong tea

da hong pao black tea

da hong pao big red robe wuyi oolong

da hong pao brewing time

da hong pao chinese tea

da hong pao clay

da hong pao caffeine

da hong pao cost

da hong pao clay teapot

da hong pao cake

da hong pao china

da hong pao clay yixing teapot

da hong pao canada

da hong pao tea for sale

da hong pao tea gift

da hong pao grades

what does da hong pao taste like

how to drink da hong pao

how much does da hong pao cost

da hong pao ebay

da hong pao oolong

da hong pao tea price

da hong pao fluid

da hong pao from 90

da hong pao fitness

da hong pao flour

da hong pao food

da hong pao effects

da hong pao expensive

da hong pao most expensive tea

da hong pao side effects

da hong pao tea ebay

why is da hong pao so expensive

da hong pao games

da hong pao gate

da hong pao for sale

da hong pao flavor

da hong pao fake

da hong pao flavour

fujian da hong pao

da hong pao health benefits

da hong pao health

da hong pao get high

da hong pao green tea

da hong pao gong fu

da hong pao brewing guide

how to grow da hong pao

1st premier grade da hong pao tea

1st premier grade da hong pao

da hong pao in english

da hong pao instagram

da hong pao images

da hong pao in springfield

da hong pao in chinese

da hong pao hotpot

da hong pao how to brew

da hong pao history

da hong pao hong kong

da hong pao high

da hong pao justice

da hong pao jobs

da hong pao japan

da hong pao in london

da hong pao ingredients

impression da hong pao

where to buy da hong pao in singapore

imperial da hong pao

what is da hong pao

what is da hong pao tea

da hong pao king

da hong pao lanterns

da hong pao hua jiao

da hong pao mandarin

da hong pao menu

da hong pao meaning

da hong pao midland

da hong pao memory

da hong pao motor

da hong pao legend

da hong pao london

da hong pao tea london

da hong pao tea legend

da hong pao malaysia

how to make da hong pao tea

how much is da hong pao

da hong pao prestige

da hong pao plant

da hong pao rare

da hong pao nixon

da hong pao richard nixon

da hong pao sale

da hong pao story

da hong pao oolong tea benefits

da hong pao original

da hong pao online

da hong pao order

da hong pao tea buy online

organic da hong pao

dahongpao wuyi rock tea

how to brew da hong pao tea

da hong pao tree

purchase da hong pao tea

buy da hong pao tea

da hong pao tea for weight loss

da hong pao tea bags

da hong pao unraveling

da hong pao updates

da hong pao usa

da hong pao urban

da hong pao university

da hong pao preparation

da hong pao web

da hong pao warrior

da hong pao wiki

da hong pao west

da hong pao weather

da hong pao winter

da hong pao review

da hong pao red tea

da hong pao red robe

da hong pao rock tea

da hong pao rock

da hong pao x-ray

da hong pao singapore

da hong pao show

da hong pao seeds

da hong pao steeping time

da hong pao tea history

da hong pao uk

da hong pao tea price uk

da hong pao tea buy uk

da hong pao buy uk

da hong pao wikipedia

da hong pao wuyi

da hong pao water temperature

da hong pao wuyi shan

da hong pao tea wiki

da hong pao tea where to buy

wuyi star da hong pao

yin xiang da hong pao

da hong pao yancha

wuyi da hong pao

zheng yan da hong pao

wu yi shan da hong pao

Mount Wuyi

mount wuyi airport

mount wuyi scenic area

why is mount wuyi a world heritage site

mount wuyi facts

mount wuyi china

mount wuyi climate

mount wuyi china tea

mount wuyi cycle classic

mt wuyi china

mount wuyi fujian china

mount wuyi cycle classics

mount wuyi china map

mount wuyi fujian

mount wuyi fuzhou

mt wuyi fujian

福建世界遗产

双语语料库构建与应用

附
录

175

wuyi rock essence tea

wuyi wusheng electric vehicle

wuyi green tea

wuyi clear water hot springs

wuyi college

koshine hotel wuyi china

wuyi forum tea

wuyi fujian

wuyi dance taipei

wuyi dahongpao

wuyi diet

wuyi diet tea reviews

wuyi green tea diet auto ship

wuyi fountain palm golf club

wuyi hot spring

wuyi hot spring resort

wuyi garden

wuyi tiandi motion apparatus

wuyi oolong tea

wuyi hot springs

wuyi hengrui stationery factory

wuyi hotspring

wuyi hotel

wuyi hotels

wuyi mountain oolong tea

wuyi mountain reserve oolong loose leaf tea

wuyi mtn oolong tea

wuyi mountain tea

wuyi mountain oolong

wuyi jinhua zhejiang china

shaolin wuyi institute

wuyi in chinese characters

wuyi iron lady

wuyi guangdong china

wuyi oolong

wuyi oolong tea bags

wuyi oolong tea loose leaf

wuyi oolong loose leaf

wuyi kung-fu

wuyi liquid tea

wuyi mountain

wuyi map

wuyi mountain map

wuyi mountain weather forecast

wuyi mount

wuyi mountain villa

wuyi mountain images

wuyi mountain hotels

wuyi mountain rock tea

wuyi mountain big red robe

wuyi mountain weather

wuyi mountains china

wuyi mountain da wang peak youth hostel

wuyi rock tea

wuyi night market

wu yi night market

wuyi national park

wuyi star tea

coconut mango wuyi oolong tea

wu-yi oolong teas weight loss

foo joy wuyi oolong tea

wuyi oolong health benefits

wuyi oolong weight loss

does wuyi oolong tea have caffeine

wuyi tea

wuyi pixie tea

附

录

wuyi shan

wuyi plaza

wuyi palace wuyishan

wuyi rock oolong

wuyi rock oolong tea

wuyi rock tea benefits

wuyi shui xian

wuyi star

wu yi shan

wu yi tea song

wuyi university wuyishan

wuyi villa

vintage wuyi oolong tea

wuyi mountain villa hotel

wu yi wiki

wuyi xiangyu tea

wuyi yan tea

Gulangyu

gulangyu architecture

gulangyu accommodation

gulangyu agoda

gulangyu attractions

gulangyu aquarium

gulangyu island attractions

gulangyu island architecture

gulangyu island accommodation

tripadvisor gulangyu

gulangyu island tourist attractions

gulangyu island xiamen

gulangyu island hotels

gulangyu map

gulangyu island xiamen map

gulangyu island china

gulangyu island facts

gulangyu beach

gulangyu beiyu hotel

gulangyu boutique hotel

gulangyu beach hotels

best gulangyu hotel

gulangyu island beach

gulangyu island blog

gulangyu travel blog

gulangyu island travel blog

gulangyu bike

gulangyu art

gulangyu beach china map

gulangyu beach hotel prices

gulangyu china

gulangyu catholic church

gulangyu concert hall

gulangyu cable car

gulangyu cats

gulangyu church

gulangyu xiamen china

gulangyu island xiamen china

gulangyu cafe

gulangyu cave

hotel gulangyu china

gulangyu china map

gulangyu district

gulangyu things to do

gulangyu subdistrict

gulangyu ferry

gulangyu ferry tickets

gulangyu ferry times

gulangyu ferry xiamen

福建世界遗产

双语语料库构建与应用

gulangyu island

gulangyu entrance fee

gulangyu real estate

gulangyu island shops

xiamen gulangyu ferry tickets

gulangyu food

gulangyu fujian

how to get to gulangyu from xiamen

xiamen to gulangyu ferry terminal

xiamen gulangyu ferry

gulangyu ferry schedule

ferry gulangyu to xiamen

gulangyu piano festival

gulangyu island ferry

gulangyu weather forecast

xiamen gulangyu garden

gulangyu guesthouse

gulangyu garden

gulangyu garden hotel

gulangyu guide

gulangyu marine garden hotel

gulangyu shuzhuang garden

gulangyu travel guide

shuzhuang garden gulangyu island

gulangyu xiamen marine garden hotel

gulangyu hostel

gulangyu hotels

gulangyu history

gulangyu hotel

xiamen gulangyu hotel

gulangyu hotel xiamen

hotel gulangyu island

hotels gulangyu island xiamen

huaijiu gulangyu museum

gulangyu island history

gulangyu island map

gulangyu island piano museum

gulangyu island ferry schedule

gulangyu xiamen

gulangyu xiamen ferry schedule

gulangyu massage

gulangyu music festival

gulangyu piano museum

gulangyu organ museum

gulangyu nightlife

xiamen gulangyu north island hotel

how to go to gulangyu island

gulangyu islet

hotels in gulangyu island

gulangyu island tourist map

gulangyu island restaurant

xiamen gulangyu map

beach gulangyu map

gulangyu lonely planet

gulangyu international youth hostel

gulangyu in chinese

gulangyu map english

gulangyu passport

gulangyu places to stay

gulangyu pictures

xiamen gulangyu piano museum

gulangyu villa hotel

gulangyu xiamen pictures

gulangyu xiamen map

hotels in gulangyu xiamen

gulangyu xiamen weather

附
录

gulangyu xiamen ferry

gulangyu international settlement

gulangyu restaurant

gulangyu service pier

gulangyu street map

gulangyu statue

gulangyu shopping

map of gulangyu island

history of gulangyu island

map of gulangyu

history of gulangyu

gulangyu tourist map

xiamen gulangyu tripadvisor

gulangyu tea shop

gulangyu travel

gulangyu tour

gulangyu tripadvisor

gulangyu paper

gulangyu wikitravel

gulangyu piano island

gulangyu photos

gulangyu pronunciation

gulangyu pearl world

gulangyu pier

gulangyu weather

gulangyu wiki

gulangyu island review

gulangyu island restaurants

gulangyu sunlight rock

gulangyu island sunlight rock

best restaurant gulangyu

gulangyu island things to do

gulangyu

gulangyu song

gulangyu subdistrict siming

starbucks gulangyu

xiamen gulangyu softtime inn

gulangyu tourism

gulangyu tunnel

gulangyu ticket

gulangyu underwater world

gulangyu villa

gulangyu villa hotel xiamen

visit gulangyu

gulangyu wikipedia

gulangyu world heritage

gulangyu island wikipedia

gulangyu island weather

gulangyu island wikitravel

gulangyu xiamen hotel

xiamen gulangyu island

xiamen gulangyu international youth hostel

gulangyu youth hostel

Zhu Xi

zhu xi analects

zhu xi and wang yangming

zhu xi amazon

how did zhu xi affect the song dynasty

zhu xi reading of the analects

zhu xi reflections on things at hand

zhu xi learning to be a sage

zhu xi book

zhang xi chinese movies

zhu xi confucian

wang xi chinese

zhang xi china

双语语料库构建与应用

福建世界遗产

zhu xi biography

zhu xi books

zhu xi buddhism

zhu xi definition

zhu xi conversations with his disciples

zhu xi china

zhu xi i ching

zhu xi and foot binding

zhu xi four books

zhu xi on basic and secondary human
    nature

zhu xi element

zhu xi song dynasty

zhu xi family rituals

zhu xi famous book

zhu xi family

zhu xi scholar officer

zhu xi's neo-confucian synthesis

zhu xi negotiation techniques

zhu xi neo confucianism

zhu xi english translation

zhu xi educational philosophy

zhu xi elementary learning

zhu xi education

zhu xi english

zhu xi divination

zhu xi facts

zhu xi famous quotes

zhu xi in china

zhuxi family precepts

zhu xi philosophy

zhu xi philosophy writings

zhu xi great learning

zhu xi quotes

zhu xi life history

zhu xi human nature

zhu xi importance

zhu xi japan

zhu xi on women

zhu xi on meditation

zhu xi pronunciation

zhu xi parental instruction

zhu xi principle

zhu xi picture

zhu xi poem

zhu xi life

zhuxi china

zhu xi meditation

zhu xi's elementary learning

zhu xi's family rituals

zhu xi reflections of things at hand

zhu universe

zhu xi wikipedia

zhu xi white deer academy

zhu xi writings

zhu xi wiki

zhu xi school of principle

zhu xi's world of thought

zhu xi poems

zhu xi poetry

zhu xi poet

zhu xi significance

zhu xi school

zhu xi sayings

zhu xi teachings

zhu xi translation

附
录

zhu xi vs wang yangming

zhu xi works

Hakka

hakka association

hakka architecture

hakka art

hakka army

hakka abacus recipe

hakka alliance

hakka building

hakka brothers

hakka ancestry

hacker alphabet

hakka arts

hakka buildings

hakka burlington

hakka chinese

hakka cooking

hakka chinese restaurant

hakka chinese food

hakka culture

hakka chilli chicken

hakka chow

hakka chow mein

hakka cookbook

hakka commercial

hakka dialect

hakka dictionary

hakka dishes

hakka definition

hakka chow menu

hakka chinese people

hakka chow restaurant

hakka earth building

hakka english translation

hakka ethnic minority

hakka egg fried rice

hakka dish

hakka cuisine

hakka food

hakka foundation

hakka fried rice

hakka folk songs

hakka flavours

hakka funeral ritual

hakka fish

hakka food recipe

hakka ethnic group

hakka ethnicity

hakka egg noodles recipe

hakka eggplant recipe

hakka food processing

hakka family relationship name

hakka fried rice pot

hakka funeral

hakka fried rice recipe

hakka garden

hakka girls

hakka grammar

hakka ground tea

hakka houses

hakka history

hakka hat

hakka hokkien

hakka homes

hakka houses xiamen

福建世界遗产

双语语料库构建与应用

hakka hut

hakka in english

hakka in china

hakka jokes

hakka kung pao chicken

hakka kung fu

hakka king

hakka kung fu styles

hakka language

hakka legend

hakka last names

hakka meaning

hakka martial arts

hakka menu

hakka magic

hakka music

hakka guangdong tulou

hakka hong kong

hakka heritage

hakka kids

hakka kitchen

hakka love song

learn hakka language online

great hakka marathon

hakka mountain songs

hakka marathon

hakka noodles

how to make hakka noodles

chicken hakka noodles

vegetable hakka noodle recipe

chinese hakka noodles

vegetable hakka noodles

hakka oil

hakka origins

learn hakka online

hakka people

famous hakka people

origin of hakka people

hakka restaurant

hakka recipes

hakka round house

traditional hakka recipes

hakka tea

hakka song

hakka style chili chicken

hakka noodles recipe

hakka tulou

hakka traditional clothing

hakka tofu recipe

hakka traditions

hakka noodles wiki

hakka villages in china

hakka village

hakka video

hakka pronunciation

hakka people of china

hakka people origin

hakka wedding

hakka walled village

hakka worship songs

hakka words

hakka writing

chinese hakka women

hakka origin

hakka opera

hakka phrases

附

录

hakka stuffed tofu	minnan dialect
hakka style eggplant	minnan dictionary
hakka quotes	xiamen min nan grand theater
hakka queen	min nan grand theatre
quick hakka noodles recipe	min nan hotel xiamen
hakka tofu	what is min nan hua
hakka translation to english	min nan hua
hakka town	xiamen min nan hotel
hakka style	min nan english dictionary
hakka style noodles	minnan ethnicity
hakka village xiamen	min nan to english translation
hakka village china	min nan international hotel
hakka and hokkien	minnan fujian
hakka xiamen	min nan furniture
xiamen hakka village	minnan food
xiamen hakka houses	minnan-flowers
xiamen hakka tulou	min nan movie
xiamen hakka tour	minnan—kaiyuan temple
hakka village xiamen china	minnan gallery
Minnan	min nan language
min nan association of usa	learn min nan language
min nan architecture	min nan language dictionary
min nan aquatic	minnan hua
min nan baidu	minnan hotel xiamen
minnan aquatic development co. ltd	minnan hotel
minnan architecture	min nan hokkien
minnan aquatic	min nan grammar
minnan aquatic development	minnan golden triangle
minnan animal names	minnan hokkien
minnan chinese	hokkien minnan
minnan china	minnan history
minnan cuisine	min nan people
minnan culture	min nan phrases

福建世界遗产 双语语料库构建与应用

minnan language

min nan xiamen

minnan international hotel

idl min nan

what is min nan

min nan songs

min nan translator

min nan tv series

min nan theatre xiamen

min nan university

minnan language dictionary

min nan music

min nan wage

min nan wikipedia

minnan river fly fishing

minnan residential complex

minnan normal university

minnan opera

minnan dictionary online

learn minnan online

minnan name origin

min nan pronunciation

minnan phrasebook

min nan prawn noodles

min nan pinyin

taiwan minnan radio

taiwanese minnan resources

minnan shipyard

minnan shipyard shanghai

minnan savusauna

minnan taiwan

minnan translator

min nan translation

min nan tones

min nan thailand

minnan taiwanese

minnan university of science and technology

minnan normal university zhangzhou

min nan vs hokkien

minnan wiki

minnan xiamen

xiamen minnan hotel

xiamen minnan hotel agoda

xiamen minnan grand theater

minnan hotel xiamen china

minnan hotel xiamen tripadvisor

zhangjiajie minnan international hotel

minnan zumba

附

录

附录 2

福建世界遗产双语语料库之术语库样例

安海路　Anhai Road

安献楼　Anxian Hall

八卦楼　Bagua Mansion

保生大帝　the God of Medicines

笔架山　Bijia Hill

博爱医院旧址　Former Pok Oi Hospital

春草堂　Chuncao Villa

大北电报公司　Great Northern Telegraph Company

大夫第　Dafudi Courtyard Mansion

番婆楼　Fanpo Mansion

福建路　Fujian Road

福州路　Fuzhou Road

鼓浪石　Kulang Stone

鼓浪屿　Kulangsu

鼓浪屿工部局遗址　Former Kulangsu Municipal Council

鼓浪屿会审公堂旧址　Kulangsu Mixed Court

鼓浪屿-万石山风景区　Kulangsu-Wanshishan Scenic Area

鼓浪屿自来水供水设施旧址　Historic Kulangsu Water Supply Facility

鼓新路　Guxin Road

海坛路　Haitan Road

海天堂构　Haitian Tanggou Mansion (Sea-Sky Mansion)

红砖厝民居　the red-brick courtyard mansion

黄赐敏别墅　Huang Cimin Villa

黄氏小宗　Huang's Ancestral Hall

黄家花园　Huang Family Villa Complex

黄荣远堂　Huang Rongyuan Villa

黄氏小宗　Huang Family Ancestral Hall

汇丰银行公馆　the former Residence of HSBC Bank

汇丰银行职员公寓旧址　Former HSBC Staff Residence

鸡母石　Jimu Stone

基督教教徒墓园　Christian Cemetery

九龙江　Chiu-lung River

救世医院和护士学校旧址　Former Hope Hospital & Nurses' School

李清泉别墅　Li Qingquan's Villa

廖家别墅　Liao Family Villas

龙头路　Longtou Road

鹿耳礁　Lu'erjiao

鹿礁路　Lujiao Road

鹭江 Lujiang

伦敦差会 London Missionary Society

美国领事馆旧址 Former American Consulate

蒙学堂旧址(吴添丁阁) Former Mengxue Preschool (Wu Tianding's House)

闽南圣教书局旧址 Former Bookstore of South Fukien Religious Tract Society

内厝澳 Neicuo'ao

泉州路 Quanzhou Road

日本警察署及宿舍旧址 Former Japanese Police Station & Staff Quarters

日本领事馆旧址 Former Japanese Consulate

日光岩 Sunlight Rock

日光岩及延平文化遗迹 Sunlight Rock & Yanping Cultural Relics

日光岩寺 Sunlight Rock Temple

三明路 Sanming Road

三丘田码头遗址 Sanqiutian Jetty

三一堂 Trinity Church

厦门港礼拜堂 Xiamen Chapel

厦门海关副税务司公馆旧址 Former Residence of Amoy Customs Deputy Commissioner

厦门海关理船厅公所旧址 Former Amoy Harbour Master Office

厦门海关通讯塔旧址 Former Amoy Customs Telecommunication Towers

厦门海关验货员公寓旧址 Former Amoy Customs Examiners' Quarters

商办厦门电话股份有限公司旧址 Former Commercial Amoy Telephone Limited Building

升旗山 Flag Raising Hill

世界文化遗产名录 the List of World Cultural Heritages

世界遗产名录 World Heritage List

菽庄花园 Shuzhuang Garden

菽庄吟社 Shuzhuang Poetry Society

四落大厝 Four-Courtyard Complex

天主堂 Catholic Church

田尾路 Tianwei Road

万国俱乐部旧址 Former Amoy Club

吴添丁阁 Wu Tianding's House

五龙屿 Five-dragon Islet

协和礼拜堂 Union Church

新街礼拜堂 Xinjie Chapel

亚细亚火油公司旧址 Former Asiatic Petroleum Company Office Building

延平文化遗迹 Yanping Cultural Relics

延平戏院旧址 Former Yanping Complex

岩仔脚 Yanzaijiao

燕尾山 Yanwei Hill

燕尾石 Yanwei Stone

杨家园 Yang Family Mansion

洋人球埔旧址 Foreigners' Football Pitch

英国领事公馆旧址 Former Residence of British Consul

英国伦敦差会女传教士宅 Women's Residence of the London Missionary Society

毓德女学校 A.R.C.M. Girls' School

长老会 the Presbyterian Church

中南银行旧址 Former China & South Sea Bank Limited Building

种德宫 The Zhongde Taoist Temple

竹树脚礼拜堂　Zhushujiao Chapel

安全疏散指示图　Evacuation Chart

安全须知　Safety Instruction

安全指南　Safety Guide

半票　Half-price Ticket

半日游　Half-day Tour

步云楼　Buyun Tulou

参观路线　Visitor Route

残疾人专用　Disabled Only

查票　Ticket Checking

禅房　Meditation Room

朝水楼　Chaoshui Tulou

成人票价　Adult Price

承启楼　Chengqi Tulou

城隍庙　Town God Temple

出口　Way Out

初溪土楼群　Chuxi Tulou Cluster

春贵楼　Chungui Tulou

祠堂　Ancestral Temple

大地土楼群　Dadi Tulou Cluster

单行线　One Way

当日使用，逾期作废　Use on Day of Issue Only

当心踏空　Mind Your Step

导览册　Guide Book

导览机　Audio Guide

导览设施　Tour Guide Facilities

导游　Tour guide

导游服务　Tour Guide Service

导游亭　Tour Guide Booth

导游图　Tourist Map

地质景观　Geological Landscape

东升楼　Dongsheng Tulou

东阳楼　Dongyang Tulou

度假村　Holiday Resort

多语言导游　Multilingual Guide

二十四小时营业　24-Hour Service

二宜楼　Eryi Tulou

藩庆楼　Fanqing Tulou

福建土楼　Fujian Tulou

福庆楼　Fuqing Tulou

福兴楼　Fuxing Tulou

高北土楼群　Gaobei Tulou Cluster

庚庆楼　Gengqing Tulou

共庆楼　Gongqing Tulou

观赏区　Viewing Area

观堂　Taoist Temple

和昌楼　Hechang Tulou

和贵楼　Hegui Tulou

洪坑土楼群　Hongkeng Tulou Cluster

华庆楼　Huaqing Tulou

怀远楼　Huaiyuan Tulou

火警出口　Fire Exit

集庆楼　Jiqing Tulou

集体票　Group Tour Tickets

接待处　Reception

仅供紧急情况下使用　Emergency Only

紧急出口　Emergency Exit

禁止摆卖　Vendors Prohibited

禁止钓鱼　No Fishing

禁止停留　No Lingering

请勿吸烟　No Smoking

禁止游泳　No Swimming

景点　Tourist Attraction

景观　Scenery

景区　Scenic Area

九曲溪　Nine-bend Stream

喀斯特景观　Karst Landscape

开放时间　Open Hours

奎聚楼　Kuiju Tulou

联合国教科文组织　UNESCO

旅行路线　Travel Route

旅行指南　Itinerary

旅游安排　Tour Arrangement

旅游目的地　Tourist Destination

旅游散客　Independent Traveler

门票　Ticket

门票价格　Ticket Price

南熏楼　Nanxun Tulou

南阳楼　Nanyang Tulou

牌楼　Memorial Archway

票价　Ticket Price

票务服务　Ticket Service

侨福楼　Qiaofu Tulou

请爱护公共财产　Cherish Public Facilities

请爱护景区设施　Please Protect Facilities

请保管好随身物品　Please Take Care
  of Your Belongings

请保护古迹　Please Protect Historical Sites

请您注意上方　Watch Your Head

请绕行　DETOUR/Vehicle By-pass

请勿触摸　Hands Off

请勿打扰　Do Not Disturb

请勿倒置　Keep Upright ↑

请勿践踏草坪　Keep off the Grass

请勿将手臂伸出车外　Keep Arms inside
  Carriage

请勿跨越　No Crossing

请勿乱扔废弃物　No Littering

请勿拍照　No Photography

请勿摄影　No Video

请勿使用闪光灯　No Flash

请勿随地吐痰　No Spitting

庆成楼　Qingcheng Tulou

入口　Way In

瑞云楼　Ruiyun Tulou

散客旅游　Independent Tour

善庆楼　Shanqing Tulou

世界文化遗产　World Cultural Heritage

世界遗产公约　World Heritage Convention

世界自然文化遗产　World Natural and
  Cultural Heritage

售票处　Ticket Office/Tickets

水上漂流　Drifting

田螺坑土楼群　Tianluokeng Tulou Cluster

团队入口　Group Tour Entrance

危险，请勿靠近　Danger! Keep Away

文昌楼　Wenchang Tulou

问询处　Information

乌龙茶　Oolong Tea

无障碍设施　Wheelchair Accessible

五云楼　Wuyun Tulou

庑殿　Hip Roof

武夷宫　Wuyi Palace

武夷山　Mount Wuyi

武夷山国家级自然保护区　Mount Wuyi
  State-level Nature Reserve

锡庆楼　Xiqing Tulou

小心碰头　Mind Your Head

小心台阶　Mind the Step

晓春楼　Xiaochun Tulou

严禁攀登　No Climbing

严禁攀折　No Picking

衍香楼　Yanxiang Tulou

阳照楼　Yangzhao Tulou

一日游　Day Excursion

遗址　Historic Relics

永贵楼　Yonggui Tulou

永庆楼　Yongqing Tulou

永荣楼　Yongrong Tulou

永盛楼　Yongsheng Tulou

游船包价旅游　Cruise Line Package

游船码头　Cruise Terminal

游客投诉电话　Complaints Hotline

游客须知　Notice to Visitors

游客止步　No Admittance

游客中心　Tourist Center

游客咨询电话　Inquiry Hotline

游览观光车　Sightseeing Trolley

余庆楼　Yuqing Tulou

裕昌楼　Yuchanag Tulou

裕兴楼　Yuxing Tulou

暂停服务　Service Suspended

赠票　Complimentary Ticket

振昌楼　Zhenchang Tulou

振成楼　Zhencheng Tulou

振福楼　Zhenfu Tulou

正在维修　Under Repair

竹筏　bamboo raft

注意上方　Watch Your Head

注意台阶　Mind Your Step

咨询服务中心　Information Center

咨询台　Information

自动售票机　Passimeter/Stamp-vending
　Machine

自然保护区　Natural Reserve

自然景观　Natural Attraction

自然文化遗产　Natural and Cultural Heritage

自由行　Free Walker

自助游　Do-it-yourself Travel

租船处　Boat Rental

租赁车　Car Rental

附录 3

福建世界遗产申遗文本句对样例

说明：共 200 句对，其中 100 句对来自土楼申遗文本，100 句对来自鼓浪屿申遗文本，均为原始文本，未修订，供进行申遗文本修订研究参考。

1. 土楼是分布在中国东南部的福建、江西、广东三省，以生土为主要建筑材料、生土与木结构相结合，并不同程度地使用石材的大型民居建筑。

Tulou ("earthen house"), mainly distributed across the southeastern part of China, namely Fujian, Jiangxi and Guangdong Provinces, is a large-scale civilian residential building built mainly with rammed earth and in a wooden framework. Stones are also used to a varying degree.

2. 它们是几次中国乃至东亚历史动荡和民众大迁徙的产物。

Tulou is closely associated with several historic upheavals and great migrations in China and East Asia.

3. 其中分布最广、数量最多、品类最丰富、保存最完好的，是福建土楼。

Among the Tulou buildings of various descriptions, Fujian Tulou is the best-preserved with the broadest coverage, largest quantity and richest variety.

4. 福建土楼分布范围以福建西南地区尤为集中，总数达 3000 多座。

Fujian Tulou concentrates in the southwestern region of Fujian Province and a total of three thousands Tulou Buildings have been found across this province.

5. 所处自然环境以丘陵谷地为主，南亚热带海洋性季风气候，气候温暖，雨水充沛，植被茂密；居住着汉民族的客家民系和福佬民系，生活方式沿续着汉民族的传统习俗，生产方式以农耕为主。

The region is full of hills and valleys covered by bushy vegetation, enjoys subtropical and marine climate and rich rainfall. The Hakka and the Fulao, two branches of the Han nationality, live in the region, carrying forward the traditional customs of the Han's and taking farming as their main mode of production.

6. 福建土楼的历史源远流长，它产生于 11—13 世纪（宋元时期），经过 14—16 世纪（明代的早、中期）的发展，至 17—20 世纪上半叶（明末、清代、民国时期）达到成熟期，并一直延续至今。

The birth of Fujian Tulou may date back to many centuries ago. It first appeared between the 11th and 13th century (the Song and Yuan dynasties of China), developed between the 14th and 16th century (the early and mid Ming Dynasty of China), reached its peak between the 17th century and the first half of the 20th century (the late Ming and Qing dynasties and Republic of China period), and is handed down up to now.

7. 福建土楼以"天圆地方"作为建筑主体造型的设计理念，以满足家族聚落群居和良好的防御功能需要来安排建筑的规模，采用夯土墙与穿斗式木构架共同承重的两层以上封闭式围合型大型民居建筑，坐落于山地间，依偎于溪流畔，耸立在田园间，宛如翠绿的原野上长出的朵朵蘑菇，巧似天外的来客留下的神奇飞碟。

Fujian Tulou is mainly built according to the concept of "round heaven and square earth" and in a certain scale to meet the needs of the whole clan living together and a sound defensive function. As an enclosed communal house with two or more storeys in double load-bearing design, i.e. rammed earth wall plus column and tie construction, it is mostly located in the mountainous regions, neighboring with streams, fields and gardens. Visitors may easily fall into a reverie and associate its delicate shape with mushrooms on the emerald plain or a fantastic UFO from the outer space.

8. 一座大型的土楼，往往聚居着一个数百人的家族，被称为"热闹的小城市"、"家族的小王国"。

A large Tulou building usually houses a clan with hundreds of members. Thus, Tulou is also called a "bustling small city" or a "little kingdom for the family".

9. 按照建筑形式，福建土楼基本可分为圆形土楼、方形土楼和府第式（又称五凤楼）土楼等，但以圆形土楼为多。

In terms of building style, Fujian Tulou can be divided into circular, square and mansion-style (five-phoenix building) ones, of which circular Tulou accounts for a large proportion.

10. 故国际间对这类建筑一度统称为"客家土圆楼"。

Therefore, Tulou was once uniformly called "the Earthen Round Hakka Building" across the world.

11. 方形土楼中又有诸多变异形式，如殿堂式方楼等。

The square ones have various types, such as palace style.

12. 按照建筑结构，福建土楼主要可分为内通廊式和单元式两类。

In terms of the construction structure, Fujian Tulou has two main designs, one with corridors and the other with separate units.

13. 内通廊式土楼，基本特征为楼内住户垂直拥有每层一个开间的房屋，楼层设通廊连通各个房间，设公共楼梯上下，院子中间多设祖堂兼作书斋，主要分布于福建省两大民系——客家民系、福佬民系之客家民系地区，体现了客家人高度注重家族内部团结的精神。

The Tulou with corridors is featured by corridors connecting the rooms on each floor. A household owns a room (equal to a bay in space) vertically on each floor. There are public stairways for accessing the rooms. An ancestral hall is built in the center of the courtyard, which may also serve as a study. This type of building is commonly seen in the Hakka community, which together with the Fulao community constitutes the two important branches of Han nationality in Fujian Province. It mirrors the high priority given by the Hakka people to the family cohesion.

14. 单元式土楼，基本特征为整座楼被平均等分成若干个单元，每单元为一户，各有独自的入口、内庭院、房间，有独用的楼梯上下，主要分布于福建省两大民系——客家民系、福佬民系之福佬民系地区，体现了福佬人在维系家族纽带的同时，注重满足各家各户居住的私密性、独立性与舒适性的要求。

The Tulou building with separate units is divided equally into units with one household owning one unit. Each unit has its own entrance, inner courtyard and stairways connecting rooms on different floors. It is commonly found in the Fulao community in the Fujian Province, giving a full expression to the Fulao's demand in privacy, independence and comfort while retaining the family cohesion.

15. 在选址上，充分重视中国传统的风水理论，注重选择向阳避风、临水近路的地方作为楼址，多坐北朝南、依山傍水，与自然环境融为一体。

In selecting sites, great importance has been attached to Chinese traditional Fengshui practices which emphasize a southern exposure, shelter from the wind and proximity to the road or river. Facing the south, most of the buildings are nestled among hills and streams, reflecting a harmony with nature.

16. 许多土楼依山势而筑，错落有致，构成村落，蔚为壮观。

Some buildings are backed against hills or mountains and gather together as villages in picturesque disorder.

17. 村内溪水有序回流，两岸绿树成荫，山坡梯田递次，种植着水稻、果树、茶树等农作物，山顶覆盖茂密的植被。

With circulatory streams and lines of trees, crops namely paddies, fruit trees and tea trees, are planted on the terraced fields. The hilltop is fully covered by vegetation.

18. 在规模上，一座土楼占地多在 1000 平方米以上，高 3～5 层。

In scale, a Tulou building complex usually covers an area of over 1,000 square meters and has 3-5 storeys.

19. 如提名地的承启楼，由四圈同心环形建筑组合而成，占地 5376.17 平方米，拥有 400 多间房屋，鼎盛时楼内居住有 600 余人。

For example, the nominated Chengqi Lou is composed of four concentric-circle shaped buildings, covering an area of 5,376.17 square meters and possessing more than 400 rooms housing over 600 residents in its heyday.

20. 其中外环楼高 4 层、直径 73 米。

Among those buildings, the one in the outer ring has four storeys and a diameter over 73 meters.

21. 在结构上，主楼以夯土墙与木构架共同承重，以鹅卵石或块石、条石为墙基。

In structure, the main building of Fujian Tulou consists of rammed earth outer wall, wooden framework inside, and the wall foundation made of stones blocks, cobble-stones or slab stones.

22. 设有祖堂的建筑都比较讲究，多为穿斗、抬梁混合式木构架。

The ancestral halls within the buildings are tasteful and mostly adopt a combined style of "column and tie construction" and "post and lintel construction".

23. 圆形土楼屋面为两面坡瓦屋顶，方形土楼、多边形土楼等的屋面为悬山顶或歇山顶，府第式土楼的屋面以歇山顶为主。

Most circular Tulou buildings have a two-side sloping roof of tiles; the square and polygon Tulou buildings have the overhanging gable roof or the hip and gable roof; and the mansion type Tulou mainly adopts the hip and gable roof.

24. 在布局上，圆形土楼和方形土楼多由外环和内院两个部分组成，内院有一两口水井。

In layout, circular and square Tulou mainly includes the outer ring and the inner court-yard where one or two wells stand.

25. 圆形土楼，外环一般以 3～5 层高的围合型夯土楼房为主体建筑，内院一般有 1～3 圈的一两层环形建筑，客家民系地区在楼内中心位置还多设单层祖堂建筑，整体呈外高内低。

福建世界遗产 双语语料库构建与应用

Circular Tulou mainly consists of a 3-5 storied enclosed rammed earth building in the outer ring and an inner courtyard enclosed by one or two-storied circular buildings in one or three rings. In the Hakka community, a one-storey ancestral hall is usually built at the center of the complex. Thus the whole complex is lower inside and higher outside.

26. 方形土楼一般都是由一重楼墙四边围合而就，内院有的设有单层的祖堂，楼外正面建有单层的辅助用房围合成外庭院。

In the case of the square Tulou, a quadrangle is enclosed by a building complex on four sides, sometimes with a single-storey ancestral hall at the center. An outer courtyard is enclosed with one-storey supporting rooms facing the main building complex.

27. 府第式土楼一般呈前低后高之势，楼外正面围以矮墙形成外庭院，左右两侧设门房进出。

In the case of the mansion-style Tulou, an outer courtyard is enclosed by low wall in front of the facade of the building and a gatehouse is built on either side for access. The whole building complex is lower in the front and higher in the back.

28. 每座土楼都有鲜明的中轴线，圆形土楼的中轴线依次为大门、祖堂、后厅。

Tulou almost always has a clear central axis. The central axis of circular Tulou runs through the main gate, ancestral hall and the back lobby.

29. 方形和府第式土楼尤为突出，大门、厅堂、主楼都置于中轴线上，横屋和附属建筑分布在左右两侧，整体两边对称极为严格。

This is especially clear in square and mansion-style Tulou. The lobby, main gate and main building are all set on the central axis flanked by wing rooms on the left and affiliated buildings on the right in strict symmetry.

30. 在功能上，每座土楼的各层都有明确的功能划分。

Each and every storey of Tulou possesses a clear-cut function.

31. 在通廊式圆形和方形的土楼中，一般主体建筑的一层为厨房、餐厅，二层为粮食仓库，三层以上为卧室，祖堂及其两廊多兼作学堂。

The main building of circular and square Tulou with corridors is usually utilized in the following ways, i.e. kitchens and dining rooms on the first storey, barns on the second, and bedrooms on the third or above. In addition, the ancestral hall and side corridor usually are used as classrooms.

32. 在单元式的土楼中，一般主体建筑的一层为杂物间，二层以上为卧室，顶层是粮食仓库，依着墙体设有隐通廊贯通，便于对外防御。

The rooms on the first storey in the main building of Tulou with separate units are used as utility rooms, the rooms on the second storey are used as bedrooms, and the rooms on the top storey are barns. Moreover, a concealed corridor is built along with the wall to make a joint defense easy.

33. 在功能上，主体建筑各层有明确的功能划分，一层为厨房、餐厅、杂物间，二层为粮食仓库等，三层以上为卧室，祖堂及两廊多兼作学堂。

In terms of function, each storey of the main building has its own concrete function, for example, the rooms on the first storey are used as kitchens, dining rooms and utility rooms, the rooms on the second storey are used as barns, and the rooms on the third storey are living rooms. In addition, the ancestral hall and side corridor usually are used as classrooms.

34. 福建土楼在建筑设计上还充分考虑到建筑的稳定性、防御性和排水系统，不仅满足了聚族而居、安全防卫、教化育人的要求，还具有防风抗震、冬暖夏凉等良好性能。

The structural stability, defensive functions and the drainage system are fully taken into consideration when the buildings are designed. They meet the needs to have the whole clan live together, fend off enemies and educate the youngsters. In addition, it is warm in winter, cool in summer, and can protect the residents from strong winds and earthquakes.

35. 在稳定性方面，土楼外墙呈下大上小，从下而上逐渐向里收拢，生土外墙底部的厚度一般是顶部的 150% ～ 200%，从而保证了建筑的整体稳定性。

In terms of structural stability, the outer wall of Tulou tapers in the upper part which is only two thirds or even one half of the thickness at the bottom. This fully ensures the overall stability of the building.

36. 墙基部分多为鹅卵石或块石、条石砌筑，高出地面 1 ～ 2 米，以防墙体被地下毛细水或地面渍水浸泡而坍塌。

Meanwhile, the base of the wall, 1-2 meters above the ground, is comprised of stone blocks, slab stones and cobblestones for the purpose of protecting the wall from soaking by the underground and surface water.

37. 屋檐出挑较长，以防夯土墙被雨水淋漓坍塌。

The eave of the building projects further to protect the rammed earth wall from rain.

38. 在防御方面，一、二层不在外墙设窗，二层以上由小到大在外墙多设置射击孔；有的土楼还在最高层外墙处设置瞭望台，用以观察敌情；大门门扇多为硬木板门、

福建世界遗产 双语语料库构建与应用

有的还包以铁板以防撞击，在门框顶部则设水槽以防火攻。

As for the defensive function, there are no windows on the first and second storeys, while the holes for shooting are placed on the external wall above the second storey. The watchtowers projecting from the wall on the highest storey are used to watch for enemies. The door leaves are mostly made of hard board, sometimes covered with iron sheet, and a water trough is set on the top of the door to protect the building from fire attacks by the enemy.

39. 土楼的排水系统十分完善，在楼外根据地形、水流条件，因地制宜设置散水通道；在内部则沿大门走向设置主排水道，呈放射状向外扩散，主排水道上多设检修孔。

The drainage system of Tulou is complete and well arranged by taking into consideration the topographical factors and flow of streams. There are some main drainage ditches along the main gates of Tulou, which radiate to the outside. There are access holes to facilitate any repair on the ditches.

40. 在排水系统的设计上，还综合考虑了传统的"风水"理念，在主排水道的走向上很少呈直线外泄。

The concept of Fengshui is also taken into consideration in the design of the main drainage ditch.

41. 因为按照"风水"理念，如果设计主排水道直线外泄，就意味着房主人的财气和运气无法聚集、容易外泄。

A straight-line discharge is avoided, which, according to the Fengshui practitioners, means that the owner can hardly accumulate wealth and luck within his house.

42. 福建土楼文化底蕴深厚。几家甚至数十家聚居于一楼，反映了传统宗族观念。

Fujian Tulou also points us to the profound Chinese culture. A large amount of horizontal inscribed boards and couplets as well as the ancestral halls within the building mirror the concept of respecting ancestors and valuing education.

43. 岁时节庆、婚丧喜庆、民间艺术、伦理道德、宗法观念、宗教信仰、穿着饮食等，处处展示了土楼人家的淳朴民风。

Traditional folkways are found in every aspect of the Hakka life, such as the celebration of birthday and festival, wedding, funeral, folk art, code of ethics, domestic discipline exercised by the clan's leaders, religious belief and clothing as well as cuisine.

44. 土楼丰富的文化内涵，集中展现了家族内部团结互助、开拓进取的精神风尚，是地方传统的宗法伦理、民俗文化的实物载体。

The cohesion, mutual help and enterprising spirit within the clans give full expression to the rich culture and well demonstrate the local customs and the patriarchal clan system.

45. 初溪土楼群位于永定县南部的下洋镇初溪村，距县城凤城镇 47 千米。

Chuxi Tulou Cluster is situated at Chuxi Village, Xiayang Town in the south of Yongding County, 47 kilometers from the county seat, Fengcheng town.

46. 2005 年住有 253 户，1686 人，均为徐氏族人，以农耕为主业。

In the year 2005, Chuxi Village had 1,686 villagers in 253 households, all members of the Xu family with farming as their main occupation.

47. 初溪土楼群位于海拔 400 ～ 500 米大山深处的山坡上，群山环抱，地形复杂，坡度较大。

Surrounded by high mountains, the Chuxi Tulou Cluster is situated on a hillside 400-500 meters above the sea level with complex terrains and big gradients.

48. 土楼群整体坐南朝北，背靠海拔 1200 多米的高山，东西面长约 500 米，南北面长约 300 米。

Measuring about 500 meters from east to west and roughly 300 meters from north to south, it faces the north on the whole, backing against high mountains more than 1,200 meters above the sea level.

49. 一条小溪自东而西从土楼群的前向横穿而过，溪中遍布大大小小的鹅卵石，水流湍急，水面距土楼群前向土楼的地面落差达 20 多米。

A creek flows rapidly across the Cluster in the front from east to west with cobbles of various sizes. The water surface is more than 20 meters below the ground in front of the Cluster.

50. 两路山涧水分别自东而西、自南而北流入村内，汇合后从村中贯穿而过，然后注入小溪。

Two mountain streams respectively from east to west and from south to north converge in the village and then flow into the creek.

51. 位于谷底的小溪，流水潺潺，清澈见底，景色迷人。

Situated at the bottom of the valley, the gurgling creek is really fascinating with its clear water and all kinds of strangely-shaped rocks.

52. 站在溪中仰望土楼群，别有一番情趣。

Standing in the creek and looking up at the Tulou Cluster, you feel as if you were in a wonderland.

53. 该村南面山势陡峭，与土楼群隔溪相望。

Separated from the Cluster by the creek, the southern part of the village is on a steep hillside.

54. 北面山势相对较为平缓，土楼群便坐落在这里。

On the contrary, the hillside of the northern part of the village is not so steep, and the Tulou Cluster is situated here.

55. 在北面山坡上，距小溪越近，所建的土楼的规模越大，年代也越久，以后建造的土楼依山就势逐渐向山势较高的南面扩展。

On the northern hillside, the nearer it is to the creek, the larger the scale of the Tulou buildings and the earlier they were built. The Tulou buildings built later are spread to the south according to the terrain of the mountainside.

56. 土楼群后向（南面）及两边为层层梯田，有上千亩之多，一直延伸到山顶，十分壮观。

Behind (south of) and to both sides of the Cluster, there are tiers and tiers of terraces, covering an area of more than 1,000 mu (1mu = 1/15 hectare) and reaching the mountain top, providing a spectacular view.

57. 山顶上的小村落还有若干座徐姓人家的大圆楼，林木掩映，从远处眺望，这个小村落在云雾之中隐隐约约，更显得神秘而充满魅力。

In the small village on the mountain top, there still exist some of the circular Tulou buildings of the Xu family which are partly hidden behind the trees. Seen from far away, the small village is sometimes visible and sometimes invisible due to clouds and mists, looking mysterious and arousing your curiosity.

58. 土楼群的前半部分靠近小溪，分布有 5 圆 1 方土楼。

The front part of the Cluster is near the creek, consisting of five circular buildings and one square Tulou.

59. 村内有 3 条以青石砌成、呈阶梯状的主干道，其中两条东西走向，另一条自南而北依山势延伸到小溪，通往对面（北山）脚下的过境村道。

There are three main terraced paths paved with blue stones, two of which are in east-west direction. The third one winds its way along the creek from south to north, leading to the village path at the foot of the opposite north mountain.

60. 楼与楼之间均以青石板小道连接贯通。

Different Tulou buildings are connected via paths paved with blue stone slates.

61. 徐氏宗祠位于村中心，其墙体以生土夯筑而成。

The ancestral hall of the Xu family is in the center of the village, with its walls made of rammed earth.

62. 村子西侧有一座装饰华丽的永丰庵，村东、西两边的村口狭小，地势险要，可谓"一夫当关，万夫莫开"。

There is also a magnificent nunnery in the west of the village. The east and west entrances to the village are rather narrow and difficult to access, which provide easy defense against enemy attacks.

63. 该土楼群周边山体植被较好。

Forestation around the Cluster is in good condition.

64. 站在位于北面山上的观景台眺望，整个初溪土楼群尽收眼底、其磅礴的气势令人为之震撼。人们可以更深切地感受到土楼、小桥、流水、青石板路与梯田、青山、蓝天、白云融为一体的客家古村落的独特韵味。

The whole Chuxi Tulou Cluster can be clearly and completely seen from the sightseeing platform on the north mountain. Seeing the Cluster, you can experience the unique lingering charm of the ancient Hakka village, where Tulou buildings, small bridges, flowing water, stone paths, terraces, green mountains, blue sky and white clouds are integrated in harmony.

65. 初溪土楼的主要类型有长方形楼、正方形楼、圆楼、椭圆形楼、六角形楼等。

Chuxi Tulou is mainly built in rectangular, square, circular, oval, hexagonal shapes.

66. 列入申报的土楼有集庆楼、余庆楼、绳庆楼、华庆楼、庚庆楼、锡庆楼、福庆楼、共庆楼、藩庆楼、善庆楼等 10 座土楼，均保存完好。

The Chuxi Tulou proposed for inclusion constitutes 10 well-preserved ones, such as Jiqing Lou, Yuqing Lou, Shengqing Lou, Huaqing Lou, Gengqing Lou, Xiqing Lou, Fuqing Lou, Gongqing Lou, Fanqing Lou and Shanqing Lou.

67. 1999 年 4 月，初溪土楼群被公布为永定县级文物保护单位。其中，集庆楼于 2006 年 5 月被公布为全国重点文物保护单位。

This Cluster was announced as a historic site under protection at the county level in April 1999, among which Jiqing Lou was classified as a historic site under protection at the state level in May, 2006.

68. 坐落在初溪村北面溪边，海拔 500 多米，高出溪面约 30 米，地势险要。

It is located beside the creek in the north of Chuxi Village. About 500 meters above the sea level, the Tulou is about 30 meters above the creek and difficult to access.

69. 圆形土楼，两环，建于明永乐年间（1403～1424 年），坐南朝北，占地 2826 平方米。

In a double-ring shape, the circular Tulou was built in 1419, the 17th year of the reign of Emperor Yongle in the Ming Dynasty. It faces the north and covers an area of 2,826 square meters.

70. 楼门为石质门框，阴刻楹联："集益都从谦处爱，庆馀只在善中求。"

The doorframe of the Tulou is made of stone, on which a couplet is engraved, reading: "Modesty is a lovable quality; wealth is pursued in goodness."

71. 横批："物华天宝。"

The horizontal hanging scroll reads: "Prosperous Material Life and Favorable Natural Condition".

72. 厚实的门扇封铁板，上方设防火水槽，可有效防止火攻。

The iron cover of the door and anti-fire trough on the top can protect the house from fire.

73. 外环土木结构，直径 66 米，高 4 层。

The four-storey-high outer ring is of earth-and-wooden structure and 66 meters in diameter.

74. 底层 53 开间，二层以上每层 56 开间。

The first floor has 53 bays and each of the upper storeys has 56 bays.

75. 底层墙厚 1.6 米，无石砌墙基，后人在墙外表用鹅卵石加砌 1 米高的石墙贴面，以防土墙被屋檐水溅湿。

The wall around the first floor is 1.6 meters thick without original stone-laid base. People of later generations built one-meter high wainscots for the wall with pebble stones to protect it from eavesdropping.

76. 建楼时只设一道比其他土楼宽敞的楼梯，位设于门厅东侧，通至四层。

When constructing this Tulou, only one staircase was set, which is wider than those of other Tulou buildings. Located on the east side of the entrance hall, the staircase leads to the 4th storey.

77. 底层为厨房，底层、二层不开窗，二层为粮仓，三层以上为卧室。

Rooms on the first floor are used as kitchens, on the 2nd floor used as barns and above the 3rd floor used as living rooms. Rooms on the first floor and the 2nd floor do not have any window.

78. 外环 1 ～ 4 层原为内通廊式，清乾隆九年（1744 年）维修该楼时，为了解决全楼数百人只靠一道楼梯上下造成诸多不便的问题和便于管理，对原来的结构稍作改变：底层不变，仍为内通廊式，二层以上改为单元式，每单元 6 个房间，各设一道楼梯，楼梯较窄，三层每单元分别在梯侧设一神龛。

The 1st to 4th storeys of the outer ring were originally inner-corridor planes. When the Tulou was repaired in 1744, the 9th year of the reign of Emperor Qianlong, its structure was slightly modified to solve the problem that there was only one staircase for hundreds of its dwellers, which brought a lot of inconvenience for daily life and management. The first floor still kept its inner-corridor type without any change while the upper floors were changed into the type of separate units. Having 6 rooms, each unit was provided with a narrower staircase. For every unit on the 3rd floor, a shrine was set on one side of the staircase.

79. 单元与单元之间的廊道以杉木板相隔。

The passages between one unit and another were separated by cedar planks.

80. 底层每单元各有一条高出天井与内环户主名下的房子相连的石砌通道。

Each unit on the first floor had a stone passage which was above the patio and led to the rooms under the name of the owner of the inner ring.

81. 外环二层以上在每单元的梯间靠外墙处，另设一道宽 50 厘米的暗梯，平时用木板盖住，外人根本无法发现，一旦遇到紧急情况时才使用。

From the 2nd storey of the outer ring above, a 50 cm-wide hidden staircase is additionally set between the staircases near the external wall for each unit. Usually covered with wooden boards, the hidden staircase cannot be discovered by outsiders at all. It is only for use in emergency.

82. 外环第四层外墙的 9 个瞭望台，木结构，向外挑出，既可瞭望又可架设土铳；大门上方的瞭望台可直接观察村口的动静，还可封锁正面的通道，凭险踞守该楼。

The external wall of the 4th storey of the outer ring was installed with nine wooden-structured overhanging lookouts, which could be used either for watching out or for supporting blunderbusses. From the lookout above the main gate, one could directly see what was going on at the village entrance and blockade the front path to the village when it was urgent to protect the Tulou from any attack by the advantage of the favorable position.

83. 这是由于初溪村地处大山深处，当时经常有土匪野兽出没，所以建楼者特别注重增强防卫功能。

As Chuxi Village lies deep in the mountains and used to be frequented by bandits and wild animals. Thus the designer of the Tulou took the defensive function into special consideration.

84. 楼后侧底层还设一秘密通道，在一个房间的外墙上预留距地面高1米、长1.6米、宽0.7米的缺口，外用夯土墙封住，因用与土墙相同的泥土，外人也发现不了破绽；其内向外凸出，平时用木板遮住，外人进入该房间亦无法发现其中奥秘。

A hidden exit is also designed on the first floor at the back of the Tulou. Actually it is a hole which is 1.6 m in height and 0.7 m in width, and reserved in the external wall of a room. The hole is sealed by rammed earth which is precisely the same material as that of the external wall and outsiders cannot tell the difference. Inside the room, it is recessed into the wall but usually covered with wooden boards. When an outsider comes into the room, he will not be able to find out this secret.

85. 当楼内居民需向外紧急疏散、逃避时，可迅速捅开这个秘密通道，直奔楼后的山坡，隐蔽在树林之中。

In case of emergency, the hidden exit can be quickly broken open and the dwellers can make their way to the mountain woods behind the Tulou.

86. 内环与外环以天井相隔，门厅至内环之间以青石板铺设通道。内环单层，砖木结构，前后向和两侧各有一条约3米宽、高于天井的石砌通道与外环的内通廊连接。

The inner and outer rings are separated by the patio. A blue stone path is paved to link the entrance hall to the inner ring which is of single-storey brick-and-wood structure. There is a 3 m-wide stone path on each of the four sides of the inner ring to link the corridor of the outer ring, and the stone path is higher than the patio.

87. 26开间，设饭厅、杂物间；房间与房间以杉木板相隔，房间前、后向地面以上1米为青砖墙，砖墙以上为杉木封板；每一两个房分别开前、后门，前门朝向祖堂，后门与外环底层贯通。

The 26-bay space is provided with a dining room and a utility room. Rooms are separated by cedar boards. Within the height of 1 meter above the ground, the front and rear walls of the room are made of grey bricks, above which are cedar boards. There is a front door and a back door for every one or two rooms, with front one facing the ancestral hall and the back one leading to the first floor of the outer ring.

88. 内、外环均为两面坡瓦屋顶，穿斗、抬梁混合式木构架。

A composite structure was designed for the inner and outer rings with a two-side sloping roof of tiles, a combination of the overhanging gable roof, column and tie construction and post and lintel construction.

89. 祖堂位于楼中心，方形，单层，土木结构，以位于后向的厅堂、厅前两侧的回廊和正面的回廊围合而成，中为天井，正面的门正对楼门。

The single-storey square ancestral hall is of earth-and-wood structure, and is in the center of the Tulou building. It is enclosed by the main hall at the back, the cloisters on both sides of the main hall and the front cloister. The patio is in the center, whose front door directly faces the Tulou gate.

90. 厅堂宽敞，供奉神座，两边各设一小门出入。

Used for honoring ancestors, the spacious ancestral hall has a God Seat, on both sides of which there is a small door for people to go through.

91. 楼内底层的通廊、天井以及楼外的门坪均以鹅卵石铺面。

The corridor on the first floor, the patio and the gateway outside are all paved with pebbles.

92. 坐落于初溪村东北部，临溪而建。

This building stands beside the creek in the northeast of Chuxi Village.

93. 圆形土楼，建于清雍正七年（1729年），坐南朝北，占地1256平方米。

Built in 1729, the 7th year of the reign of Emperor Yongzheng of the Qing Dynasty, the circular Tulou faces the north, covering an area of 1,256 square meters.

94. 直径41.6米，主楼高3层，每层34开间，设4部楼梯，内通廊式。

41.6 meters in diameter and 3 storeys in height, the main building of inner ring corridor design has 34 bays and is equipped with four staircases.

95. 坐落于初溪村西北部，临溪而建。

It is situated beside the creek in the northwest of Chuxi Village.

96. 由内外两个方形楼组合而成，外楼宽39米，深27米，高4层，设1个大门；内楼高2层。

It is composed of two square buildings, one of which is the inner building and the other is the outer building. The outer building is 39 meters in width, 27 meters in depth and 4 storeys in height, provided with a main gate, while the inner building is 2 storeys high.

97. 内通廊式。全楼168个房间、两个厅堂，设4部楼梯。

In an inner ring corridor pattern, the whole Tulou has 168 rooms, 2 halls and 4 staircases.

98. 坐落于初溪村中部，西为藩庆楼、东与福庆楼为邻。

It is located in the central part of Chuxi Village, neighboring Fanqing Lou on the west and Fuqing Lou on the east.

99. 长方形土楼，建于清道光九年（1829 年），坐南朝北，占地约 480 平方米。

Constructed in 1829, the 9th year of the reign of Emperor Daoguang of the Qing Dynasty, the rectangular Tulou facing the north covers an area of 480 square meters.

100. 高 2 层，宽 19.5 米、5 开间，深 20.5 米、6 开间。

Two storeys in height, the Tulou is 19.5 meters in width, equaling to five bays, and 20.5 meters in depth equaling to six bays.

101. 鼓浪屿位于中国厦门市的九龙江出海口，是一座面积 1.88 平方公里的海岛，与厦门市区隔着 600 余米宽的鹭江海峡遥遥相望。

Kulangsu, located at the estuary of Chiu-lung River, is a tiny island with an area of only 1.88 square kilometers and faces the city of Xiamen across the 600-meter-wide Lujiang Strait.

102. 随着 1843 年厦门开埠和 1903 年鼓浪屿公共地界的确立，这个位于帝国南部海疆的小岛突变为一扇中外交流的重要窗口，见证了清王朝晚期的中国在全球化早期浪潮冲击下步入近代化的曲折历程。

With the opening as a commercial port at Xiamen in 1843 and the establishment of Kulangsu as an international settlement in 1903, the island in the southern coastal areas of Chinese empire suddenly became an important window for Sino-foreign exchanges, and also witnessed China's twists and turns to modernization in the early pinching globalization waves.

103. 鼓浪屿的发展和建设成就，是中外多元文化在社会治理、人居环境营造、建筑与园林艺术、文化生活等领域广泛、深入交流的物证。

The development and construction achievements of Kulangsu are the tangible evidence for the extensive and profound exchanges of diverse Chinese and foreign cultures in all aspects including social management, habitat cultivation, architecture and garden art, material and cultural life.

104. 在这不到百年的时间内，鼓浪屿经历了从传统聚落到殖民风格居留地，再到兼具国际化与本土化特征的现代社区的跨越发展；其岛上保存完好的历史遗存真实完整地记录了这一曲折的发展进程和鲜明的风格转变，浓缩了一个激烈变革的时代，显现出主导了鼓浪屿不同阶段更新发展的群体特质。

Through a period less than a century, Kulangsu had experienced a leap development from a traditional settlement, through a colonial settlement, to a modern community with international and local characteristics. The well-preserved historical remains in

Kulangsu offer an authentic and integral record of its tortuous development process and vivid style changes, a crystalized reflection of the history of an era with intense reforms and a unique witness to the different characteristics of the leading force at various stages in its renovation and evolution.

105. 这不但使鼓浪屿成为全球化早期阶段多元文化交流、碰撞、互鉴的典范，也为当今世界不同文化间价值观的相互理解与共同发展提供了宝贵的历史经验。

Thus, Kulangsu not only becomes a model for exchanges of diverse cultures at the early globalization stage but also offers us today valuable historical experience for mutual understanding and joint development among different cultures and values across the world.

106. 在 19 世纪中叶到 20 世纪中叶的百年间，鼓浪屿是东亚和东南亚区域独具特色的对外交流窗口。

Kulangsu had been an outstanding international cultural exchange window with unique chracteristic in East Asia and South-east Asia from the mid-19th century to the mid-20th century.

107. 鼓浪屿位于中国南部海疆的九龙江出海口，特殊的地理区位造就了其远离政治的宽松环境，也使这里成为历史悠久的海上门户；至 19 世纪早期全球化进程开始，大量的移民流动和贸易往来，进一步促使这个小小的岛屿成为东亚和东南亚区域的贸易焦点与中外多元文化的集聚地。

Kulangsu is located at the estuary of the Chiu-lung River in China's southern coastal area. Its unique geographical location shaped its relaxed environment far from politics and made this place an important portal for maritime activities with a long history. In the early 19th century, the course of globalization began. Driven by a large migrant population and trading exchange, this small island became a focus of trade in East Asia and Southeast Asia and a hub of diverse Chinese and foreign cultures.

108. 鼓浪屿丰富的物质遗产——特色各异的街区肌理、功能完善的公共建筑、风格多样的居住建筑、宅园设计等，鲜明地反映了中外多元文化在社会生活、建筑和园林景观设计、营造技术等方面的接触、互鉴、碰撞和融合，是这百余年间人类价值观广泛而深刻交流的典型见证。

Kulangsu's abundant material heritage including urban fabrics of distinctive features, public buildings with all functions, residential buildings and home garden designs of various styles, etc. clearly reflects the contact, interaction, collision and fusion of diverse Chinese and foreign cultures with respect to social life, architecture and garden scenery designs and construction techniques, and is a typical witness to the extensive and in-depth exchange of human values in this period of more than 100 years.

109. 有宋以降，鼓浪屿凭借其地理优势便与日本、东南亚沿海区域保持着密切的商业往来，至19世纪中叶厦门开埠，鼓浪屿因"环境以及自然风光的迷人，有优美的港口，还有群山的环抱，沿着整个中国海岸再找不到比这里更美的地方"，得到西方和日本的普遍关注，迅速成为多国机构的驻地和多国侨民的居住地。

Due to the unique geographic location, since the Song dynasty, Kulangsu has maintained close business relations with the coastal areas of Japan, and Southeast Asia. By the mid-19th century when Xiamen was opened up as a commercial port, Kulangsu gained the attention from many western countries and Japan which were attracted by its beautiful and pleasant natural landscape and made it the location for their institutions and residences —"No other place along the China coastline is better than the island of great atmosphere and beautiful landscape with ports and mountains".

110. 曾先后有英国、法国、西班牙、美国、日本等13个国家在鼓浪屿设立领事机构，建造领事公馆或职员宿舍。

A total of 13 countries have set up consulates, consular residences or staff quarters on Kulangsu, such as Britain, France, Spain, America and Japan, etc.

111. 可以说正是由于鼓浪屿政治力量的多元化，多元文化以相对均衡、平等的姿态出现、交流，并始终温和地融入鼓浪屿社区公共生活的营造和革新之中，形成了其独特的建成环境。

Only because of the diverse political powers and relatively balanced cultures which always exerted impact on the creation and renovation of public life made the unique built environment of Kulangsu.

112. 在物质层面上，鼓浪屿由道路网络、街区肌理、历史建筑、宅园景观共同构成的建成环境，在空间布局上多从地形地貌条件和生活需要出发，并没有因文化或社会阶层差异而产生严格的边界，呈现出有机、自由散布而开放的特点。

In terms of the physical composition, the built environment of Kulangsu which comprised by the road network, urban fabrics, historic buildings and home gardens is arranged in an organic manner, free and open, following the topographic and geomorphic conditions and catering to the need for a convenient life. No strict boundary was made to reflect the differences of cultures or stratums.

113. 随后的20年中，美国归正教、美部会、英国长老会和西班牙天主教的传教士也纷纷来到鼓浪屿并建造教堂、传播福音。

In the following 20 years, many missionaries from the American Reformed Church, American Board of Commissioners for Foreign Missions, Presbyterian Church of England, and Roman Catholicism of Spain arrived at Kulangsu to build churches and spread gospel.

114. 现存英国领事公馆、美国领事馆、日本领事馆、丹麦大北电报公司办公楼等历史建筑，从一个侧面展现出鼓浪屿早期受到的外国文化影响。

The existing Former Residence of British Consular, former American Consulate, former Japanese Consulate, Former Office of Great Northern Telegraph Company (Denmark) are the historic buildings reflecting the cultural impact of various foreign countries on Kulangsu in early days.

115. 由协和礼拜堂和天主堂构成的三角地，即是 20 世纪初多种宗教流派在鼓浪屿和谐共存的三角地，即是 20 世纪初多种宗教流派在鼓浪屿和谐共存的有力见证：协和礼拜堂于 1863 年由伦敦差会、长老会共同兴建；而临近的天主堂则于 1917 年由西班牙天主教士修建，两者建筑风格迥异却互不干扰。

The triangle square between the Union Church and the Catholic Church are the reflection of the harmonious atmosphere among different religious sects on Kulangsu in the early 20th century. The Union Church was built in 1863 under the joint effort of London Missionary Society and the Presbyterian Church; the nearby Catholic Church was constructed by missionaries of the Roman Catholicism of Spain in 1917. These two religious buildings are totally different in architectural style, but the usages are not contradictory to each other.

116. 以上数量众多且属于不同信仰、不同时期、不同建筑风格的宗教建筑，生动地展现了多元文化的开放性及其在鼓浪屿的和谐同存。

All the religious buildings built in different times of different styles serving different religious purposes are vivid reflection of the openness and harmony of diverse cultures on Kulangsu.

117. 中西方住区的选址原则的转变及不同街区肌理的相互杂糅，生动地展现了鼓浪屿中西方文化的相互影响和融合。

The transformation of criteria on selecting good place for residential houses and the mixed fabric of different cultural patterns both represent the mutual influence and fusion between Chinese and western cultures on Kulangsu.

118. 旧时鼓浪屿被当地中国社区称为"五龙屿"，以强调其地貌形态中多个小山丘形成的交叉山岭。

In the past Kulangsu was called "Five-dragon Islet" by the Chinese community at that time as there were crossing ridges formed by several small hills.

119. 而在早期到达鼓浪屿的西方人眼中，鼓浪屿连绵的山丘恰似船帆，因而将其比喻为"帆船岛"。

While for the westerners who arrived at Kulangsu at an early stage, it was called an "island of sailing boat"— as they looked at the continuous hills on Kulangsu like a sailing boat.

120. 如此，鼓浪屿狭小的岛屿空间密集地汇聚了大量风格迥异，却颇具文化特色和时代特征的建筑形式，体现出多元文化的和谐共存。

Therefore, a large quantity of architectures with different characters of culture and time were crowded on the tiny island space of Kulangsu, representing the harmony and coexistence of diverse cultures.

121. 而随着早期传教士、洋行老板、领事登岛，盛行于南亚、东南亚区域的殖民地外廊式建筑则被引入鼓浪屿，成为早期西方建筑风格的代表。

With the arriving of missionaries, Tai-pan of foreign firms and consuls, the architecture of colonial veranda style popular in South Asia and Southeast Asia appeared on the island, becoming the early representative instance of western architecture styles and life mode.

122. 与之相对，西方古典复兴样式、早期现代主义建筑风格及装饰艺术风格，也被作为二十世纪初欧美国家流行文化的一部分传入鼓浪屿，前者的代表如协和礼拜堂、美国领事馆、救世医院、八卦楼，后者则如博爱医院、日本警察署等建筑。

Meanwhile, western neoclassical style architecture (the Union Church, the former American Consulate, the former Hope Hospital, Bagua Mansion), early modernism and Art Deco style architecture (the former Pok Oi Hospital, the former Japanese Police Station) were also introduced to Kulangsu as kind of expression of popular cultures in western countries.

123. 华侨洋楼建筑设计的发展经历了外廊式建筑的本土化和厦门装饰风格两个阶段，无疑是鼓浪屿多元文化交流与融合最杰出的见证。

Western-style buildings of overseas Chinese were developed in two phases—localization of veranda style and Amoy-Deco Style, best representing communication and fusion of diverse cultures of Kulangsu.

附录

124. 鼓浪屿的早期西方建筑多由西方建筑师设计，或采用从东南亚带来的范例图纸加以改造，然后由本地工匠进行施工。

The structures of most early western buildings on Kulangsu were designed by architects from western countries, or adopted and revised the drawings brought from the Southeast Asia, but were constructed by local craftsmen.

125. 而鼓浪屿独立的海岛环境，使其遗产区、缓冲区的保护管理要求得到了很好的执行，有效限制和管理了缓冲区内海域活动；另一方面，政府也通过控制性规划和保护条例的颁布，对厦门岛鹭江沿岸城市的建设提出了控制性要求，尽可能地保护了遗产地的视觉完整性。

The location of Kulangsu as an indepedent island contributes to the effective implementation of the protection and management requirements of the property area and the buffer zone, and the effective limitation and management of activities in the sea waters of the buffer zone. On the other hand, the government's promulgation of regulatory plans and protection regulations propose control requirements on the construction of the coastal cities along the Lujiang River in the Xiamen Island to protect the visual integrity of the nominated property as much as possible.

126. 鼓浪屿作为历史城镇类型遗产，由岛屿自然景观要素、历史道路、典型街区肌理、历史建筑和宅园景观等遗产要素共同构成了完整的城市历史景观，整个遗产地的真实性突出地体现在以下几个方面：延续至今的住区功能和性质、保存完好的城市空间格局与道路体系、特色鲜明的片区形态和完整延续的历史建筑与宅院景观。

Kulangsu, as a historic settlement, possesses an integrated historical urban landscape consisting of natural landscape elements, historic roads, typical block fabrics, historic buildings, gardens and other heritage components. The authenticity of the entire property is obviously embodied through the continuous residential function and nature, well-preserved urban spatial layout and road network, featured forms of urban blocks and historic buildings and gardens continuously used till today.

127. 首先，在社区功能方面，鼓浪屿作为理想居所的住区功能通过城市规划层面上对鼓浪屿的城市功能定位延续了下来，并至今仍保持着文化与教育等方面的发展特色。

First, in terms of function, Kulangsu has continued its urban functions as an ideal residential area through defining and regulating this in urban planning, and kept its historic development features in culture, education and other aspects.

128. 其次，在城市结构的整体保护和片区肌理特色层面，鼓浪屿目前采取以控制性详细规划为导向的小规模城市更新策略，有效地保持自然景观要素的历史形态，相关文化遗迹的位置、形态、材料的历史特征，历史道路的网络形态、空间尺度、街道界面的历史材料和空间感受，以及典型街区肌理的原有功能、建筑密度和空间尺度等历史特征。这使历史线索在今天的整体环境中清晰可读，并成为当代城市设计的根据和基础。

Second, in terms of the integrated maintenance of the overall urban structure and texture, a small-scale urban renewal strategy, based on detailed regulatory plans, has been adopted to effectively preserve the historic outlook of natural landscapes, the locations, forms and materials of related cultural heritage sites; the layout, spatial dimensions, original materials and image of historical roads; as well as the original functions, building density, and spatial dimensions of typical districts. It enables the historical clues to be clearly read and understood in the overall context today and used as reference for contemporary sustainable urban development.

129. 其深厚的民族特性、宽阔的文化包容力和强大的自我更新能力，随着 20 世纪后还乡移民群体在鼓浪屿推动的社区治理、公共设施建设、经济活动、文化创新等多个层面的近代化变革，以及对后世的深远影响中得到了充分的体现。

The profound national characteristics, great cultural inclusiveness and powerful self-upgrading capability have been fully exhibited in the modern reforms at multiple aspects such as the community governance, public facility construction, economic activities and cultural innovations boosted by the returned Chinese in Kulangsu after the 20th century, and in its far-reaching influence to the later generations.

130. 由此，发生在鼓浪屿的文化交流才变得急剧而迅猛。

It was not until then that the cultural exchange taking place on Kulangsu became dramatic and rapid.

131. 外来多元文化和相对先进的社会治理理念，通过外国领事、洋行商人和传教士传入鼓浪屿，迅速在这个有着开放文化传统的小岛上生根发芽，促进了其经济和社会生活的繁荣。

Diverse cultures and relatively advanced concepts of social governance brought to Kulangsu by the consuls, foreign merchants and missionaries quickly rooted and geminated on this small island with the traditions of an open culture, and promoted the prosperity of its economy and social life.

132. 甲午战争后，日本的力量在亚太地区进一步扩张，与之相对，鼓浪屿相对安全、宽松的社会环境与良好的人居环境，成为大批爱国台胞、海外华侨回国寻求发展的理想选择。

Japan began to expand its influence after the Sino-Japanese War in 1894-1895 (the jia-wu war). A great number of patriotic Chinese from overseas found Kulangsu safe and relaxed with a good living environment, an ideal place to pursue personal dreams.

133. 20 世纪初期，鼓浪屿岛内居住的华人数量已远远超过外国侨民，而随着 20 世纪初华人社会地位的不断提高，还乡华侨已不满足于个人生活环境的提升和营造，他们开始更为积极地参与到推动鼓浪屿社区治理、公共设施、房地产开发、文化教育等各个层面的革新和提升之中，成为鼓浪屿城市发展的核心推动力。

In the early 20th century, the number of Chinese living on Kulangsu was much larger than foreign residents. With the rising social status of Chinese at that time, returned overseas Chinese has gradually put more efforts on promoting and improving the settlement governance, public facilities, real estate development, cultural and educational affairs instead of their personal life. They were the key impetus to Kulangsu's urban development.

134. 据统计，从 1924 年至 1936 年间，鼓浪屿工部局颁发的建筑执照中华人占 75%，而这十几年中，华人在岛上新建建筑则逾千座。

Statistics showed that from 1924 to 1936, local and returned Chinese obtained 75% of the construction licenses issued by Former Kulangsu Municipal Council and altogether they had built more than 1,000 buildings during the decades.

135. 在社区治理方面，还乡华侨群体对于鼓浪屿社区公共事务的参与和革新表现在推动华人社会地位的提升。

In term of settlement governance, returned overseas Chinese made great contribution to raising the social status of Chinese as they fully participated in public affairs.

136. 在社区公共生活方面，还乡华侨群体吸取了西方社区建设理念中对公共生活的重视，将社区基础设施、文体娱乐、医疗、教育设施的营造和提升作为推动社会革新的工具，追求社区生活品质的提升，这将鼓浪屿社区的近代化转型推向高潮。

In term of the public life of the settlement, learning from the western philosophy to focus on community life, returned overseas Chinese invested in infrastructures, recreational venues, medical and educational facilities for a better living quality, pushing the modernization transformation of Kulangsu into a climax.

137. 现存由印尼华侨巨商黄奕住兴建的鼓浪屿自来水公司旧址，以其办公和供

福建世界遗产　双语语料库构建与应用

水设施完整地展示了20世纪20年代亚太地区处于技术领先地位的自来水处理技术。

The existing former Kulangsu Water Supply Facility established by the great Indonesian merchant Huang Yizhu, with the intact office building and water-supply equipment, manifested the advanced water-processing technology of the Asian-Pacific region in the 1920s.

138. 同样由黄奕住投资兴建的鼓浪屿电话公司，于1924年率先实现了厦鼓之间通话，翌年将电话服务覆盖至福建漳州地区。

The former Office of Kulangsu Telephone Company, also invested and established by Huang Yizhu in 1924, enabled the telephone communication between Xiamen and Kulangsu for the first time in history. Telephone service was further expanded to Zhangzhou of Fujian in 1925.

139. 1927年由鼓浪屿华人议事者会众多医院牵头筹备，以越南黄仲训主动捐献日光岩附近地产改造而成的延平公园，为厦门第一处公园，至今仍是最受欢迎的游览场所。

Yanping Park, the first park in Xiamen and still a place most visited today, was an initiative led by Kulangsu Chinese Council, and built on the land near Sunlight Rock which was donated by the Indonesian Overseas Chinese Huang Zhongxun in 1927.

140. 1928年由缅甸华侨王紫如、王其华兄弟投资兴建的鼓浪屿市场和延平戏院，集菜市场、戏院、影院等多种功能于一身，成为鼓浪屿新兴龙头路商业街的核心。

The former Yanping Complex invested by the Burmese Overseas Chinese Wang Ziru and his brother Wang Qihua in 1928 encompassed market, theater and cinemas under one single roof, becoming the center of the new business street Longtou Road of Kulangsu.

141. 印尼归侨黄奕住在鼓浪屿期间积极投资房地产开发，与郭映春一起开发了龙头路商业街区，不久，越南华侨黄仲训所创办的房地产公司"黄荣远堂"又兴建黄家渡码头。据工部局记载，黄家渡码头的兴建带动了龙头路一带商业的繁荣，修建当年码头周边就新建100多间商店，极大地促进了鼓浪屿商业的繁荣和生活的便利。

The returned overseas Chinese Huang Yizhu from Indonesia actively involved in real estate investment, together with Guo Yingchun, they invested in forming the new Longtou Road business street. The real estate company "Huang Rongyuan Villa" established by Vietnam overseas Chinese Huang Zhongxun, constructed the Huang's

Jetty, which helped drive the growth of business in Longtou Road. As recorded by the Municipal Council, more than 100 shops were set up around the new jetty on the very year when it was constructed, which greatly promoted the prosperity of business and convenience of life.

142. 至今龙头路片区仍旧是鼓浪屿最为繁华的商业街区，是岛上市井生活的生动写照。

Nowadays, Longtou Road is still the most bustling business street on Kulangsu, the most vivid reflection of people's everyday life.

143. 20世纪20年代特殊的政治环境，经济和文化的繁荣，不仅使鼓浪屿聚集了一批经济实力雄厚的华侨实业家、政治家，如前文提到的林尔嘉、黄秀烺、黄仲训、黄奕住等人，还产生了许多学贯中西的学者，其作品和成就对中国文化开放和文化进步做出积极贡献。

The specific political environment, thriving economy and culture in the 1920s not only attracted a group of financially strong overseas Chinese businessmen and politicians to return to Kulangsu, such as Lin Erjia, Huang Xiulang, Huang Zhongxun, Huang Yizhu as mentioned above, but also created many scholars well versed in both Chinese and Western, whose works and achievements had made aspiring contributions to China's cultural openness and progress.

144. 鼓浪屿是汉语拼音早期原型的诞生地，被称为"从事切音运动第一人"的卢戆章生活并埋葬在这里。

Kulangsu was the birthplace for the primary model of Pinyin. Lu Zhuangzhang, the "first person of the Pinyin Campaign" lived and is buried on Kulangsu.

145. 中国当代著名学者、文学家、语言学家林语堂出生于鼓浪屿一个基督教牧师家庭，岛上至今仍保留着林语堂及其夫人生活过的旧居。

Lin Yutang, the famous scholar, litterateur and linguist in modern China, was born into a Presbyterian minister family on Kulangsu. The former residence of Lin Yutang and his wife is still kept intact.

146. 开创中国体育教育和理论研究的第一人，马约翰，早年也生活在鼓浪屿，他将西方体育基本的训练理念引入中国高等教育，而后推广普及大众，在中国体育理论、体育教学、运动训练等方面都做出了开创性的贡献。

Ma Yuehan, who was regarded as the pioneer in China's physical education and theoretical study, also lived his early days on Kulangsu. His efforts to introduce western physical training theories into Chinese higher education and later to public sphere exhibited his great creative contribution in theory, teaching, exercise and training of China's physical education.

147. 纵观 19 世纪至 20 世纪的亚太地区，如鼓浪屿这样短期近代化的历史城区实例并不罕见，可以说其成长历程在近代跨区域文化交流的背景下具有普遍性——反映出西方文化的传播对于相对封闭、落后的传统社会形态带来的巨大冲击。

During the 19th-20th century, there are many historic towns like Kulangsu in the Asian-Pacific region which went through the modernization process in a short period. The growth of Kulangsu, to some extent, bears testimony to the quite universal fact that western culture has brought tremendous impact on traditional societies, which were relatively closed and backward, under the context of emerging trans-regional cultural communication in early modern times.

148. 鼓浪屿是近代东亚和东南亚地区具有高品质和早期现代性特征国际社区的独特范例。

Kulangsu is a unique example of an international settlement with high living quality and initial modernization characteristics in East Asia and Southeast Asia in modern times.

149. 经由多元文化群库参与管理和共同营建的鼓浪屿，在有限的岛屿空间内，组织出有机且功能完善的城镇空间结构，建造了风格多样且时尚的建筑宅园，引入了同时代最先进的社区公共设施，构成了完整且保存完好的岛屿历史景观，从而突出地展现了引领理念。

Within a limited island, Kulangsu has developed organic urban spatial structure with complete functions, erected fashionable architectures and gardens of various styles, and introduced the most advanced public facilities at that time. Thus it constitutes an integrated and well-preserved historical island landscape, presenting distinctively the modernity that took the lead in those days and the modern habitat concept integrating Chinese and foreign cultures.

150. 随着 1843 年厦门开埠，鼓浪屿虽然有着繁荣的港口贸易，但并非一个纯粹的贸易城市，而是自建设之初即以高品质住区作为发展目标。

Although Kulangsu has prosperous port trade after opening as a commericial port in 1843, it aimed to develop into a high quality settlement since the early stage of construction, instead of a pure trading port.

151. 在 19 世纪中叶到 20 世纪中叶的一百年间，鼓浪屿凭借其优美宜人的海岛自然环境，鲜明的地方自治特点，以及由多元文化群体参与的管理机制，形成了有机且丰富的街区肌理、完善且先进的服务设施，以及鲜明且时尚的居住建筑，成为亚太地区近代国际社区的独特范例。

From the mid-19th century to the mid-20th century, with graceful and pleasant natural island environment, distinct local autonomous and joint managed by multicultural groups, Kulangsu has formed organic and rich urban fabric, advanced service facilities with sound functions, distinctive and fashion residential architectures, which became a unique example of modern international settlement in the Asian-Pacific region.

152. 鼓浪屿整体的城市历史景观保存至今仍具有较高的真实性和完整性，展示出其高品质的人居环境特色。

The entire historic urban landscape of Kulangsu is still well-preserved with high authenticity and integrity, which shows high-quality living environment of modern settlement.

153. 20世纪初的鼓浪屿形成了华洋共管、具有地方自治色彩的特殊社区管理模式。

In early 20th century, Kulangsu was under a special management system jointly governed by Chinese and foreigners with the feature of local self-government.

154. 鼓浪屿特殊的社区管理模式源自中国近代历史中独特的时代、政治、社会和文化环境。

Kulangsu's special management system was originated from the unique political, social and cultural environment of Chinese modern history at that time.

155. 从管理机构和主导群体力量的变化来看，鼓浪屿的社区管理先后经历了由西方多国侨民主导的"鼓浪屿道路墓地基金委员"，以洋人纳税者会主导的工部局，以及由华人议事者会和洋人纳税者会共同主导的工部局三个不同的发展阶段。

Judging from the change of management organizations and the leading groups, Kulangsu was successively managed in three development stages —" Kulangsu Road and Cemetery Fund Committee" made up by multi-national western foreign residents, the Municipal Council led by the Foreign Taxpayer Committee, and the Municipal Council jointly governed by Chinese Councilors and Foreign Taxpayer Committee.

156. 在20世纪20年代，鼓浪屿形成了华洋共管的管理模式，西方多国侨民和华侨群体的地位相对平等，和谐共处，这为鼓浪屿的社会革新、经济繁荣和文化自由提供了基础。

In 1920s, a management system was formed on Kulangsu, which was jointly managed by multi-national foreign residents and Chinese groups. With relatively equal status, western foreign residents from different countries, returned overseas and local Chinese were in harmonious coexistence, which laid a foundation for social reform, economic prosperity and cultural liberty of Kulangsu.

157. 鼓浪屿保存有社区完整的行政、司法、警察署等管理机构旧址，包括鼓浪屿工部局遗址、会审公堂旧址、日本警察署及宿舍旧址等历史建筑或遗址，集中地展示出 20 世纪初期鼓浪屿的管理模式，具有一定的时代领先性。

All former office buildings or sites of public authorities (administrative, judicial, police station) have been kept intact on Kulangsu, including sites of Kulangsu Municipal Council, Former Kulangsu Mixed Court, the Japanese Police Station and Staff Quarters that demonstrated Kulangsu's unique management system in the early 20th century as a pioneering attempt of the times.

158. 鼓浪屿国际社区具有与自然景观有机结合且功能多样的城市空间结构，体现出注重自然环境与建成环境有机结合的现代人居理念。

Kulangsu international settlement has a diversified urban spatial structure organically integrated with the natural landscape, demonstrating the modern human settlement ideas focusing on organic combination of natural evironment and built environment.

159. 鼓浪屿在城市发展之初即注意到岛屿环境中优美宜人的山形地貌、沙滩礁石，城市的发展讲求与自然景观要素的有机融合，注重景观视野的通畅和入画。

During the early stage of urban development, Kulangsu had focused on beautiful and pleasant mountains and landforms, beaches and reefs. Urban development stresses the organic integration of built environment and natural landscapes, as well as unobstructive and picturesque landscape views.

160. 19 世纪 70 年代鼓浪屿道路墓地基金委员会最初开辟的道路网络即注意和地形地貌的结合，道路依山形变化而蜿蜒曲折、高低起伏，尽可能减少对自然景观的破坏。

In the 1870s, Kulangsu Road and Cemetery Fund Committee paid attention to the combination of terrains and landforms during the early stage of road construction. Roads experienced twists and turns in terms of changes of mountains, trying to reduce destruction to natural landscapes.

161. 同时，工部局时期还在《鼓浪屿工部局规例》中特意将日光岩、鼓浪石、鸡母石、笔架山、燕尾石等标志性的自然景观要素认定为"名胜石"，明确提出不得对其进行破坏。

During the period of the Municipal Council, Kulangsu Municipal Council Regulations specially regarded Sunlight Rock, Kulang Stone, Jimu Stone, Bacon Hill, Yanwei Stone and other symbolic natural landscape elements as "Scenic Stones", clearly indicating that no damage was allowed to these stones.

162. 如今，鼓浪屿的早期历史道路网络仍在社区交通体系中承担着核心作用，与自然景观紧密结合而蜿蜒曲折的道路走向并未改变；而标志性的自然景观要素除去因战乱而受到损失的，均保留至今，并随着历史的发展，被当地居民赋予了更加多重的文化内涵，以城市公园绿地的形态成为鼓浪屿城市空间结构的重要组成部分。

Now, the historic road network of Kulangsu built in the early stage still plays a key role in the settlement's traffic system and the twist-and-turn roads closely integrated with natural landscapes keep unchanged. Except destruction caused by natural disasters, the symbolic natural landscape elements have been preserved till today, and were endowed with more cultural connotations by local residents with the development of history, becoming an important part of Kulangsu urban spatial structure in the form of urban green areas or parks.

163. 与此同时，至 20 世纪 30 年代，鼓浪屿基本形成了若干片功能明确且肌理特征具有差异性的街区，反映出近代社区具有的复合功能。

Until 1930s, Kulangsu's urban fabric was formed by several areas with distinctive features and functions, reflecting the composite functions of a modern settlement.

164. 这些典型的街区紧密联系、相互交错的状态，展示出不同历史时期、不同文化力量对于社区建设的贡献，以及鼓浪屿社区具有的文化多样性和开放性。

Such typical areas were in the state of close connection and interaction, presenting contributions of different cultures in different times, presenting the cultural diversity and openness of Kulangsu.

165. 鼓浪屿具有功能完善且同时代最先进的社区公共设施。

Kulangsu has a full range of public facilities of a modern settlement with the most advanced functions in that period.

166. 鼓浪屿保留有数量众多且功能完善的社区服务设施，从类别上包括：宗教建筑、医疗设施、文教机构、文体娱乐设施、基础设施、商贸机构、交通设施、墓地；以及反映公共意识发展的活动场所，如球埔、公园等。

Kulangsu kept a large number of well-functioning public facilities in different categories: including religious, medical, cultural and educational, recreational, infrastructure, commerce and trade, transportation, cemetery; as well as public places such as football fields and parks.

167. 这些公共设施的丰富性、完备性和先进性在近代亚太社区中是首屈一指的，也为鼓浪屿高品质生活图卷的描绘提供了清晰的佐证。

The diverse, complete and advanced public facilities are second to none and very rare among modern Asia-Pacific settlements, providing clear evidence for depicting Kulangsu's picture of high-quality life.

168. 鼓浪屿的先进性突出地体现在医疗卫生、文教水平和基础设施技术等方面。

Kulangsu's advanced nature is prominently reflected by aspects such as medical care, the cultural and educational level and infrastructure techniques.

169. 由"幼稚园—小学—中学—职业教育"共同构成的教育体系使鼓浪屿人才辈出，并在20世纪的很长时间中代表了福建最高的教育水平。

A galaxy of talents had been cultivated thanks to the educational system covering "kindergarten, primary school, secondary school and vocational education", which represented the highest level of education in Fujian in a long period of the 20th century.

170. 鼓浪屿的基础设施条件和设备，包括电报电话设施、自来水供水设施、电灯电力设施等均于20世纪前引入鼓浪屿，不仅时间上是国内最早的一批，设备上也处于近代亚太地区先进水平。

Kulangsu's infrastructure and equipment conditions, including telegraph and telephone facilities, water supply facilities and electric light and power facilities, were all introduced before the 20th century. They were the earliest ones to be introduced into China, and the equipment also reached the advanced level of the Asia-Pacific region in modern times.

171. 鼓浪屿保存有大量反映近代特定历史时代特征的居住建筑，构成了高品质居住社区的主题。

Kulangsu keeps a large number of residential architecture reflecting the specific period of modern times, rendering the theme of high-quality settlement.

172. 此外，由于鼓浪屿相对独立的地理环境，以及长期以来岛屿内实施较为温和的小规模城市更新策略，在近半个世纪中，它没有受到太多战争或城市建设等人为破坏，较好地保存了其形成、发展各个历史阶段代表性的建成环境要素，特别是数量众多且各具特点的历史建筑。

In addition, due to the unique geographical environment and long-term mild and small-scale urban renewal strategies implemented on Kulangsu, in nearly 50 years

Kulangsu did not suffer too much man-made damages brought by wars or urban development. The built environment was well preserved showing the development in different historical stages, especially a large number of historic buildings of distinct styles.

173. 鼓浪屿现存城市历史景观真实且完整地反映出近代社会在社区管理、公共生活营造、居住模式等方面的成就。

The existing historic urban landscape of Kulangsu truly and comprehensively reflect the achievements in management, public life building and residential environment of a modern settlement.

174. 综上所述，作为近代由多国侨民共同营建的社区实例，鼓浪屿在亚太地区是罕见的——它以有限的地理单元，集中地容纳了丰富而完整的城市历史景观，形成了具有现代性特征的高品质社区，成为该遗产主题历史城区的独特范例。

To sum up, Kulangsu is a rare example of modern settlement in Asia Pacific jointly constructed by the residents from different countries. In a limited geographic space, Kulangsu intensively accomodates rich and complete urban historic landscapes, gradually developed into a modern settlement with high-quality, and became a unique example of heritage-oriented historic town.

175. 鼓浪屿作为 19 世纪中叶至 20 世纪中叶亚太地区多元文化共同影响下形成发展的历史城镇历史城区，具有极高的完整性，具体表现在：

As a historic town in the Asian-Pacific region developed from the mid-19th century to the mid-20th century under influence from diverse cultures, Kulangsu bears testimony to the integrity, which expresses in the following aspects:

176. 鼓浪屿各种文化之间的地位相对平等，和谐共存，最终相互融合。

Different cultures on Kulangsu are equal, harmonious and integrated.

177. 鼓浪屿包含有表达突出普遍价值的所有遗产构成要素。

Kulangsu includes all heritage attributes expressing the Outstanding Universal Value.

178. 鼓浪屿的突出普遍价值通过其完整的城市历史景观整体得以表达，后者包含有岛屿自然景观要素，由历史道路和典型街区肌理构成的城市空间结构，社区公共管理机构、驻岛机构、各类社区公共服务设施，居住建筑和宅园等遗产构成要素。

The Outstanding Universal Value of Kulangsu are expressed through the complete urban historic landscape, including the natural landscape elements, urban spatial structures comprising of historic roads and urban fabrics, public management offices, institutions and various public service facilities, residential buildings and home gardens.

179. 多种类型的遗产构成要素以其保存完好的状态，全面地展示出 19 世纪中叶至 20 世纪中叶百年间，鼓浪屿国际社区在社会治理、公共生活、居住环境的营建等方面取得的巨大成就，展示出中国传统文化与外来多元文化多方面的交流与融合。

All heritage attributes are under well conserved and intact conditions, which fully exhibit the great achievements of Kulangsu international settlement in social governance, social life, and living conditions during the century-long period from the mid-19th century to the mid-20th century, reflecting the communication and fusion between traditional Chinese culture and diverse foreign cultures.

180. 遗产要素的选择涵盖鼓浪屿的所有代表性特征和历史时期。

The selection of heritage attributes covers the representative characters and historic periods of Kulangsu.

181. 鼓浪屿完整地保存有代表性的自然景观要素和城市空间结构。

Typical natural landscape elements and urban spatial structure are well preserved on Kulangsu.

182. 鼓浪屿的地貌景观包括两道十字相交的山岭，这些山丘不仅具有重要的空间标识作用，与其社区的发展演变息息相关，而且和一些重要的历史事件相关，从而被赋予了丰富的文化内涵。

The geomorphologic landscape on Kulangsu formed by two cross-shaped ridges are key marks for location identification, which are closely associated with the settlement development and significant historic events.

183. 鼓浪屿城市空间结构包括：与岛屿地貌特征有机结合的历史道路网络，丰富且各具特色的街区肌理等遗产构成要素。

Urban spatial structure comprises the historic roads built along the geographic features, the rich and distinct urban fabrics.

184. 在 20 世纪后半叶的建设中，鼓浪屿形成于 19 世纪末的历史道路完整地得到保存，这可以通过各个历史时期地图的比对得以印证。

Historic roads constructed by the end of the 19th century were well reserved during the urban construction carried out in the late 20th century, which was testified through the different maps of historic periods.

185. 鼓浪屿保留有见证社区公共管理体系的完整历史遗存。

Complete historic sites of settlement public management system are well preserved on

Kulangsu.

186. 20世纪初成为公共地界后，鼓浪屿在社区管理方面形成了具有地方自治特点的行政管理机构与司法审判机构，设置有工部局和会审公堂。

After identified as an international settlement in the early 20th century, a self-governance management system has been established on Kulangsu, including administrative system, judicial institutions, the Municipal Council and the Mixed Court were set up.

187. 鼓浪屿现存有工部局遗址、会审公堂旧址两处历史遗存，这是其特殊社区管理体系的历史见证。

The existing sites of the former Kulangsu Municipal Council and former Kulangsu Mixed Court are the historical testimony to the unique settlement management system.

188. 鼓浪屿保存有表现文化多元性及繁荣经济社会生活的代表性驻岛机构。

Consulates representing diverse cultures, booming economy and social life are well preserved on Kulangsu.

189. 鼓浪屿早在19世纪下半叶，即建成多处领事或代理领事机构、海关机构办公与其职员居住的建筑，以及多处商贸金融机构，不仅反映出当时鼓浪屿所受到的多国文化影响，更反映出其政治、经济生活的繁荣景象。

Many consulates or agents, customs offices and quarters for staff, and trading and financial institutions have been established on Kulangsu during the late 19th century, representing diverse cultures and booming political, economic and social life.

190. 时至今日，鼓浪屿仍保存了多处具有代表性的领事馆建筑，如美国领事馆旧址、日本领事馆旧址等；领事官邸，如英国领事公馆旧址；海关不同办事机构要员官邸和职员宿舍，如厦门海关理船厅公所旧址、厦门海关副税务司公馆旧址、厦门海关验货员公寓旧址；由外商和华商兴办的工商业机构，如英商亚细亚火油公司旧址、中南银行旧址等。

Many typical buildings are well-preserved today, such as the consulates—former American Consulate, former Japanese Consulate; mansions of the customs officials and staff quarters—former Amoy Maritime Affairs Office, Residences of Amoy Deputy Commissioner of Customs, former Amoy Customs Tax Officers' Quarters; industry and commerce buildings set up by foreign merchants and Chinese merchants—former Office Building of British Asiatic Petroleum Company, and former Building of China & South Sea Bank Limited.

191. 鼓浪屿保存有反映近代社区公共设施完善性和先进性的代表性历史建筑。

Historic buildings representing community facilities are well preserved on Kulangsu.

192. 特殊的地理位置，相对温和的社会环境，外来多元文化的影响，以及华侨群体对社区近代化所做的多方面努力，使得鼓浪屿在 20 世纪初期迅速地由传统住区向近代国际社区转变。

In the early 20th century, Kulangsu witnessed rapid transformation from a traditional society to a modern international settlement, due to its special geographic location, moderate social environment, impact from diverse foreign cultures, and the efforts made by the returned overseas Chinese.

193. 每类设施均保存有不同历史时期、代表不同文化群体修建的代表性历史建筑，总量达 20 余处，完整地表达了鼓浪屿近代社区在公共设施建设方面取得的卓越成就。

There are a total of more than 20 historic buildings built in different periods by different cultural groups, reflecting the excellent achievements of Kulangsu in public facilities.

194. 鼓浪屿完整地保存有大量风格多样的居住建筑和宅园景观。

Residential buildings and home gardens of different styles are well preserved on Kulangsu.

195. 鼓浪屿完整地保存了 3 个代表性历史时期的建设成果。

Constructions in 3 typical historic periods are well preserved on Kulangsu.

196. 鼓浪屿现存城市历史景观完整地保留有各代表性历史时期的建设成果，突出地反映了社区历史转变过程和文化特征的演变。

The constructions in different historic periods are well preserved on Kulangsu, reflecting the transformation of the settlement and the culture.

197. 多元文化影响下，初步具有近代特征的国际社区：鼓浪屿保留有建于 19 世纪后半叶的核心历史道路，典型街区肌理，一系列领事馆、商业金融机构等驻岛机构，多由外国人建造的社区服务设施及别墅洋楼。

International modern settlement during the period of diverse cultures: Most of the important historic roads, urban fabrics, consulates, commercial/financial institutions during the late 19th century were public service facilities, villas and western-style buildings built by foreigners.

198. 华侨主导下的公共设施和华侨洋楼建筑：鼓浪屿保存有建于 20 世纪后的社区公共管理机构，由华侨群体兴建了大量的文教、医疗、戏院、基础设施等社区公共设施，以及大量华侨洋楼和宅园。

Public facilities and Western-style buildings built by returned overseas Chinese: Many public facilities (culture and education facilities, medical centers, theaters, and infrastructure), Western-style buildings and home gardens built by the returned overseas Chinese during late 20th century were well preserved on Kulangsu.

199. 在理念和设备技术方面具有区域性的先进性社区公共设施，如宏宁医院、延平戏院、鼓浪屿自来水公司、鼓浪屿电话公司、中南银行旧址等，均表现出华侨群体对于近代化和社会变革的追求。

The advanced facilities in terms of construction ideas and skills are the former Hong-ning Hospital, former Yanping Complex, former Kulangsu Water Supply Facility, former Office of Kulangsu Telephone Company, and former Building of China & South Sea Bank Limited, manifesting the returned overseas Chinese's pursuit of modernity and social transformation.

200. 鼓浪屿岛屿内长期实行小规模有机更新的城市发展策略，有效控制了岛内新建筑、历史建筑改造项目的高度、体量和形态，使整体的城市历史景观的完整性得到了有效保护。

Small scale renovation mechanism have been implemented on Kulangsu to control the height, scale and forms of the new buildings on the Island, and the renovation on historic buildings, making it an effective way to protect the entire historic urban landscape.